Entrepreneur®
MAGAZINE'S

COMPLETE GUIDE TO OWNING A HOME-BASED BUSINESS

BANTAM BUSINESS BOOKS

Ask your bookseller for the titles you have missed

Entrepreneur®
MAGAZINE'S

COMPLETE GUIDE
TO OWNING
A HOME-BASED
BUSINESS

THE EDITORS OF
Entrepreneur®

A
BANTAM
TRADE
PAPERBACK

BANTAM BOOKS
NEW YORK • TORONTO • LONDON • SYDNEY • AUCKLAND

Acknowledgments

Thousands and thousands of hours of research have gone into creating this book. For much of it, we are indebted to the staff, past and present, of *Entrepreneur®* magazine. Particular thanks go to Maria Anton, Christine Forbes, Charles Fuller, Frances Huffman, Maria Johnson, Erika Kotite, Kevin McLaughlin, Frank Mixson, and Gayle Sato.

We'd also like to express our gratitude to Barbara Alpert of Bantam, a wonderful editor, who had the vision to bring these books to life.

—Rieva Lesonsky, Editor
Clare N. Thain, Publisher
Entrepreneur® magazine

ENTREPRENEUR MAGAZINE'S COMPLETE GUIDE TO OWNING A HOME-BASED
BUSINESS
A Bantam Book / August 1990

Library of Congress Cataloging-in-Publication Data
Entrepreneur magazine's complete guide to owning a home-based business
/ the editors of Entrepreneur.—Bantam ed.
    p.   cm.
  ISBN 0-553-34919-8
  1. Home-based businesses. I. Entrepreneur. II. Title: Complete
guide to owning a home-based business.
HD2333.E571   1990
658'.041—dc20   90-30192
                                                                CIP

Published simultaneously in the United States and Canada

PRINTED IN THE UNITED STATES OF AMERICA

OPM   0 9 8 7 6 5 4 3 2

CONTENTS

I

GEARING UP

II

SETTING UP SHOP

V

GROWTH AND EXPANSION

VI

OPPORTUNITIES

I

GEARING UP

1

THE HOME-BASED-
BUSINESS PHENOMENON:

WHY AMERICANS ARE COMING HOME TO
START BUSINESSES

Working from home. Sounds good, doesn't it? For millions of people, it not only sounds good, it *is* good. In the last ten years, so many people have traded their office jobs for a home-based business, it's beginning to look like a definite trend.

We're not talking just about sideline businesses or hobbies that bring in a few extra dollars. On the other hand, many successful businesses start out as a hobby and turn into full-time operations. The point is, some people have an outdated notion of what it's like to work at home. Many consider it a half-baked, last-resort, no-frills attempt to make a little money until a "real" job comes along.

The fact is that while few home-based entrepreneurs strike it rich, many have found that they can make the same income they would have in their former positions. What they leave behind are long commutes, office politics, vituperative bosses, and lost time with spouse and family. It's a business trend to be taken seriously.

The idea of running a business in the privacy of your own home is extremely appealing to many people. According to a recent study from a national marketing-research firm, nearly one third of all American workers would like to work at home. Just take a look at all of the examples we have on prime-time television—*Who's the Boss?, The Bob Newhart Show,* and *Cheers* all contain major and minor characters who run businesses from their homes. In your job you've probably run across a few people who have quit to start home-based businesses. You will also be joining an illustrious circle of real-life entrepreneurs who started from their homes—Lillian Vernon, Hewlett and Packard, Milton Hershey, and Steven Jobs—and went on to make business history. In other words, we are all surrounded with solid proof that there is truly something phenomenal going on in home-based business. The question is, What brought on this wave of home-based entrepreneurship? Why is it happening now?

A MODERN-DAY RENAISSANCE

Once upon a time, the home-based business was a fact of life. Most people were farmers or ranchers who raised their food, made their clothes, and handled their book-keeping at home. It wasn't until the Industrial Revolution of the nineteenth century, when the first factories appeared in Europe, that there began a steady move toward industry decentralization. People no longer spun cloth on their home looms; instead, they went to work at textile factories and were paid wages for their labor. By World War II, cottage industries were a thing of the past. Home-based business was no more than a sideline or hobby to bring in a little extra money.

Today, home-based businesses are enjoying a renaissance. And they aren't the sweatshops of yesteryear but legitimate, professionally run businesses like consulting firms, advertising agencies, publishing companies, bed-and-breakfast inns, photography studios, free-lance writing businesses, and event-planning services.

There are no official statistics on the number of home-based businesses in existence, but it's estimated that anywhere from 15 to 25 million people are currently working from their homes. By 1990, 12 to 20 percent of the U.S. work force will be working full-time at home. These figures include both home-based entrepreneurs and "telecommuters," or corporate employees who work out of their homes and communicate with the office via telephone and computer.

Recent government decisions reaffirm this growing trend. Last year, for example, the federal Industrial Home Work Act of 1943 was repealed. The rule had outlawed the practice of manufacturing certain types of apparel in the home, in an effort to protect workers from exploitation by their employers. Now, home workers are allowed to manufacture apparel such as gloves, buttons, handkerchiefs, and certain kinds of jewelry in their homes.

Home-based businesses are started by both men and women, but it seems to be especially prevalent among women. According to the National Center for Policy Analysis, 70 percent of home-based businesses are run by women, due in part to the growing number of women who want to have a career and stay at home to raise their children.

Another work force that's turning the home into a place of business is retirees. Because many corporations are giving early retirement to their employees in order to cut down on payroll costs, many people in their fifties and early sixties still have the energy and drive to run their own companies. Daniel, a college professor who plans to retire in a few years, has already started a desktop publishing business in his home; Belinda accepted early retirement at the steel company she worked for and started her own antiques-refinishing business.

Home-based entrepreneurship is proving that there is an alternative to the corporate rat race, high office rents, and answering to an employer. The possibilities are endless.

ELECTRONIC COTTAGES

The home-based business movement could not have happened so fast without computerization. The personal computer has made so many tasks possible to do at home, better and in less time than ever before. They have made it possible for one man or woman to do the work of two or three people. Computers, specialized software, facsimile machines, and modems mean that "being at home" no longer means "being without." Manufacturers of business equipment have all recognized the lucrative home-based-business market; after all, it's worth about $20 billion! In response, they're making equipment that's compact, feature-rich, and very affordable. Also, equipment is easier to buy now that more retail outlets sell discounted office equipment.

The mighty yet humble telephone has also come of age with the home-based-business phenomenon. Both local and long-distance companies offer inexpensive services such as call waiting, 800 numbers, and call forwarding to their business and residential customers. These services bring home telephones much closer to sophisticated office systems at a fraction of the cost. The simple answering machine enables a one-person operation to survive without missing important phone calls. And don't forget the cellular telephone, which in the past ten years has revolutionized both the corporate office and the home-based office.

Now, close your eyes and picture a home office. If you see a cramped spare room with poor lighting, an old manual typewriter, and a card table, you're way behind the times. Today's home-based office can also be a paragon of design and technology. You can take advantage of furniture, lighting, and fabrics designed specifically for offices that need to make the most of every inch of space.

In chapter 8, we will discuss the newest developments in home-office furniture and the impact it has on both your personal comfort and professional image. Setting up your office right means investing in the right equipment, which you will read about in chapter 9. You'll see what's available for the home-based business, from copiers to telephones, facsimile machines to electronic typewriters; what features to look for, how they will help your business, and approximately how much they will cost. And in chapter 10, you will learn about the world of personal computers, probably the most important development of all for home-based businesses.

THE BOOMING SERVICE INDUSTRY

In conjunction with the personal computer, the service age has ushered in an entirely new way of doing business. And it has opened up marvelous new inroads for the home-based entrepreneur. Services are the perfect "products" to sell from home!

It's a well-known fact that we are a service economy. It seems that almost everyone you meet is in marketing or sales or consulting. The service sector is growing faster than either the agricultural or manufacturing sectors: It brings in billions of dollars in revenues and accounts for more than two thirds of our gross national product. The Bureau of Labor Statistics estimates that by 1995, nine out of ten new jobs will be created in the service sector. Service businesses make ideal home-based businesses because they generally cost less to start and require less equipment—many are run on a desk and a telephone!

If you offer a service, you don't have to worry about storing inventory on the premises or having big delivery trucks parked in front of your home. In many areas, zoning regulations allow home-based businesses as long as they don't create excessive noise or cause an increase in traffic. Many service businesses have none of these disruptive side effects. Your neighbors may never know that you're in business.

The increasing need for services can be seen as a major contributing factor to the growing number of home-based businesses. Today, home-based entrepreneurs are everywhere, in every neighborhood, running hundreds of different businesses. They are living proof that, while not without its challenges, working out of one's home can be fulfilling and profitable.

REASONS FOR LEAVING . . .

Corporate Flight
If you remember the forties and fifties—or if you grew up watching *Leave It to Beaver* reruns—it seemed that

everyone donned a starched white shirt, grabbed a briefcase, and headed off into the vague world of tall office
buildings and typing pools. Being a company man was a
way of life; if you played your cards right, worked hard,
and got along with the boss, you'd be assured of a decent
salary, good health benefits, and a retirement pension for
your golden years.

But there's a dark side to the corporate American
dream. Because of a recent bout of corporate buyouts,
mergers, and reorganizations, thousands of "company
men"—and women—are being laid off. Early retirement
is also a common occurrence today. As a way of "hu-
manely" (and legally) reducing their staffs, companies will
offer employees between the ages of fifty and sixty-five
continued health coverage and full pensions if they agree
to retire early. And although it isn't mandatory to accept
early retirement, companies can make it hard to say no.
Employees who are offered "voluntary" retirement have
the choice of accepting what is offered them and keeping
quiet or taking the chance that their job will be phased
out later on, leaving them with nothing. After working at
a company for years, many run the risk of being "kicked
out" for their efforts. It's no wonder that ex-corporate
employees are turning to other sources of income.

Another reason people are leaving the corporate workplace is simple burnout. Because of high housing costs,
many people are forced to live far away from their jobs.
This means thirty-minute, one-hour, even two-hour commutes each way. Many of the tasks one performs in an
office could be done just as easily at home. Meredith, an
executive recruiter, found that she was spending many
hours on the train commuting from her home in Con-
necticut to New York City . . . instead of with her one-year
old son. "There was no point in going all the way to New
York for a job I did almost exclusively by telephone," she
says. "I didn't need an office or a supervisor—I had my
own clients." Meredith now has a successful executive
recruiting agency out of her own home.

Burnout can also come from too many late-night meetings, where little is accomplished. It comes from constant
interruption from coworkers who stop by your office "for

just a few minutes" to chat. It may also stem from an agonizingly slow decision-making process you have to muddle through every time you want to do something. "Being a corporate man held a lot of frustrations for me," says Ben, formerly of AT&T. "The decision-making process takes so long, and you need about ten thousand signatures to get anything done." Ben eventually went out on his own and started a computer training service.

The home-based-business movement is filled with people who have had enough of the corporate life and its many headaches. Do you fit the description?

Stumbling Into It

Many industries, such as engineering, computer programming, and designing, make it easy to stumble into a home-based business. Southern California, a mecca for space and aeronautics engineering, employs literally tens of thousands of engineers. During slow periods or between projects, however, many engineers get laid off. Some, like Sebastian of Santa Ana, California, develop free-lance businesses in the interim. Sebastian, in order to support two young children, started doing free-lance projects for several companies from his apartment. Soon, he found that he was busier, making more money, and had a steadier income than when he worked for a multi-billion-dollar aeronautics firm. "I miss the employee benefits," he says, "but I'm with my kids and I'm surviving."

The advantage of starting a home-based business in your own field is obvious. You already have expertise to sell and, presumably, some important contacts and clients from your old job. A high percentage of today's home-based entrepreneurs are doing some form of what they did in the corporate world—consulting, marketing, research, law, writing, and sales.

On the other hand, what you do as a hobby or a sideline interest may make a good business, too. Do your homemade cakes take blue ribbons at the county fair every year? Are your neighbors begging you to help them get their backyards looking like yours? These are marketable talents you can build a business around.

Nancy used to bake puff pastries for her family's annual Christmas parties. They were such a hit, she decided to try marketing them commercially. In five years, her gourmet-food company has become a $6 million business.

This doesn't mean you can't start a business with an idea completely unrelated to what you were doing before or that you don't know very much about. If your community has a specific need for something—a word-processing service or an image consultant, for example—you can fulfill that need. It just requires some extra time and effort to learn about the business, perfect your skills, and find clients.

THE REWARDS

Economies of Scale

Everyone knows that starting a business takes money. The key is finding a way to get started with the least amount of capital and a minimum of overhead. A home-based business could be the answer!

Saving money is one of the biggest reasons for working from home. On the average, the rent for a 500 square foot office is around $2 per square foot, or $1,000 a month. This doesn't even include extras like association fees, maintenance fees, etc.

With a home-based business, you not only save money on office rent, you can also deduct a portion of your mortgage or rent at tax time. Let's say you use a room such as a den, study, garage, or spare bedroom exclusively as a studio or office. The room is 10 feet by 12 feet, or 120 square feet. If your home is 1,200 square feet, you can deduct 10 percent of your total mortgage or rent payments on your tax return.

In addition to saving rent, you will also save on overhead. Your telephone and electricity are already installed. You don't have extra association or maintenance fees. Your decorating and maintenance costs will be much lower. Commuting costs, of course, are nonexistent! For the beginning business, a low overhead can be the difference between surviving that first year and . . . not surviving.

The Gift of Time

Working at home gives you the gift of time—the time you would have spent driving to work, which could add up to a couple of weeks in one year. Time to do the things you want to do—play with the kids, run errands, organize the files, read the paper—and still use your work time productively.

Besides getting more time, home-based entrepreneurs get what many people only dream of—a flexible work schedule. Tests have proven time and time again that a nine-to-five workday is extremely unproductive for some people. Some people don't "wake up" until ten-thirty. Others are raring to go at six A.M., and lose steam by three P.M. Still others do their best work while burning the midnight oil.

Most home-based entrepreneurs can set any kind of work schedule they want. Two hours in the morning for correspondence and telephone calls. Three hours in the afternoon for errands and meetings with clients. Three hours at night to write and do bookkeeping. You can work four days a week or seven. You can give yourself the afternoon off for your child's school play. You can clean your desk and watch *Good Morning, America* at the same time. Even if you end up working more than eight hours a day, you'll be less stressed, because you have control over which hours you work and how many. Many people who experienced lack of motivation and productivity during their years in an office have blossomed under the freedom of running a home-based business.

Personal Satisfaction

Maybe you're not interested in the rent savings or the extra time you'll have working from home. Maybe what you're looking for is extra satisfaction. Well, you'll get that too. In these days of dual-income families, no one has as much time as he or she would like for personal pursuits. With a home-based business, you have the option of staying home and building a profitable business at the same time.

You'll get to know your neighborhood, too. Think about it—in all the years you've lived where you are, how many neighbors do you know well? Can you name three good lunch places within five miles? Most of us spend more time away from our homes than in them. With a home-based business, you'll become familiar with everything that goes on during the day on your street: when kids come home from school, what time the mail comes, how fresh the doughnuts are at the convenience store down the street . . . it gives you more of an interest in your own neighborhood. Many people find themselves more involved in community organizations and activities as a result of being home all day.

And last, but certainly not least, being at home means you'll be able to spend more time with your family. This is the advantage most home-based women feel is most important, but men are enjoying it too. Men are beginning to realize that they can enjoy their children and run a business at the same time.

We'll probably never return to the days of the single breadwinner and the housewife/mother's being the normal household pattern. The number of dual-income households will continue to increase. People will continue to buy homes that are far away from the city in which they work. As long as these patterns continue, so will the trend toward small businesses' returning to the home.

2

THE RIGHT STUFF

IS HOME-BASED ENTREPRENEURSHIP FOR YOU?

Although the lure of being able to work at home captures more and more Americans these days, running a home-based business is not for everyone. In many ways, it's not as easy as it sounds.

Tom, an English professor, decided he needed more free time in which to finish his nearly completed novel. Tom quit his job and opened an English tutoring service, which he ran out of his home. For the first few weeks, things were great. Tom would get out of bed, write for five hours, and then begin seeing students. The tutoring service brought in enough money to pay the bills and also afforded Tom enough free time to write.

But then, things started going downhill.

Gradually, Tom's friends, neighbors, and even former students found out that Tom was at home (and, they thought, at their service) all day long. The hours Tom had set aside for writing began to be interrupted by unexpected phone calls and knocks at the door. What was worse, Tom, who had begun to feel just a little bit lonely without the hordes of students who had previously surrounded him, was happy to answer the phone and let visitors in to chat. But he wasn't so happy when all his socializing started to cut into his tutoring time—and put a crimp in his cash flow. A few months later, Tom found himself out of money and was forced back into the classroom, his novel still unfinished.

Maintaining a successful home-based business may sound like it's a simple proposition, but it isn't. There are many factors involved in working at home, not the least of which are psychological: isolation, lack of motivation, workaholism, and lack of concentration. Working at home requires a great deal of independence and self-discipline, two characteristics that may not be critical when you are working in a corporate environment but that must be present when you are on your own.

All your life, your home has been a place to . . . well, come home to. As a student, you got up, ate breakfast, and went to class. You did your work and then came home. Going to the office, you followed pretty much the same routine. You don't associate your living room or spare bedroom with a workplace.

Now the rules are changed. You get up, eat breakfast . . . and then clear the dishes off your desk and get to work. What time is it? Should you get dressed? "The best part about working out of my home is that I can hang around in my pajamas," says John, who runs a children's clothing mail order business. "I always hated wearing a suit and tie to work." On the other hand, some find it difficult to feel businesslike in a robe and slippers.

In other words, working at home means making a lot of adjustments, both psychologically and logistically. There are certain personality types that adjust faster and better to working at home. Some have to work at it, and some should probably not try it at all. The more you can examine your motives in advance, the more prepared you'll be to start a successful venture from home.

THE PERSONALITY TEST

To a certain extent, having an "entrepreneurial" personality means you will also have the traits necessary for working at home. Some of these traits are inherent; others can be picked up along the way. Some, however, cannot be learned. You should be aware of what you have and don't have before you get started.

Independence

The biggest common denominator in every entrepreneur is independence. You have to want to be your own boss and rely only on yourself to get things done. In the normal workplace, there are always people around you to supervise your work, give you advice, praise a job well done, and share the responsibilities. At home, you're on your own.

"I never realized how much my secretary did for me until I didn't have her anymore," mourns Jim, president of a home-based software design and marketing firm. "I'm learning all over again how to take care of my correspondence and remember appointments."

Few home-based entrepreneurs have the resources to hire a secretary, at least in the beginning. For those who have been in managerial positions for most of their adult life, accustomed to clerical support, it can be a very difficult adjustment.

Independence means being able to (and wanting to) take care of problems and projects by yourself. When you talk to successful home-based entrepreneurs, most of them will say that during their years of working in an office, it was hard for them to submit to the orders of someone else. "The only jobs I liked in the outside world were those where I was given free rein to run my own department," claims Janice, a home-based writer.

In other words, for those who have always felt stifled by uncreative bosses, working at home is the ultimate chance to prove their independence.

Self-Discipline

Most of us, since we've been old enough to understand the concept, have been told to "practice a little self-discipline," whether it's cleaning our rooms without being told, staying out of the cookie jar just before a meal, or turning off the television set to do our homework. The same holds true for us as adults. Self-discipline is simply the way we govern ourselves in order to accomplish certain goals.

Because of the old Puritan work ethic, Americans have put self-discipline high up on a pedestal. Some critics say we place too much of an emphasis on self-discipline, causing undue stress. Diets, exercise regimes, New Year's resolutions, and timetables are all ways in which we try to make ourselves adhere to reaching goals that will benefit us, even if the road to these goals is not smooth or easygoing.

Everyone has self-discipline to a certain extent—after all, we all get up in the morning and put on our clothes, right? But running a business takes much more than that. Your livelihood and your future rest on how well you discipline yourself to get your work done, solicit more clients, or develop good marketing techniques.

A good way to figure out how much of a self-disciplinarian you are is to examine your past record. Are you more productive when you have someone watching to make sure you finish that report on time? Are you a notorious procrastinator, always putting off until tomorrow what you should have done today? If you answered yes to either of these questions, then you may find it hard to work without the motivating force of other people around.

Concentration

The ability to concentrate on one task at a time is important for anyone, but especially for someone running a business. Good concentration means you can filter out distracting forces like ringing telephones, an empty stomach, or a beautiful sunny day in order to get something accomplished.

When you trade an office job for a home-based business, you're often trading one set of distractions for another. At the office, you try to tune out the chatter from the halls; at home, you might be dealing with your next door neighbor's powerful stereo system. It takes patience and, yes, self-discipline to develop good powers of concentration. Without it, though, the pressing concerns of a small business would not be attended to and everything would founder.

Persistence

Getting any business off the ground takes persistence. But when you are home-based, you'll come up against obstacles that may require an extra dose of perseverance.

Laura, a home-based greeting-card designer and manufacturer, considers persistence the most vital quality she has. "It has taken me through many a rough spot," she laughs. As a young woman struggling to get her business off the ground, Laura has spent months trying to attract investors to her business. "The interest is there, but the money may not be readily available," she explains. Her bank has also refused to issue her a business checking account. Laura believes in her product and is convinced it can fill a market void. This conviction helps her keep trying in spite of discouragement.

Lately, however, things are looking up. Laura's highest investor handed her a check for $25,000, enough to get her cards printed in volume and for her to purchase the computer and part-time help that she needs.

The biggest challenge is to be persistent without being a pest. We've all been hounded by aggressive, insensitive salespeople on the phone and in stores. This isn't the kind of persistence that will gain you respect and attention—instead, you could alienate everyone around you. The kind of persistence we're talking about is never showing discouragement, always thinking of new ways to approach a problem . . . and acting on your ideas.

Other Useful Personality Traits

- Hard Work: This goes without saying. If you try to cut corners on every project so you can go to the beach earlier, forget about running a home-based business. Not only should you be capable of doing hard work, but you should enjoy it, too.
- Creativity: Depending on the kind of business you run,

creativity can play a minor or a major role in your daily activities. Creativity is one of the personality traits that cannot be taught; you either have it or you don't.

- A Businesslike Attitude: This means having some knowledge of how a business is run and knowing how to conduct yourself in a businesslike manner. Some people look on a home-based business as homegrown, not to be taken seriously. You have to have the attitude of a professional at all times, no matter how often you lounge in your pajamas while talking on the telephone.

Do You Have to Be a Superperson?

With all of these personality requirements, it's hard to imagine that any ordinary person can run a successful home-based business. But keep in mind that most "ordinary" people have some, if not all, of these personality traits; they may just have to work on them a little or draw them out of hiding. If someone is deficient in a certain trait, such as creativity or business knowledge, then it's a matter of finding a business that requires different traits. For example, a word-processing service doesn't require a lot of creativity, but it does take precision and stick-to-itiveness.

And no matter what kind of business you run, you will always have matters like taxes, billing, budgeting, and marketing to handle. You may make the best chocolate-rum layer cake in town, but if you don't know how to work out a fair price or find customers, your business is over before you've even begun.

The point is that when you're home-based, you need to have a lot of inner resources. There's no one else around to make up for your shortcomings.

THE DARK SIDE

Loneliness

As we mentioned earlier, working at home has its disadvantages. The biggest problem mentioned by home-based entrepreneurs is loneliness. Because many home-based businesses are one-person ventures, being the boss also means being the entire corporate ladder. This often leads to a feeling of isolation and may have serious consequences on the kind of business you will build.

Dick left a prosperous position as marketing director for a large computer manufacturing company to start his own image consulting business. After a few weeks, Dick, who has an outgoing, friendly personality, began to miss the social interaction at his old job. "I never realized how much satisfaction and motivation I got from talking to my colleagues over a cup of coffee," he says. "It took me a long time to adjust."

If the prospect of working alone scares you, you should think twice about working at home. But there are several ways entrepreneurs can combat feelings of loneliness and isolation should they arise. Here are a few suggestions:

- Make a point of scheduling business lunches a few times a week. These will not only get you out of the house, they will also build a network of contacts with whom you share common interests.
- Join clubs and associations. Trade and professional organizations sponsor dinners, seminars, and meetings. You can also join a club that centers around a hobby—fishing, for instance, or photography.
- Arrange for your business to take you out of the house occasionally. Even if it is a little inconvenient, go out and meet some of your clients face to face.
- Make good use of the time you spend away from work. Keep up your social contacts and go out and interact with new people. (For more tips on dealing with home-based isolation, consult chapter 19 of this book.)

Motivation

Motivation stems from interaction with other people; seeing them at work, listening to suggestions from a supervisor, and getting praise for a job well done. Human beings are social animals, for the most part, and crave attention from the people around them in order to perform at their best. Without people around to witness and validate your work, it may be difficult to get motivated.

There's another motivational sand trap in a home-based business. In a work environment that includes a refrigerator, a television, possibly a spouse and kids, and a telephone number that friends know by heart, only the most rigidly self-controlled of us can resist temptation. "Many of us are not socialized to take care of business in a home environment," says Jean Coyle, a home-based-business activist. "In our school system, a schedule's set up—the bells ring, and you go from one place to another. We get our first taste of freedom in college, but even so, there's a certain amount of discipline imposed. [At home], there are much greater temptations to get involved with other things."

So there's a potential problem of losing motivation, but what about the other extreme? Workaholism runs rampant in the home-based-business industry. When Susan ran her newspaper publishing company from her home, she got so involved in team meetings and printing deadlines, she had to check into a hotel when she came down with a cold.

Due to the long hours and intense commitment needed to start a business, many people who work at home find the boundaries between business and private life disappearing. For some, working hours expand from a manageable eight to twelve- or fourteen-hour days, until the business swallows up all free time. These extremely long hours not only make a well-balanced life impossible, they can also lead to burnout, which can kill the desire of even the most self-motivated.

The best way to stay motivated and keep your business under control is to get organized and follow a daily routine. If you're not an organized person, you could be in for trouble. Most home-based businesspeople make a point of instilling some kind of structure into their days. Structure keeps them from working too little—or too much—and ensures a proper balance between business and home life.

Tip: Fake It If You Have To
Linda, a home business consultant and the co-owner of a home-based clock shop, points out the importance of structure. "One [home-based] businessman I know

doesn't feel like he's gone to work if he's at home. So he gets in his car every morning, drives around the block, and comes back to his house. That makes him feel like he's actually at work."

Here's another example: A man who had a similar problem associating home with work puts on a pin-striped suit, walks out the front door, around the house, and in the basement door to his office. Then, he starts work. It's a simple but effective use of self-psychology.

The Right Image

Having some kind of structure also helps the home-based entrepreneur develop a positive self-image. Right-fully or not, many people see a home-based business as nothing more than a part-time hobby. For years, corporate America has looked at the home-based businessper-son as something less than professional. The fact is that home-based entrepreneurs are just as professional as anyone else. But if they're not careful, the lack of corpo-rate trappings like a sleek office, secretary, and fancy telephone can sometimes make them feel that they and their businesses aren't really worth much.

Marilyn, who ten years ago founded a home-based janitorial service that is now a multi-million-dollar com-pany, recalls how difficult it was to be taken seriously. "As soon as vendors found out I worked out of my home, they insisted on payment up front, and then I had to wait until my check cleared!" A home-based entrepreneur may en-counter banks who refuse to open a business account for them, customers who balk at someone who doesn't have a "proper storefront," and even friends who smile conde-scendingly and say how much they would love to "stay at home" if only they weren't so busy in the "real world."

Only time and truth will change the stereotype of the humble home business. In the meantime, there are many ways to enhance your image, some of which are discussed in further detail in chapters 9 and 23. The question here is whether you feel you have what it takes to build up a good image for yourself and your business.

LOGISTICAL PROBLEMS

Inadequate Space/Equipment

Although being home-based is the most economical way to start a business, there are still some basic requirements. You can't just clean out the hall closet and call it an office. And you may need more than the home telephone and an old college typewriter for equipment. A little bit of history may illuminate this point.

During the Industrial Revolution, factories hired cheap labor to piece together their products. Many of the employees did their work at home, in cramped quarters with insufficient heat and lighting. They were forced to work as fast and as long as they could, as they were paid by the piece. After World War II, a federal law was passed forbidding certain kinds of manufacturing work done in the home.

Recently, however, this law was repealed, because factory and worker conditions have improved considerably. But the law drove home the idea that the home is not equipped to be a workplace . . . unless you make it that way. If you live in a tiny one-bedroom apartment with no garage, it isn't likely that you'll have enough room to set up an office. A busy street with no parking may be an obstacle for businesses that have drive-up customers or that require frequent deliveries.

We will talk about space and equipment requirements in future chapters. Here, it should be pointed out that a business can limp along and "do without" for a while, but it will suffer in the long run. We've heard complaints from so many home-based-business owners about how they waited too long to get a computer; they could have made twice as much money if they had invested in one sooner. Or maybe they tried to fit an office onto a dining-room table and weren't able to cope with the disorganized mess their files had become.

These are important criteria for determining whether you are ready to assume the big responsibility of starting a home-based business that has a good chance of succeeding. Don't cut corners if you'll also cut into your potential profitability.

Separating Professional and Personal Lives

When you drive to the office, it's easy to separate your professional and personal lives. But when office and home are the same, your two lives will almost certainly clash. It takes a superhuman effort to block out distractions like your child clamoring for attention, the dog that's begging to be walked, or the piled-up dirty laundry. At the same time, knowing when to put it all away and get back to your personal life is just as big a challenge.

Once again, how well you organize these two parts of your life depends on how much self-discipline and what organizational skills you have. There are some personality types that won't be able to handle the juggling act. They need that physical division of separate office and home in order to maintain their priorities.

ARE YOU A GOOD CANDIDATE FOR A HOME-BASED BUSINESS?

The following questions may help you decide whether you have the right kind of personality and life-style to be a home-based entrepreneur. Remember, just because you don't answer everything "right," it doesn't mean you should give up the idea of starting a business. This is just a way to help you examine your motives and figure out whether working at home is something you really want to do.

1. Do you find that you work better in the early morning and late afternoon, when no one else is at the office?

2. Can you concentrate on a project whether you're in a restaurant, a hotel room, or by the pool?

3. Do you have to have everything just right—sharpened pencils arranged in a row, fresh-brewed coffee, a neat stack of papers, your chair tilted at the proper angle—before you can begin your work?

4. Would you miss getting response and comments from colleagues or supervisors?

5. Can you rely on your own inner resources for criticism and praise?

6. Can you find a million little errands to take up the hours you've set aside to finish an important project?

7. Is it easy for you to block out the sound of the television and the neighborhood children playing next door? Can you take your home seriously as a place of business?

8. Do you get bored easily?

9. If your neighbor asked you to do some errands for him during the day "while you're home," would you be able to say no?

10. Do you consider the time you spend on the phone valuable, and do you know how to place a time limit on your calls?

11. Do you enjoy doing things alone?

12. Can you manage a dozen different tasks through the course of a day?

Answers

1. **Yes**—if you do your job better when you are alone, you should be able to adapt to working at home.

2. **Yes**—working at home means you have to have high powers of concentration, as well as good adaptability.

3. **No**—if you're a perfectionist about your working environment, watch out. Working at home can be a comfortable, rewarding experience, but it won't be the epitome of streamlined efficiency. You have to be flexible.

4. **No**—no one will be at your house telling you what to do . . . except yourself.

5. **Yes**—inner resources will be your biggest strength in developing a home-based business. The more you can rely on yourself, the more successful you will be.

6. **No**—those little tasks may seem important, but they mask the real projects you may be avoiding for whatever reason.

7. **Yes**—it's crucial to feel that your home-based business is serious. Again, concentration on the job at hand to the exclusion of all else is very important.

8. **No**—don't work at home if you always need to chat with someone, or go out on long lunches, to feel revived.

9. **Yes**—it may happen. If your neighbors see that you're home all day "with nothing to do," they may ask for

favors beyond the call of friendship. You have to have the fortitude to say no.

10. **Yes**—the minutes can tick away while you make (or receive) dozens of unimportant phone calls.

11. **Yes**—you will most likely be working alone and spending a lot of time by yourself. If you don't like that, you won't like having a home-based business.

12. **Yes**—do you notice how some people have a million things to do yet they always get it all done? These people make great home based entrepreneurs.

3

TAKING THE PLUNGE

PLANNING MAKES YOUR TRANSITION EASIER

PREPARE THYSELF

A lot of people talk about "getting away from it all" and starting a business in their home. But how many people actually do it? Thinking about a big step like leaving your job is easy and fun. The realities, however, are a bit harsher.

Once you've typed up that letter of resignation and the guests at your going-away/good-luck party have all left, the enormity of what you are doing will hit like a ton of bricks.

"It's kind of like stepping off a cliff," says Carol, an antiques restorer in Indiana. "No more guaranteed income or benefits or company cars!" Carol accepted voluntary retirement from her job with a coal company to start her own home-based business. She had been restoring antiques as a hobby for ten years, but making it a full-time business was a tough transition. "I wasn't used to doing my own bookkeeping and figuring out taxes," she says.

Starting a home-based business means making a number of important decisions, so preparation is essential. Here are some of the points you need to consider:

- How will you make the transition from your current job to working at home?
- Will you work full-time or part-time from home?
- Where will you work until you are able to set up a home office?
- How much business should you have lined up before you start?
- How much start-up capital do you need to keep you going?

MAKING THE TRANSITION

There are a couple of ways people leave their jobs: They quit, get laid off, or get fired. Being laid off or fired is almost a blessing, because the agony of deciding when to take the plunge isn't relevant. The decision was made for you! However, when you have a good job and are making decent money, you're well liked by everyone in the company, and you're comfortable, the decision can be more difficult.

What's the best time to get started? Here is a simple way to evaluate your circumstances:

Step One: Sit down with a pad and pencil.

Step Two: Examine both your professional and personal lives. Write down each major event in your professional career in chronological order. How often did you change jobs? Has there been any pattern to the positions you've held? Did you like one kind of project more than another? What did you do best?

Step Three: Recall major events in your personal life and write them down. What were the most important? Your marriage? Having children? Buying a house? Write down the year in which each of these events occurred.

Step Four: Look at what you've written. (Your paper should look like a detailed résumé.) You should be able to see a pattern. Did change come easily into your life (indicated by frequent job promotions and new responsibilities)? Does each job last about a year? Two years? Five? Have there been a lot of "circumstances beyond your control," or have you been in complete control of your life's pattern?

Step Five: Now, make a time line for the future. Based on what you have already accomplished, make a chronological list of those goals you'd like to achieve in the next five or ten years, both in your professional and personal lives. This may include having more children, saving a certain amount of money, moving from a condo into a home—and, yes, starting your own home-based business.

Once you see how well the steps fit together and how solidly each one is based on a pattern you have already established, you will have a good idea of just the right time to start a home-based business. In other words, if you go through major changes in your life roughly every two years, then you may want to date your entrance into home-based entrepreneurship two years from your last big change.

This first phase is extremely simplified, however; there are other factors that will guide your decision. For example, if you're an expectant mother, you may want to begin working at home after the baby is born. The company where you currently work may offer anywhere from three to six weeks' unpaid maternity leave (laws vary from state to state), as well as comprehensive medical insurance, which will pay just about all your hospital bills when you have the baby. It would be foolish to leave your job when you still need these benefits.

Some companies may let you work part-time for six to twelve months after the baby is born. Many women take advantage of this, since it provides them with a steady income while allowing them time to adjust.

Another time that many people begin home-based businesses is when they retire. It can be an ideal time to start one, especially for people who have retired early. Many government and city employees, military personnel, and professional athletes retire well before they are sixty-five years old. They still have twenty years or longer in which to start and run a business of their own.

So the time to take the plunge into a home-based business can hinge on either a pattern of major changes in your life or on a one-time circumstance. It may be hard to decide in advance; most likely, the vast majority of home-based businesses are started without much forethought; they just kind of happen. That's fine, too. Just be sure that you give yourself enough time to research the business you want to start and plan how you are going to get started.

FULL-TIME OR PART-TIME?

One of the biggest advantages of starting a home-based business is the control you have over your hours. You can literally choose how many hours you want to put into the business, as well as which hours during the day you will work. This means that you can start part-time and work your way up to full-time . . . or just keep it as a part-time business indefinitely! Millions of people work from their homes for just ten or fifteen hours a week.

Mothers or fathers with young children often start their businesses on a part-time basis. This way, they can build their businesses slowly and still have time to play with and care for their kids. Melissa started a home-based gift-basket service after the birth of her son five years ago. She wanted something creative but extremely flexible, so that she could be with her son. "I could make five baskets a day, or ten, whatever I wanted," she says. "I, not my customers, controlled the output."

Starting a part-time home-based business may also be the result of your deciding to hang on to your day job a little while longer. Giving up a steady paycheck cold turkey before you have built up an adequate clientele can be a lot like jumping out of an airplane without checking to see if your parachute is intact. Most people just don't want to take the risk. You can run your home-based business on evenings and weekends. When it starts making enough money for you to live on, you will then have the option of quitting your job and expanding your business to a full-time operation.

With plum advantages like extra flexibility and bringing home a steady paycheck, is there any reason to start out as a full-time home-based business? Yes, most definitely. For one thing, trying to get your business going while holding down a full-time job is very difficult. You often feel like there aren't enough hours in the day, and you could experience burnout. Also, some businesses take off from the very beginning, leaving the owners little choice but to work long hours to keep up. A woman in Northern California wasn't allowed to start slowly. She designed a "whodunit" computer game, showed it to a computer retailer, and before she knew it, she was staying up half the night with her husband to fulfill all the orders they received.

Of course, we'd all like to have problems like that, wouldn't we? Nevertheless, starting full-time too fast also has potential dangers—not enough manpower, a crippled cash flow, disorganized bookkeeping—that can stop a business almost before it's started.

How you should start your home-based business depends on your individual situation. Are you in between jobs or retired, with nothing to do? Do you have enough savings or capital to keep you afloat for the next six months? Are you convinced that your product or service will be an instant winner on the market? If so, you may want to jump in full-time right away. Start more slowly if you are just testing the market, if you have big expenses to meet (such as a mortgage, car payments, child support, etc.), or if you don't feel ready to give up your job yet.

WHERE TO WORK AT HOME

One of the most important considerations in starting a home-based business is space. You have to have adequate space to work in, where you are comfortable and have enough room to set up a typewriter, store files, and keep the books. This may be your garage, the spare bedroom, the attic, or a portion of the dining room. If you're starting on a shoestring, you may have to make do with less than ideal arrangements. Until you have a chance (and the money!) to fix up your home office the way you want it, try to make your temporary work space as livable as possible.

John, an interior designer in New York, started his business at the dining-room table until he was able to turn one of his bedrooms into an office. "It was embarrassing to have such a humble place to work when I was trying to sell my clients on redesigning their homes or offices," he laughs. "In a business like mine, you have to practice what you preach." Fortunately, John's new office was completed soon after he started his business, and he uses it as a showroom for new accounts, designing home-based office space.

Not everyone is able to realize his or her dream home office so quickly (or elaborately), however. You may be working in a "temporary" office for a year or more. That's why it's important to make it as efficient and comfortable as possible. If your dining-room table is the only space you have, then get to work. Plan where you will eat your meals (the kitchen table? the opposite end of the dining room table?). Make sure you have enough light: If there isn't an overhead light, try placing a study lamp behind you. And, of course, you'll need enough electrical outlets to handle the typewriter, computer, and any other necessary equipment.

If you plan to use the garage, you'll need a little extra preparation. For one thing, it probably has inadequate lighting and no heat. Also, you'll have to devise some kind of work space, whether it's an old desk from the attic or a plywood carpenter's workbench built into a corner.

In other words, you can start your business before you get the office of your dreams, but you still have to put some thought and preparation into it. Trying to conduct business on the kitchen counter or spreading papers in every room of the house will not allow you to stay organized or grow in the right direction. Treat your temporary office as if it were permanent!

STAYING AFLOAT

You may have your desk ready to go, a fresh cartridge in the typewriter, and a spanking-new set of business cards . . . but where are the customers?

The home-based entrepreneur who continues to work in the same field as the job he or she left usually lines up a few projects in advance. But those who are starting a new line of work are often unsure of how much work they should have to get started . . . and where they can find it.

The answer to the first part of the question differs from business to business. Ideally, you should have enough work lined up for the next two to three months. For businesses that have long-term projects such as landscaping, child care, or event planning, then six months' worth of work should be about right.

Get the word out among your friends and business associates that you are starting a home-based business and are looking for projects. At the beginning, the best way to get business is through word-of-mouth referrals. Pin your business card on the bulletin board in your local supermarket; take out a small ad in your local advertising-supported free newspaper (such as the *Pennysaver*).

MONEY IN THE BANK

Having enough money to cover your expenses while you build up your business is important. If you don't have enough money to live on until you are making enough money from the business, you'll find yourself scrambling to make ends meet. You could spend so much time worrying about paying the bills, you won't have enough energy left to work on your business.

But how much is enough? Ideally, you should have enough reserve capital to cover your expenses for a year, even if you don't make any money from your business during that time. It's easy to figure out how much that would be: Simply write down all of your monthly obligations, such as rent, insurance, bills, groceries, and gas, as well as a miscellaneous fund for variable expenses like entertainment, car maintenance and repair, clothing, gifts, travel, etc. Multiply the number by twelve, and you have your capital requirement for the year.

The best way to get this money is to save it yourself. Set up a fund earmarked for home-based business and put aside a certain amount from every paycheck. It's a good idea to open a business checking account early; that way, you can keep your start-up fund separate from your personal account, and by the time you have officially started your business, you will already have a good relationship with your bank. You will need your dba (doing business as . . .) filing and your business license to open a business account. Once your dba filing is published in the newspaper (in the same county as your bank), the bank will want to see it as "proof of publication."

Of course, many people have started their home-based businesses with a less than ideal nest egg. For them, testing their idea as soon as possible was worth taking the risk of not having enough capital. Laura, a greeting-card designer, started her business with not much more than the next month's rent and a few hundred dollars extra for incidentals.

"I knew I was taking a big chance," she says, "but so many people were asking for my cards, I thought I could sell enough along the way to keep my business going." Laura has been able to get by, selling her cards at small shows and a local bookshop, while she works on finding investors to help her expand.

Some lucky individuals have spouses or family members who are willing to subsidize their business efforts. Rent, food, and monthly bills are taken care of, as are business expenses, until they start making money. This is great, if you can swing it. You can offer compensation, either in the form of an interest in the business or by treating the money as a loan, which you will pay back with interest.

THE BETTER THE PLAN, THE BETTER THE PLUNGE!

Home-based business is looked at by many as a fly-by-night, better-than-nothing enterprise. This is far from the truth, especially these days, but a good way to make sure your home-based business gets off to the right start is planning:

- Plan a time line for when you'd like to open your business. Give yourself deadlines: By the end of Week One, you will have a clear idea of the kind of business you will run; by Week Four, you will have finished your market research and checked out the competition; by Week Six, you will have completed a business plan, and so on.

- Plan how many hours a week you'd like to work, as well as what times and which days. If you plan this in advance, you will feel like you have more of a commitment to the business.

- Plan for the space in which you will work, even if it's only temporary. Make a list of the essential equipment you'll need to buy, rearrange the furniture, get a new telephone jack installed, etc.

- Plan ahead by lining up a few projects *before* you quit your job. Remember to give your clients a realistic deadline; it may take you a little longer to complete a project at first when you are still settling in to your "home environment."

- Plan how much money you will need to save before opening your business. Develop a new budget that allocates a certain amount each month for your home-based-business fund. Get a business checking account opened as soon as possible.

Most people find that the more planning they put into a project, the fewer unforeseen problems they have later on. The same holds true for starting a home-based business. Good planning gives credence to a business and helps you make better decisions on where you want the business to go. Putting everything on paper will keep you organized and will motivate you to achieve each project and goal you've written down.

Taking the plunge into a home-based business can be a scary, exhilarating experience. But some of the fear can be taken out of the experience if you use some proactive strategies such as research, planning, and lining up some projects in advance.

Like any entrepreneurial endeavor, starting a home-based business involves risk. No matter how much you plan, you are always vulnerable to obstacles and problems along the way. The object is to take as much risk out of the enterprise as you can and to work intelligently with the problems you didn't anticipate.

4

PREPARING YOUR FAMILY

GAIN THE SUPPORT OF YOUR LOVED ONES FROM THE START

THE ANNOUNCEMENT

The cry "Hi, honey, I'm home," will take on a whole new meaning in your household when you announce to the family that you plan to start your own home-based business. You will see quickly that making the decision to work out of your home not only involves you but also your entire family.

When Peter told his wife he was leaving his $100,000-a-year job with an insurance company to start a consulting business out of their home, she was shocked—and afraid. "We had grown accustomed to a certain standard of living that my wife knew she couldn't afford on her own salary," he explains. "She wanted to support my decision, but she was also concerned about the future, especially where our kids were concerned."

This is a common problem when one of the breadwinners in a family decides to "throw it all away on an entrepreneurial whim." Preparing your family for such a

36

big change in the way you earn your living can either be relatively easy . . . or an arduous, ongoing process.

ANXIETY RUNS RAMPANT

In a society like ours, where the way you earn your living is just as important as how much money you make, leaving a steady, well-paying job to start a home-based business is often seen as utter insanity. Your family can be the most supportive people in your life, yet they will also be the most vulnerable to anxiety. Your spouse may wonder how much thought and preparation you've put into your decision. Your parents may wonder if it's just an excuse to get out of holding down a "real job." And your kids may have a hard time understanding what you will be doing and how you are going to make money.

In a classic episode of *The Dick Van Dyke Show*, Rob Petrie discovers that his son, Richie, is supposed to bring his father to class to describe what he does for a living. Richie hasn't said anything about it. When Rob asks Richie why he's been silent, Richie tearfully says he is embarrassed because his dad doesn't have a job like other dads. He's afraid his friends will laugh. Rob is a comedy writer for a television show; all of Richie's friends have fathers in real estate, insurance, or other more predictable and "safe" occupations.

Your children may be similarly confused and upset when you leave your job to start a business at home. Although they will welcome the fact that you will be at home more often, they may worry about how you will make money or how it will look to their friends. They need to be prepared. This is a big change both for you and for them.

A spouse may experience the same doubt and worry, but he or she may also have feelings of resentment. Your spouse may need reassurance that you are committed to your new business and that you will continue to share in the household, as well as the financial, responsibilities.

THE EXPLANATION

Chances are your family has been hearing of your plans to start a home-based business for some time now. Even so, the reality is an entirely different matter. You are going to leave your job, your "other life" of commuting, office politics, and steady paychecks for a telephone and Rolodex file on the kitchen table. How do you explain it?

Once again, advance planning is just the ticket. If you have all the details worked out and written down, you will indicate to your family that you are in control of the situation and know what you are doing.

The next step is to gather everyone for a family meeting. Armed with your business plan and time line, start explaining.

Accentuate the Positive

There are a lot of advantages your family will enjoy with you as a home-based entrepreneur. It's up to you to point them out:

- You will be home now for most of the day! You will be there when your children come home from school; you can schedule an afternoon off for a Little League game, parent/teacher day, or to take the whole gang to a matinee. Even when you are working, your family can appreciate your presence at home.
- You will no longer be so frazzled from freeway traffic or congested trains that you come home seething and ready to yell at anyone who gets in your way. By working at home, the tremendous stress of a daily commute is virtually eliminated, leaving you much more time and energy to spend on your family.
- Your family will have the advantage of seeing what you do for a living. They can participate indirectly in your day-to-day operations—the kind of mail you get, how much time you spend on the phone or at the computer, and the kind of reports and correspondence that come out of your printer.
- You will be happier at home, doing what you enjoy, working the hours you want to work. The advantages to your family here are obvious—a happy spouse/parent means a happier, more peaceful home life.

After describing what kind of business you plan to run, and the advantages that working at home will give to your family, ask them if they have any questions or problems. Answer them as clearly as you can, but be honest as well; if you don't know the answer, say so. Emphasize that you are counting on their help and encouragement to keep you going through the rough spots.

In other words, give 'em your best pep talk!

WORKING OUT NEW SCHEDULES

One of the biggest battles ahead of you is convincing everyone that you are *not* at their beck and call. Just because you will be at home all day doesn't mean you have nothing to do but run your family's and neighbors' errands. A new chore schedule should be worked out in advance so that everyone knows what is expected of them.

- It will probably be easier for you to pick up the children from school or day care. You may also offer to assume more of the cooking responsibilities. In return, your family can clear the table and do the dishes, as well as a few extra chores on weekends when you want to get some extra work done. You may agree to walk the dog if someone else is responsible for feeding it. Try to give most of the evening and weekend chores to others and retain the morning or daytime chores for yourself.

- If your children get home from school at two o'clock and you wish to work until four, schedule that time as outdoor playtime or quiet indoor play. Tell them you should be interrupted only in emergencies, especially if you are with a client. Once you "leave" the office, remember to schedule free time with the kids. "If my kids know that Dad is working until three o'clock but they also know he is free to horseplay after that, they respect the rules," says one home-based businessperson.

The tricky part of juggling a schedule is managing errands. These can be anything from picking up the dry cleaning to chauffeuring the kids to cheerleading practice, paying bills in person, or going to the bank. To further complicate matters, neighbors may start asking you to take their clothes to the cleaners "while you're at it."

While it's true that you have more mobility and flexibility by working at home, it is not true that you have more time. Your deadlines are just as important as anyone else's. You won't make your business a success if you spend your days running around town. Tell people politely but firmly that you do not have the time.

As far as your family's errands are concerned, you shouldn't be expected to do them all. One possibility is to limit your errands to the places that close early, such as the bank and the post office. Leave the video returns, milk runs, and fill-ups to your commuting spouse. Take turns with other parents chauffeuring the kids to school and sporting events. It's better to have a longer trip once a week than short trips five days a week.

If you write down all of the events and errands that are a regular part of your routine, you can delegate them equally and with a minimum of confusion. Make a colorful chart, color-coding all of the chores according to the person responsible for them—yours in red, your spouse's in blue, and so on. Hang it up in the kitchen or family room for everyone to see. The spirit of cooperation will make your family more aware that there is a business in their midst and that you can't run it properly without their help. (For more tips on scheduling and family conflicts, see chapter 18.)

ANTICIPATING PROBLEMS

In chapter 21, we discuss in more detail how family considerations will affect your home-based business. Here, let us just touch upon some of the problems you may face in the future and ways to alleviate or eliminate them before they get serious.

- Confusion. Your kids do not know what working at home means. All they know is what they see around them, and chances are most of their friends' parents do not work at home. If you don't set a precedent about interruptions right away, it will be hard to correct your kids' behavior in the future.

- Anxiety. Your kids will worry about you even if they don't say anything. They may feel you have failed in the "real world," and that's why you've come home. Or they may worry that your new venture won't fly.
- Resentment. Both spouse and children may resent the changes in the household. They may feel frustrated because you are at home yet inaccessible. They may also resent clients' walking in and out, having to be quiet, and not being able to visit you in your office.

Your children will have the unique experience of not only seeing you as a parent but also as a professional running a business. They will be excited but also confused—which person is their parent? Sometimes, verbal explanations aren't enough.

That's why many parents try to show their children what they do. For example, they may give them a project, such as fitting letters into envelopes, and explain why they are sending letters to these people. Or if their work is more visual, such as furniture refinishing, graphic arts, or landscaping, they may allow their children to watch them work. Children can grasp ideas much better if they see something with their own eyes.

Once you've established when and where you are going to work, stick to the plan and see that everyone else does too. Your children will naturally test your boundaries to see how far they can go. If you relax your "no-interruptions" rule in the beginning, it will be difficult to enforce later on.

Make sure your children (and your spouse) know they can come to you at any time if they are worried or upset about something. Encourage them to ask questions about your work, and share with them your successes. Judy, an interior designer, says her family worried when she went for a few months without any large projects. "They didn't say anything, but I knew they thought my business was going under," she says. "I wasn't worried, because I know my business has a lot of ups and downs; they didn't know that." Soon afterward, Judy won a large project redesigning a chain of restaurants; that evening, she brought home some sparkling cider and a huge smoked turkey to celebrate. "When they saw how confident I was," she says, "they realized that I had everything under control and they stopped worrying so much."

Your family may be so excited to have you at home, they will "forget" you are running a business. Then, when they see you shut the door or talking to your clients all day and "ignoring" them, they may resent the work that is taking you away. Some of this resentment may be alleviated by the initial family meeting, but it won't stop there. You need to keep reinforcing the reasons why you are working at home, why you need quiet and privacy, and why you are not always available to your family. Remember, it's going to take some time for everyone to adjust, so be patient.

A GROUP EFFORT

Your home-based business should be a growing experience for you and your family. They, too, can learn what it's like to run a business by watching and helping you. So to prepare your family, you should also discuss what part each of them will play in your new entrepreneurial adventure.

Your spouse will play a crucial role in the success of your business. Every day, he or she will be your live-in consultant, discussing with you every aspect of the business, from your letterhead design to setting up your bookkeeping system. You will rely on your spouse for support, to encourage you during the rough spots, and to congratulate you for your successes.

Your spouse will need to know that he or she is an important part of your business whether you are legal business partners or not. After all, you are already legal partners, right? Emphasize how much you value your spouse's opinions and suggestions on how to improve the business. Use his or her knowledge to help you incorporate the business, formulate a business plan, conduct research, design business cards, and so on. Think about the future, when your business grows so big, you may want to "make it legal" by signing your spouse on as vice-president. The move involved your spouse has been with the business over the years, the more committed he or she will be to helping you make it work.

Your kids should also become involved. They too, want to know what you do all day and to feel that they are an important part of your professional life. Here are some suggestions for making them a part of the group effort:

- Promise them they can help you out with projects from time to time. These can be anything from stuffing envelopes to helping you clean your office after work or even letting them choose which suit you should wear to an important client meeting. It doesn't have to be something big—just enough so that they feel they are helping you run the business.
- If you have an older child, ask for his or her help in minding the younger children while you are working. Pay him an hourly wage, and emphasize his contribution to the family. Make sure that this arrangement is acceptable to everyone; the younger kids may resent being "bossed around" by their older sibling. Or maybe big sister has better things to do than baby-sit.
- If you're driving around running errands, bring your kids with you. They can drop off packages, pick up printing jobs, and help you load supplies into the trunk. They'll just enjoy being with you during the day, when you are usually too busy to spend time with them.

Remember that working at home means a big change in your life and in the life of every person in your family. No amount of preparation is going to solve every issue that will come up in the first year. You are going to make mistakes; some of the things you thought might happen won't, and many unexpected problems will.

But this doesn't mean that preparing your family is an exercise in futility. Try to help them understand why you are starting your own business, how you will start it, what you will be doing, and how they fit into the picture. Even if you don't know all the variables in advance, you do know a certain number of givens:

- you will rely on their love and support;
- you count on them to tell you when something is bothering them;
- you know that they will respect the hours when you need to work;
- the more involved they are with your business, the better;
- the more they understand what you do, the less anxious they will be;
- you are still a (husband/wife/father/mother) no matter what happens.

If you keep these points in mind, you will be able to give the right message to your family, excite them about your new business, and motivate them to help you in any way they can. Once you have the support of your family, you can work wonders.

5

CHOOSING A BUSINESS

YOU CAN FIND THE PERFECT MATCH FOR YOUR SKILLS AND AMBITIONS

Maybe you're sold on working at home and you're willing to accept the risks and responsibilities of starting your own business. Now comes the big question: What kind of business is right for you? Thoughts of service, manufacturing, consulting, and free-lance work are rolling through your head, but you're not really sure which is the right type of business for you. Entrepreneurship can mean opening the door to success, but it can also spell disaster if you try to start a business that doesn't suit your personality, experience, or financial ability.

Let's say you're a very shy person who isn't comfortable meeting new people but you've always fancied the idea of becoming an image consultant. Before setting up shop, you should realize that spending your day as an image consultant means working closely with your clients—and presenting a confident and outgoing personality. If you aren't comfortable saying, "This color isn't right for you," or "You should avoid double-breasted suits; they aren't flattering to your figure," then you are going to have problems.

On the other hand, what if you're a real "people person" and thrive on personal contact? If you start a business that keeps you isolated at home, you will probably go crazy. This may sound like common sense—and it is. But each year, thousands of people start businesses that simply don't suit their personality.

Starting the wrong home-based business may cause a number of problems. Losing your investment by going out of business is the greatest risk you run as a new entrepreneur. If you start a business and discover three months later that you despise what you are doing, you won't be very enthusiastic or energetic about succeeding. According to Roderick Crandall, Ph.D., if you start a business that isn't right for you, "you may end up dragging yourself to work or even worse, sabotaging your success. Some people [succeed at businesses they don't enjoy], but it's terribly difficult." Crandall, who is executive director of the Community Entrepreneurs Organization, a San Rafael, California-based networking and support group for entrepreneurs, has counseled hundreds of future entrepreneurs on finding the right business.

A great product or service does not guarantee business success. "The person is really the key, not the business," says Gus Berle, formerly marketing director at the Service Corps of Retired Executives (SCORE), a Washington, D.C.-based volunteer organization of former executives who offer their advice and expertise to small business owners free. Even if you have the best product around, it simply won't sell if you have the wrong attitude.

If you don't believe in your business and can't commit yourself wholeheartedly to promoting it and making it work, your chances of survival are slim. In fact, you may lose your investment. You could find yourself with stacks of inventory that you'll have to liquidate. You could lose your life savings or even find yourself with a $100,000 bank loan and no revenues with which to pay it back.

Not only do you risk losing your investment, you also

risk losing your own happiness and self-confidence. Most people want to start their own business because they're dissatisfied with what they're doing. What a waste to go to all that trouble and then find that you still hate what you're doing.

You can avoid this disaster. Before you sink any money into a new business venture, you should do some serious soul searching to determine what your interests are and which type of business would best suit your abilities and character. Unfortunately, there is no quiz that will tell you whether or not a computer-consulting service or a gift-basket service is the business that will make you successful. However, taking an honest look at your own personality and background will at least steer you in the right direction.

THE PERSONALITY TEST

Businesses are as varied and unique as the people who run them. If you have the entrepreneurial bug, it doesn't matter whether you are outgoing or bookish, aggressive or laid back; there is a business for you. However, in order to succeed, there are a couple of personality traits that every entrepreneur needs—for instance, persistence and drive. Without the determination to succeed despite adversity, you won't go far.

You also have to know what you want to succeed at. Simply wanting to be an entrepreneur isn't enough; you have to know what kind of business you want to go into. Crandall says many potential entrepreneurs seek his advice because they don't have any idea of what sort of business they would like to start. "Often, they end up researching a dozen fields and wasting a lot of time. Learning everything about eight different industries is nearly impossible," he notes.

"If someone doesn't know what business to go into, I tell them to look at the things they like to do in their free time," Crandall adds. "Usually, this will give them a picture of where their interests lie."

It's really very simple. For example, if you love to cook, then a business that involves food might be appropriate.

But what kind of business? A brownie mail-order service? A catering company? A wholesale pie company? A gourmet-meal-preparation service? Cooking classes? There are a whole range of possibilities, each one involving a different focus and different creative talents. How do you know which one would be best?

Your personality can help you determine which type of business would be best for you. Are you a perfectionist? Do you like working with your hands? Do you love the outdoors, or do you prefer an office environment? Are you a good writer? Do you like meeting new people? Are you a born salesperson? Your answers to questions like these will help you make your choice.

For example, if you enjoy the outdoors and like meeting new people, then organizing bicycle tours may be the business for you. If you are a natural seller, then perhaps you might start your own advertising-sales office.

Once you've narrowed down what you enjoy doing, then what? This is where your background and experience come into play. If you have had courses in photography and enjoy wandering around your community taking pictures and developing them in your own darkroom, then you should turn your interest and skills into a business.

On the other hand, suppose you think that starting a newsletter would be fun but you have no writing or publishing experience. Should you go ahead with a desktop-publishing business anyway? Yes—and no. While you might succeed in publishing with no prior experience, it might be wiser to gain some background first.

There are a number of ways to make yourself an expert. Berle cites just a few of the ways a determined individual can tackle a new subject. No matter which field piques your interest, numerous books on the matter can probably enlighten you. But reading books isn't enough. "Contact people in the business and ask them for advice," Berle says. This way, you'll get the real story on what it's like to run the business. You'll hear about the late nights, the bounced checks, the busy and slow seasons, etc.

In addition to just talking with business owners about their work, go a step further. Try to get a firsthand look at the business yourself. You can either arrange to visit someone who has started a similar business at home or do some free-lance work for a company in your industry. After seeing for yourself the way the business works, you'll get a better feeling for what you're getting yourself into.

There is no substitute for on-the-job training. If you don't have any experience in your field of interest, then get some. That's the bottom line.

CHOOSE YOUR INDUSTRY

Most home-based businesses fall into either the service, retail, or manufacturing industries. Service businesses are probably in the majority. However, Barbara Brabec, a home-based-business consultant and publisher of the *National Home Business Report* newsletter in Naperville, Illinois, says that most of the businesses she works with are product-oriented, particularly crafts and book/newsletter publishing.

In a service-oriented business, you are providing a service, not a product. Plan on a lot of contact with your clients, in addition to conducting a lot of marketing. Taking care of your clients and smoothing over any potential problems are essential for the owner of a service business.

Brenda found her niche in a service business: She is founder and president of a home-based nanny-placement service. Brenda had worked for a major airline as a recruiter for several years, and the interviewing skills she learned there have come in handy when she matches up families with nannies.

Brenda thinks her business is perfectly suited to her past experience and her interests. "My interest was in quality child care. And with my background in personnel, the nanny-placement service was just right for me," she says.

This successful entrepreneur thinks that everyone can find a business that suits his or her personality. "Everyone has some strength," she contends. "Look within to find your interests, and you'll discover something you would enjoy doing."

The retail industry is not normally associated with a home-based business in the classic sense, i.e., a storefront that displays and sells retail goods. But some home-based businesses are based on sales—selling advertising space, food, business opportunities, or brokering transportation, even writing books or a newsletter. All of these businesses involve selling a product to the public or business community. Sales is a satisfying, challenging, and often lucrative business. It is also difficult, stressful, and volatile. More than for any other occupation, you need a special personality—outgoing, resilient, confident, intuitive, and patient—to be a successful salesperson.

Of course, any business you choose will involve selling to some extent. But a business based on sales means you are constantly on the telephone, giving presentations and entertaining clients, trying to sell your product, day after day. If you don't have the "sales personality," you are going to get burned out fast.

Morton, a food broker in New Jersey, had about twenty years' experience in sales with big brokerage companies before starting out on his own. "I knew I was good at it," he says, "and I had the contacts in the industry. It didn't make any sense to start a business totally different from everything I knew." People do, of course, and are often successful; but it takes a certain type of person to really get out there and sell.

If you are more comfortable producing something tangible—something with your own hands—then manufacturing may be the industry for you. Manufacturing covers everything from the smallest craft to space-shuttle assembly (although we don't know of any home-based aeronautic businesses). Thousands of people are making everything from Christmas ornaments to quilts, art and sculpture, rocking chairs, children's clothing, toys, draperies, paper goods, wedding apparel, and glassware. They enjoy what they do and are happy to be making money at it.

Manufacturing also has some special requirements. For one thing, it is often more costly to start a manufacturing business, since you need to invest in materials and machinery. You may also need more hired help to fulfill large orders. All of this adds considerably to your initial investment and your monthly overhead costs.

Also, remember that making the same thing over and over again can get tedious unless you are wholeheartedly committed to your craft. Consider what happened to Thom, a college student who started a diploma-framing business from his apartment a few years ago. He didn't particularly enjoy gluing wood pieces together and cutting glass to fit inside, but he couldn't afford to contract out the work or hire anyone to help him. The frames were very popular, and the student store was even interested in ordering several hundred units . . . but Thom lost interest. He delivered fewer frames than the store had ordered, and many of the frames were poorly made and were returned to him. He simply wasn't equal to the detail work and the patience involved in getting a manufacturing business off the ground.

THE TIME FACTOR

To some extent, the amount of time you are willing to commit to your new venture will dictate the type of business you start. Most people who hope to spend only a portion of their day working choose some sort of service business they can run on a part-time basis. And in general, it's much easier to make your own hours when you operate a home-based business.

Remember, though, that the less time you spend working, the less money you can potentially make. Even if you don't base your fees on an hourly schedule, more hours usually translate into more income. Let's say you are a wedding consultant and you only want to work twenty hours a week. You figure that each wedding takes about forty hours to plan and execute; therefore, you will be able to do two weddings a month and would net $2,000 in fees. If you had worked full-time, you might have earned $4,000.

If you are starting a home-based business to cut down on the grueling schedule you had as a corporate executive, then be realistic about the kind of business you can run and the income you expect to derive from it. For instance, a day-care center has to be open a certain number of hours in order to attract working parents. If you don't know how many hours of work are required for the business you are interested in, make sure you find out from someone who does know.

THE DOLLARS AND CENTS OF IT ALL

Once you know where your interests lie and how much time you are willing to devote to your business, you may think you're home free. Wait, though—there's one more thing: money.

Suppose you've decided that a desktop-publishing business is something to which you're willing to devote all your time and energy. You love writing, you've had some copyediting and production experience, and your neighbor's law firm wants to hire you to produce its employee newsletter. A business made in heaven, right?

Hold on! There is one final hurdle you'll have to surmount before becoming the proud owner of a desktop-publishing business—money. The all-important question is, Do you have enough money to invest in the computer equipment you will need? Producing a newsletter requires at least several thousand dollars' worth of computer equipment, software, accessories, and paper goods.

Your dream may be shattered when you see the price tag of all of this equipment and then contemplate your slim savings account. So if you have little to invest other than your time and enthusiasm, you'll either have to borrow the money or consider a business that's less costly to start.

BEING A ROUND PEG IN A ROUND HOLD

When you are deciding what kind of business would be best for you, take the time to write down everything you want out of your business and the skills you will contribute. The list might look like this:

- All of your previous jobs: What were your responsibilities, where were your strengths and weaknesses, and how long did you stay at each one?

- Any businesses you have owned or operated in the past: Were they successful? What did you like and dislike about them? Did they fail? Why?
- Your family: What does your spouse do? What kind of hours does he/she work? How do you spend personal time together? What are his/her hobbies and interests? How many children do you have? What kind of personalities and temperaments do they have? Are they in school?
- Your personal interests: What are your hobbies, special talents, hidden skills?
- Your own personality: What do you like to do? How do you react in emotional or emergency situations? Are you attentive, social, creative, methodical, irritable, sensitive? Think of all the adjectives that best capture your personality.
- Your goals: What do you hope to accomplish within the year? Within five to ten years?
- How much time do you want to invest in a home-based business?
- How much money do you want to make from a home-based business?

If you think of any other facets of your life that may shed some light on choosing the right business, include them in your list. Your political or religious beliefs, for example, may be important influences. Or you may have a physical limitation that will affect your choices.

YOU WON'T SELL MUCH ICE IN ALASKA

The most exciting, most suitable business in the world won't be a business for very long if you are selling something that isn't needed or wanted by your potential customers. This may sound obvious, but many businesses have foundered because of inadequate market research. Don't just hope that customers will love your business—find out for sure.

You must gather as much information as you can in advance to really know which kinds of businesses have a fighting chance in your area. Know the demographics of people in your area—age, income, blue collar or professionals, family and marital status—as well as general life-style trends. Is your area a bedroom community for a large city? Is it mostly rural farms and cottages or "yuppie" condominiums? Are there a lot of elderly retirees? Recent immigrants? College students? Do you live in a ski-resort area that empties out in the summer?

Once you have a general idea of who your target market is and what their special needs might be, then make a list of the products or services that would interest them. After that, drive around or look in the Yellow Pages and determine how many companies are already fulfilling that need and whether there's room in the market for you.

If you start a mail-order business, your customer base won't necessarily be limited to people in your area. But before you crank out five thousand hand-painted scarves, you still need to test the market first. Start small, with a local crafts show or swap meet, and see what kind of people stop to buy. Ask them for their comments on the design, fabric, selection, price, etc. Find out if they are buying the scarf for themselves or as a gift. Some mail-order hopefuls take out a small ad describing their product and analyze the number and type of orders that come in. If the scarves sell well to the working woman thirty-five years old and up, you will be able to tailor your mailing list specifically to this market.

STATE YOUR BUSINESS

In chapter 27, we've outlined twenty-one businesses that work as home-based businesses. Most of them are service oriented and don't require a lot of start-up capital. They rely heavily on your own ingenuity and "elbow grease."

But the list doesn't stop there. You may be able to think of dozens of other successful home-based businesses we didn't mention. When you have narrowed your choice down to two or three, remember all the factors you should consider:

- personality
- life-style

- family
- strengths and weaknesses
- work experience
- industry (service, sales, or manufacturing)
- number of hours
- expected income
- market research

You might feel there are a number of possible businesses that would be right for you! Unfortunately, you can only choose one. The more preparation and thought you put into your choice, the better the chance you will succeed. Remember, you will be the most important asset to your business, so make sure you choose something you will be good at and will enjoy doing for a long time to come.

II

SETTING UP SHOP

6

OWNER, PARTNER, CORPORATION

CHOOSING THE LEGAL FORM OF YOUR HOME-BASED BUSINESS

E ven if your new home-based business is going to be modest, now is a good time to start thinking about legalities. Should you incorporate? Are you starting the business with a partner? What changes will you need to make if the business expands?

Right now, forming a corporation or drawing up a detailed partnership agreement may seem unnecessarily formal—after all, you may have little more than a desk and chair to work with. Still, ironing out legal details early on will save you the hassle of reorganizing later—and it may prevent you from making costly mistakes.

Before we get started, though, let us recommend that you consult an attorney. In this chapter, we offer some basic information that will prepare you for discussing matters with your attorney. But the information here is not a substitute for the advice of a qualified attorney. Your attorney can help you choose the best form for your particular needs. He or she can also help you comply with any local regulations or ordinances.

In the following pages, we discuss five different types of businesses: sole proprietorships, general partnerships, limited partnerships, corporations, and subchapter S corporations. Each has its own benefits and costs. Among the considerations you may be taking into account: tax savings, liability, cost, and the number of people involved in your business. Again, your lawyer can help you determine what's best for you.

SOLE PROPRIETORSHIP

The simplest and most common form for the home-based business is the sole proprietorship. If you are the sole owner of your business, you automatically end up as sole proprietor if you do not establish yourself in another structure. If you operate using any name other than your own, you will have to file a fictitious business name statement in your local paper. This puts the public on notice that you are the owner of that business. The only other steps you must take are to secure a business license and apply for federal and state payroll ID numbers. (The federal employer identification number is secured by filing a form SS-4 with the Internal Revenue Service.)

As a sole proprietor, you will use Schedule C on income tax Form 1040 to report your income or loss. You will also be required to pay self-employment tax. This tax should be paid in quarterly installments, along with your income taxes, using form 1040ES.

As a sole proprietor, your personal assets are subject to any legal liabilities you might encounter while operating the business. Therefore, to guard against potential lawsuits from your customers, you should secure general liability insurance.

GENERAL PARTNERSHIP

If you're starting your business with other people, you may operate as a general partnership. Partnerships exist through oral or written agreement. However, it's wise to put your terms in writing. That way, each partner knows what he or she is responsible for. And you will have a plan of action in case the partnership does not work out.

Before you enter into a general partnership agreement with anyone—including friends and family members— make sure you're confident in your partners' honesty and business ability. Unless you stipulate otherwise, any partner in a general partnership may legally bind the partnership in a contract. Each partner is liable for any and all partnership debts. That means that a creditor can collect amounts due from the individual personal assets of any partner.

Each partner will report his or her share of the partnership's income each year on form 1040. Generally, all partnerships must operate using a calendar year and file form 1065 with the IRS reporting partnership income and expenses. That form includes form H-1, which reports each partner's share of the income or loss.

Like a sole proprietorship, a general partnership is subject to unlimited liability. To that end, it is wise to secure good liability insurance for the partnership and partners. General partnerships operating under fictitious names must file fictitious business-name statements.

A good general-partnership agreement is complex. It should cover all situations that the partners may encounter, and work to resolve any conflicts that may result between them.

Some of the many items that should be covered in a partnership agreement include: capital contribution; profit-and-loss sharing; voting rights; delegation of management authority to partners; disposition of a partner's interest upon death of that person; methods to resolve possible tie votes between partners on a crucial partnership decision; admission of new partners; signature authority and number of signatures on partnership bank accounts; option to purchase a selling partner's interest and a method to determine the purchase price of that interest.

A general partnership, under most state laws, automatically dissolves upon the death of a partner or if more than 50 percent of the partnership interests changes hands. Partnership law is complex. Ask an attorney to review your agreement if you write it yourself, or have your lawyer draw the agreement up for you.

LIMITED PARTNERSHIP

A limited partnership is similar to a general partnership, except that it has two classes of partners. The general partners have full management and control of the business but also accept full personal liability for partnership liabilities. Limited partners have no personal liability beyond their investment in the partnership interest. Limited partners do not participate in the general management or daily operations of the business. Because of size limitations, home-based businesses are rarely formed as limited partnerships.

CORPORATION

Most people associate corporations with big business. Indeed, it may be hard to imagine your new home-based company issuing stock, electing directors, or holding annual meetings. Yet many small companies decide to incorporate for legal or tax reasons. Depending on your field of business, your personal finances, and your long-term goals, you may want to consider taking the corporate plunge—either now or down the road.

You can incorporate your business by filing articles of incorporation with the appropriate state agency. One hitch you might encounter is your company name: Usually, only one corporation in the state may use a given name. Check with your attorney for other specific requirements you will have to meet.

A corporation is not a simple operation. It is a separate legal entity from its shareholders. It issues stock in exchange for cash or other assets transferred to the company. Shareholders elect a board of directors annually, who then meet to guide corporate affairs anywhere from once a month to once a year. Each year, the directors elect a president, vice-president, and other officers to conduct day-to-day operations. Furthermore, directors and shareholders usually adopt bylaws that govern the powers and authority of the directors, officers, and shareholders.

If all this bureaucracy sounds like a major disadvantage, consider the advantages involved in incorporating. Corporations limit the liability of their shareholders. Unlike a partnership, a corporation protects your personal assets. Even if the corporation's business is not successful—or if it is held liable for damages in a lawsuit—the most you can lose is your stock investment. Your personal assets are not on the line for corporate liabilities. If you're going into a business that has a lot of potential liability, incorporating may be the answer for you.

Operating as a corporation may lend your business credibility. In some cases, it may show that you're serious about your business—and even suggest that you're a relatively large company. Another advantage of incorporating is that, as a legal entity, a corporation can outlive you. In the event of your (or your partner's) death, the corporation can live on. The same is true if you or your partner wish to leave the business.

The main disadvantage to incorporating is possible double taxation: You may pay taxes on the corporation's net income and again on the dividends you receive from the company. For this reason, business owners often increase their own salaries in order to reduce or wipe out corporate profits. This lowers the possibility of having those profits taxed twice.

If a corporation is small, the shareholders should sign a buy-sell agreement. This contract provides that if a shareholder dies or desires to sell his or her stock, it must first be offered to the remaining shareholders. It also may provide for a method to determine a fair price for these shares. Such agreements are usually funded with life insurance to purchase the stock of deceased shareholders.

A corporation with only a few shareholders can issue shares without formal Securities and Exchange Commission registration under private offering exemptions.

SUBCHAPTER S CORPORATION

For small and mid-sized companies, subchapter S election is an attractive alternative to the standard corporation. Through subchapter S, the possibility of double federal taxation is virtually eliminated (state tax laws vary: Some states regard subchapter-S corporations as they do regular ones).

A subchapter-S structure allows profits or losses to travel directly through the corporation to you and other shareholders. If you earn other income during the first year and the corporation has a loss, you can deduct that loss against your income.

Subchapter-S corporations elect not to be taxed as corporations. Instead, the shareholders include their portion of the company's profits and losses in their individual gross incomes. If your company produces a substantial profit, you can add those profits to your personal income and be taxed at an individual rate, which may be lower than the regular corporate rate on that income.

To qualify for subchapter S, a corporation must meet the following requirements:

- It must be a domestic corporation.
- It must not be a member of an affiliated group.
- It must not have more than thirty-five shareholders— all of whom are either individuals or estates.
- It must not have a nonresident alien as a shareholder.
- It may only have one class of outstanding stock.

A subchapter-S corporation may have unlimited passive income from rents, royalties, and interest. For details—and to find out about any recent changes in laws governing subchapter-S corporations—call your local IRS office.

FILING A FICTITIOUS-NAME STATEMENT

Sole proprietorships and partnerships have the option of choosing distinctive names for their businesses. If you want to operate under a business name (e.g., Jamie Doe doing business as The Bread Pantry), you may be required by the county, city, or state to register that fictitious name.

Procedures vary. In many states, you need only go to the county office and pay a registration fee to the county clerk. Other states require placing a fictitious-name statement in a local newspaper. Generally, the newspaper that prints will file the necessary papers with the county for a small fee.

The cost of filing a fictitious name notice ranges from $10 to $100. The easiest way to determine the procedure for your area is to call your bank and ask if it requires a fictitious-name registry or certificate in order to open a business account. If so, inquire where you should go to obtain one.

Fictitious-name filings do not apply to corporations in most states unless the corporation is doing business under a name other than its own. Documents of incorporation have the same effect for the corporate business as fictitious-name filings have for sole proprietorships and partnerships.

FINDING A LAWYER

Finding the right lawyer early is a critical task for you. A lawyer who can meet your needs should possess several key qualities. Among the most important are honesty, experience in your field, and availability. Make sure your lawyer can follow through on your problems. If he can't provide his service on time and in good order, at a price consistent with its value, find one who will.

Make certain you understand your attorney's fee schedule. This is the biggest area of misunderstanding between clients and lawyers. Put the agreement in writing. In today's complex business world, you have to be alert to the legal consequences of all your business decisions.

LICENSES AND PERMITS

Basic Business Licenses

Obtaining a license for your business is relatively simple, but it does require some homework. As a rule, home-based businesses have more local regulations to deal with than office- or shop-based companies. Why? Most communities want to keep residential neighborhoods livable. If, for example, you decided to open an all-night pool hall in your garage, your neighbors would have to contend with late-night noise, traffic, lack of parking—all kinds of problems that would make normal family life difficult.

What this means for you, the aspiring home-based business owner, is that you'll have to comply with local ordinances. And to do that, you'll have to figure out what the requirements are. Depending on your business, you may need a variety of permits and licenses. Contact your city's business licensing or planning department for specific regulations in your community.

In most communities, you'll need a home-occupation permit and a business license to conduct business from your home. Fees vary from community to community, but the typical cost for a home permit is about $50; business licenses cost about $100. If a building inspection is required, you will have to pay for it. Even in communities with high fees, the combined cost of these two permits rarely exceeds $500. Once you've paid for these initial licenses, you'll probably have to renew them yearly.

Restrictions vary widely from area to area. Most center around the preservation of the neighborhood's residential atmosphere. Here are a few common regulations:

1. *Noise:* Your neighbors should hear no evidence of work being performed on your premises. Sound restrictions may or may not be expressed in decibel levels, but as a rule, your neighbors should not be disturbed by the sound of your work—whether hammering, pounding, operating machinery, ringing bells, blowing whistles, or tending to barking dogs. Time limits may apply: for instance, no music lessons after 5:00 P.M.

2. *Odor:* Smells should not be wafting from your home-based firm. Again, your neighbors are your chief concern. If you must work with malodorous chemicals in your business, try to find an unobtrusive way of doing so.

3. *Employees:* Your local government will dictate how many employees you may have working in your home. Three employees, other than yourself, seems to be a com-

mon limit. Some communities also restrict employees to residents of the house or to immediate relatives.

4. *Traffic:* Any noticeable increase in car, truck, or pedestrian traffic—including delivery vehicles—may be illegal. Increased vehicle traffic may also violate standards of noise and odor.

5. *Electronic interference:* Running industrial machinery or electronic equipment can readily disrupt your neighbor's right to sit home and enjoy the television or stereo.

6. *Signs:* Some communities allow 9-by-12-inch window signs; others allow signs no larger than a standard real-estate yard board. Worse, some cities have abolished any signage whatsoever. In just about any community, neon or lighted signs are out of the question.

7. *Sales showrooms:* Normally, you may only sell what you make on the premises. Many towns enforce a rule that says you cannot sell at home except by phone or drop shipment.

8. *Odds and ends:* Additional charges may apply for running a consulting business at home. Health codes prohibit cooking or baking in home kitchens. There may be a limit on the number of phone lines you can have installed in your home. Other community-specific regulations probably apply: Check your local government for details.

Note that if your business is established, you may be protected by a grandmother clause, permitting the business practices you have established to continue but restricting any further development of the same business.

City business-license departments are operated as tax-collecting bureaus and do not perform any public service. You simply pay a fee to operate your business in that city. In addition to the license fee, some cities receive a percentage of your gross sales.

When you apply for a license, it will probably be processed through the planning or zoning department. It will check to make sure that the zone covering your property allows the proposed home-based use. You will not be allowed to operate in an area not zoned for your business unless you first have a variance or conditional-use permit.

You are well advised to obtain a license as soon as possible if you're serious about running a business from your home. If you have no customers coming to your door and you have all business correspondence delivered to private postal-box services, chances are that you can operate under a regular license with no problem.

Seller's Permits

With a few exceptions, almost every state has a sales tax. These sales taxes usually are collected from the ultimate user or consumer of a product only. A seller's permit is the license you must secure if you are required to charge your buyers sales tax. If you plan to sell any item retail (to the ultimate consumer), you must get this permit from your local state-sales-tax agency and collect sales tax from all of your customers. To get a permit, you must give the agency financial data and sometimes make a deposit or post a bond against which the state can proceed if you fail to pay the taxes you collect. When you apply for a seller's permit, estimate your sales low. This may reduce the amount of the bond or deposit required.

You will then have to file monthly or quarterly sales-tax returns with the state and turn over the taxes you have collected. Failure to collect and pay sales tax may result in severe penalties and interest. Request an informational pamphlet on sales-tax rules and regulations from your state-tax agency.

Resale Permit

Depending on the state, a resale permit may be the same as the sales-tax permit or is a separate license secured from the state-sales-tax department. A resale permit allows you to purchase goods without paying sales tax. It is used by retailers who collect sales tax from their customers, and by manufacturers and wholesalers who do not sell to end users and therefore do not collect sales tax from their customers.

Buyers must show their resale permit numbers to avoid paying sales tax. If sellers do not get resale numbers from resale customers, they may be obligated to pay the sales tax they should have collected.

Health-Department Permit

Purveying and distributing food requires a county health-department permit. The health department will want to inspect your facilities before issuing the permit. The fee for such a permit will start at about $25, depending on the size of the operation and the quantity of equipment.

Be sure to check with the health department before starting any home-based food-related business. Permits are restricted in many residential areas. This is done to keep commercial kitchens from starting up in quiet suburban areas.

Liquor, Wine, and Beer Licenses

In most states, one type of license is required to serve wine and beer and another to serve hard liquor. A liquor license is difficult to obtain. In some areas, no new liquor licenses are being issued at all—you can only obtain one by buying it from an existing license holder. Although the original licenses cost less than a hundred dollars, competition has forced the going price from two thousand dollars to tens of thousands of dollars, depending on the location.

You are required to have a liquor license if you sell liquor through the mail—for instance, through a home-based gift-basket company. The white pages of your phone directory will have the number for the nearest beverage-control agency, which can supply you with the information you need.

Fire-Department Permit

Many fire departments require your business to obtain a permit if it uses any flammable materials or if your premises will be occupied by the public at large. In some cities, you must secure a permit before you open for business. Other jurisdictions don't require a permit; instead, periodic inspections of the premises are scheduled to see if they meet regulations. If you have not complied with safety regulations, they will issue a citation. Home-based businesses that use super-strength glues or other chemicals may have to notify the local fire department that they are storing possibly toxic materials.

Air- and Water-Pollution-Control Permit

Many cities now supervise the control of air and water pollution. If you burn any material, discharge anything into the sewers or waterways, or use gas-producing products (such as paint sprayers), you may be required to obtain a special permit from this department of your city or county.

Environmental protection regulations may require you to obtain approval before construction or operation. Check with your state agency regarding federal or state regulations that may apply to your business.

Sign Permit

Recently, many cities have instituted sign ordinances that restrict the size, location, and sometimes the lighting and type of sign used. These laws are much more restrictive for the home-based business in the suburbs. To avoid costly mistakes, be sure to check city and county regulations before you buy a sign.

County Permits

Many times, county governments require the same types of permits and licenses that cities require. These apply to commercial enterprises located outside city limits. Educate yourself about county ordinances that apply to your business if you are located outside a city or town's jurisdiction. County regulations often are less strict than those of adjoining cities.

State Licenses

Many states require a license or occupational permit for persons engaged in certain occupations. Often, these persons must pass state examinations before they can conduct business. Licensing is commonly required for the following types of workers: auto mechanics, plumbers, electricians, building contractors, collection agents, insurance agents, real-estate brokers, repossessors, and those providing services to the human body (barbers, cosmetologists, doctors, nurses, etc.). Your state government can provide a complete list of occupations that require licensing in your state.

Federal Licenses

A few trades require federal licensing, including meat processors, common carriers, radio and television stations, and investment advisory services. The Federal Trade Commission can tell you if your business will require a federal license.

ZONING ORDINANCES

If your new business is small and only occupies one room in the house, zoning regulations will probably not be a problem. However, if an existing building—such as a garage—is used for a purpose other than what was originally intended or extensive remodeling is required, local building and zoning codes should be checked carefully. If zoning regulations do not allow the type of business you wish to open, you may file for a zoning variance, a conditional-use permit, or a zone change.

A variance or conditional-use permit grants you the conditional privilege of operating a business on land not zoned for that purpose. The filing fee may be as high as $1,200, and it may take ninety days or more to get a decision. A zone change, on the other hand, is a permanent change in the way a particular area is zoned and, therefore, in the way it will be used long into the future. It involves a lengthy procedure—six months or more—of filing a petition with the city-planning commission, issuing notice, presenting your case at public hearings, and finally getting the city council or other governing body to make a decision.

In some cases, any change in land use—whether permanent (by zone change) or temporary (by variance or conditional-use permit)—will require environmental clearance. Local planning or zoning departments can tell you whether your project is exempt from the law or whether you should seek a negative declaration from its regulations. If your project will displace residents, generate a lot of traffic, or impact natural habitat, some municipalities will require you to prepare an environmental-impact report. This can be a costly and time-consuming procedure for which you will need expert help.

If your request for a zoning variance or change is approved, many restrictions still apply. In addition to meeting local building codes, you will probably be required to observe minimum setbacks at the front, side, and rear of the structure; maximum floor space in relation to land area; maximum heights; minimum provisions for parking; and other factors. We cannot generalize on this subject since each government entity has its own specific policies.

Essentially, zoning is a way of ensuring that the community's land development is sufficiently open to permit light, air, and privacy for persons living and working in the area.

OTHER REGULATIONS

In addition to licenses and permits, other regulations may apply to your business. Federal and state laws designed to encourage competition prohibit practices such as contracts, combinations, and conspiracies and restraint of trade; they prohibit discrimination in price between different purchasers of commodities similar in grade and quality that may injure competition; they make unlawful "unfair methods of competition" and "unfair or deceptive practices."

Any firm conducting business across state lines is subject to federal regulations—usually, those of the Federal Trade Commission (FTC). Any business that advertises in more than one state is subject to FTC regulations. Even the smallest mail-order business comes under FTC jurisdiction.

Because of the complexities of these regulations and the penalties imposed for violations, we recommend that you consult a lawyer. Starting your business on the right legal footing may not guarantee success, but it's an important safeguard against failure.

7

Establishing Your Public Identity

CREATING AN EFFECTIVE NAME AND LOGO FOR YOUR BUSINESS

Regular businesses have it easy. When you open a store on Main Street, you can put up a sign, hang banners, construct fabulous window displays, and hire a brass band to play in your doorway. Home-based companies have no such luxury. If yours is like most home-based businesses, customers won't know you for your fabulous location—they'll know your business through letters, ads, and business cards. That's why creating an effective business identity through your company name and logo is a major task and one that should not be taken lightly.

Having a meaningful moniker and an attractive logo is important in any business. Yet for home-based businesses, it's even more important. A well-designed, creatively conceived name and logo will tell people that you're serious about your business. They ensure that, on paper at least, your business will look as good as your competitors'. In fact, with a little planning, it can look better.

The implicit messages that your name and logo convey are marketing assets. Simple as they are, names and logos can tell a lot about your business—what you do, how you do it, your personality and style. A good combination is catchy, meaningful, and lingers in the mind. If it does its job properly, it can save you time and money in making your product known.

Here, in a nutshell, are a few basics on giving your business a proper name and logo.

A NAME FOR ALL SEASONS

What's in a name? More than you think, if you're talking about the name of your business. Once you've come up with a brilliant new product or service and raised the start-up capital you'll need, you still have a few hurdles to overcome. And one of the most important is choosing your name.

A simple task, you say. Unfortunately, it isn't so. Finding a name that conveys your new product or service and your philosophy of doing business isn't as easy as it may seem. With some sixty thousand trademarks registered in 1987 alone, finding a name that hasn't already been copyrighted is becoming more difficult with each passing year.

A rose by any other name may smell as sweet, but in business, choosing the wrong name costs money. Your name can virtually make or break your new business. So selecting a good name is important right from the start.

There is a lot of controversy over what makes a good name: Few experts agree on the subject. Some say it's one that attracts the attention of the target market, is memorable, easy to pronounce, and meaningful. For a gift-basket service, they might suggest the name Basket Case. Others claim that suggestive names, ones that aren't too descriptive, are best. They might argue that the same service use the name Baskorp, to allow for future expansion.

Experts can't make up their minds about using coined

words or real words, either. Some swear by made-up
names, while others only stand behind names you can
find in the dictionary. And what about initials? Most
name-makers say to steer clear from them, but who's
going to tell that to IBM or AT&T?

Giving Yourself a Bad Name

A truly effective name can be a most important marketing tool. It can attract new customers to your business,
create a good image for your business, and decrease the
amount of money you'll have to spend on advertising.
Take a look at one entrepreneur in Texas who discovered
the benefits of choosing the right name.

Before Charlene Mason started her wedding-planning
service, she went through at least a dozen names before
landing on the perfect one: What A Wedding! Since she
worked from her home, she had no sign to attract customers. Her name had to say it all. After placing a small ad in
the yellow pages and sending a direct-mail flyer to young
women in the community, Charlene exclaims, "I started
getting calls almost immediately."

Susie Johnson, her competition, wasn't doing as well.
The name of her business, The Beautiful Bride, made
potential customers think that she did makeup or hair
styling for brides. "I kept getting calls from future brides
who wanted me to do their hair or makeup," she laments.
While Johnson was wasting her time with these calls,
Mason racked up new clients for wedding consulting.

Eventually, Johnson changed the name of her business to Wedding Planning by Susie. Granted, it wasn't the
most creative name, but it did the trick. She stopped
fielding calls about hair and makeup and started receiving calls from potential customers.

Spending time and money to develop a good name
right from the start can save you money in the end. A
good name should help a limited budget work to its best
advantage. An effective name leverages advertising and
promotion costs so that after just a few exposures in the
media, consumers remember your name. And with advertising costs at an all-time high, that kind of efficiency
should not be overlooked.

Take No Names in Vain

Every day, consumers are bombarded with hundreds of thousands of company names whether in the newspaper, on television, on billboards, in supermarkets, or in shopping centers. In today's competitive market, a good name can give you an edge simply by sticking in the consumer's memory.

Additionally, the right name can help you build a positive image and convey your company's personality. Are you state-of-the-art like Compaq computers? Fresh like Surf detergent? Done properly, even a simple name can communicate a lot.

Similarly, an ill-conceived name can turn customers off. One problem is pronounceability. Janice, a Washington entrepreneur, ran into this problem with her gift-basket service. She wanted to give her business a foreign flair by using a French name that implied sophistication and style. But even though La Boîte Des Rêves (literally, the Box of Dreams) means what she wanted to say, the name left shoppers in the dark. When referring to her business, they'd say, "You know, that Boyt . . . whatever it's called." No one could pronounce the name, so they rarely recommended the service to their friends or colleagues.

"I ended up wasting a lot of time thinking up a new name," she recalls. Luckily, the new name, Le Basket Sophistique, did the trick. Janice currently delivers about fifty baskets a week at $35 to $50 each. That translates into gross weekly sales of $1,750 to $2,500.

The Moniker-Makers

For the potential entrepreneur, choosing a name can prove to be very confusing. However, by following the same basic methods that professional namers use, you can arrive at that perfect moniker. Naming is an art, not a science, so don't think that plugging in a formula will replace human creativity.

But what can you do if you are too busy with other aspects of your business to devote a sufficient amount of time to the naming process? Or you simply feel incapable of finding a catchy name that will attract customers? Or you don't have the eye to know whether the name you choose will be visually attractive or not? If this is the case, then hiring a professional may be the answer.

Although this can mean spending a few thousand dollars of your start-up capital, it can save you countless dollars down the road. Naming firms can save you a lot of time and money by approaching the name game in a professional manner. They know the kinds of names that are popular and effective, and they know the ins and outs of trademark registration.

You might think up a brilliant name, start pouring your money into stationery, a logo, and business cards only to discover too late that the name is already registered. If you make the discovery, the cost of renaming your business will include buying new stationery, new business cards, and additional ad space to introduce the new name. You will also lose time, momentum, and credibility. You could even find yourself faced with a lawsuit and attorney's fees. And for many businesses, that can mean closing your doors permanently.

A professional naming firm has vast resources at its disposal. Professional moniker-makers have elaborate systems for creating names. First and foremost, they conduct extensive preliminary research to understand the target market as well as the business owner's goals and long-term strategies.

They study the competitive environment of the product or company in question. Then they talk with the business owner to see what the name needs to say about the company—does it need to suggest quality or low prices? Innovation or tradition?

Once they have this background information, they start brainstorming and looking in dictionaries, books, and magazines to generate ideas. A naming firm can normally generate about seven hundred to a thousand names. From there, they review the possibilities and narrow the field to a small group.

With just a handful of names left, they screen them for registration availability, which usually leaves only three to five names. These are the names that are presented to the business owner, and it's up to the entrepreneur to decide which is most appropriate for the business. Once a decision is made, the naming firm should do a preliminary test on consumers to see how they react to the name you've chosen. A positive reaction means you've found your name.

Finding that perfect name usually takes anywhere from six weeks to six months. And while you may not have that much time to devote to the process, you should plan on spending at least a few days to a few weeks choosing your moniker. If you're doing it on your own, try following the same techniques used by big naming firms.

For the entrepreneur who's going it alone, there are naming guides and computer-software programs to help you. For those who simply don't have the cash to hire a professional, this type of computer program can help. Of course, a computer cannot replace human creativity. What it can do is leave you with maybe a dozen good names at the end instead of one or two, which is what most people come up with on their own.

Once you've made your decision and found that perfect name for your business, start putting it to use immediately. While giving a name to your business may have seemed overwhelming at first, your efforts will be well rewarded in the long run. Your new name is the first step to building a company image that will stay with you as long as you're in business.

YOU'VE GOT THE LOOK

Nobody would go into a professional job interview naked, and no new business should plunge into the marketplace without a graphic identity. Just as a good suit and brief-case will enhance your professional image, a graphic identity will spruce up your corporate image.

When you forge ahead in the corporate world with a new business, you're going to be a bit nervous about how your new baby will be perceived in the marketplace. But you don't have to leave your image to chance. You can make sure that consumers and suppliers see your business in its true light with your graphic identity—your logo.

What your graphic identity should do is communicate to the outside world what your business is all about. A successful logo should communicate a fine mix of information and image quickly. Think of your logo as a sort of visual shorthand—a little glyph that tells a great deal about your company.

And since it will be included in every bit of business correspondence you mail and on every business card you hand out, it has to be attractive and appropriate. Make sure that it accurately conveys the essence of your business. With a home-based business, the logo carries even greater importance, since it is often the only thing potential clients will have to judge you on.

A graphic identity is just one of the elements that a company uses to communicate who it is and what it's about to its various key audiences. That includes its employees, its suppliers, regular customers, and potential customers.

If you take the time to dress your business for success with a well-designed logo, you will create a powerful marketing tool. This means that your message will attract your target market effectively and you won't waste advertising or promotion money on the wrong audience. And you'll avoid any confusion with consumers or suppliers.

For example, let's say you run a catering service that specializes in appetizers only, although you also offer a few assorted desserts. And let's say you go to a designer who draws a terrific-looking cake and a so-so appetizer tray as logo possibilities. Don't pick the cake logo simply because it's prettier. If you use the cake as your logo, you'll have more calls from clients who want baked goods than about the appetizers you are really trying to promote. While a logo may be attractive, it will be ineffective if it doesn't reflect what your business is all about.

A Closer Look

Before you design your logo, do some soul-searching. The real issue is finding out what your company stands for. When you look at many small-business failures, they are due to the fact that the entrepreneur doesn't have a clear idea of what he or she is and where he or she is going with the business.

A well-planned identity means that the owner knows what the goals of the business are. If your identity is clear, it will send out the right message to your customers and suppliers—in fact, it will impress everyone who comes into contact with it, including lenders. And every entrepreneur knows the value of presenting a good image to potential investors.

Once you've pinpointed your goals, there are a few other elements you should look at before putting a pencil to paper. Look at your competitors and try to zero in on what differentiates you from them. Does your business provide the best quality? Is it the only business of its kind in the region? Do you provide the fastest turnaround on your services? Whatever it is that makes your business unique, try to convey that quality in your graphic identity.

Once you have all of these criteria, you're ready for a brainstorming session. One thing you should remember is that when it comes to logos, the simpler, the better. With the thousands of images consumers face each day, the less the eye has to take in, the more the mind will remember.

But what kind of logos are popular today? Should you come up with some abstract symbol or a logotype (a stylized rendition of your name) or a combination of both?

There is no right answer. However, some experts warn that promoting an abstract symbol can prove to be very costly, especially for a small business with a limited budget. In addition, people can't remember something they can't relate to, and abstractions are sometimes hard to relate to. A logotype or word mark is much easier to recall. This may explain why we're seeing more typographical identities than symbols these days.

Abstract symbols came into vogue in the 1960s and 1970s mainly because corporations were diversifying and expanding past their original product lines and services. To stay general, the corporations introduced new logos that didn't symbolize a single product or service. But it took years and millions of dollars in advertising for Americans to grow accustomed to their new looks. A new company may not have that kind of budget to make its symbol known.

However, the abstract symbol should not be dismissed as a relic from the past. It is probably beyond a small business's budget to promote a symbol that stands alone. You can, however, use a symbol with your typeset name and get the best of both worlds. In fact, most experts agree that if you use a symbol, you should always use it in conjunction with your name.

Entrepreneurs are waking up to the importance of corporate identity. Although small-business owners don't have the vast financial resources of large corporations, they do have one advantage. With small businesses, there's room for experimentation and innovation that large companies can't allow themselves. Large, well-known companies have reputations to uphold. You are just creating yours. You have a lot more independence and a vast sea of possibilities to explore.

Help!

Creating an effective logo can be pretty confusing. Unless you're an artist, you'll need to hire the services of a graphic designer at some point. Plan on setting aside a certain amount of money from your start-up capital to cover the expense. Depending on your needs, a designer will charge anywhere from $500 to several thousand dollars for a logo design.

For a first-rate design firm, you can expect to pay at least a few thousand dollars. Do you go first-class and shell out more money in the beginning? Or do you cut corners and end up with a second-rate logo? While it may be hard to go first-class with limited funds, experts agree that it pays off and makes sense to do it right the first time. Of course, a designer's fee doesn't always match his or her talents. Shop for a bargain, but don't be afraid to pay for quality.

Don't despair if you don't have a lot of money to invest. There are several options available to you. Try going to a design school in your area and soliciting help from the faculty or students. Students eager for real work experience are usually willing to charge less than professional designers. Or look for a free-lance or one-person design firm that can take care of your needs for a reasonable fee.

More Than Just a Pretty Face

Coming up with an effective graphic identity means more than just having an attractive logo. You should look at graphic identity as part of your overall image. In addition, consider how your logo will work if you eventually move to an office location or if you expand your services.

Take a look at Karen, a New York entrepreneur who started a grocery-shopping service. Karen found what she thought was the perfect logo—a shopping cart full of groceries on a doorstep. But six months down the road, she discovered that there was a much bigger market for baby products-shopping than for groceries.

So Karen switched her specialty to baby products. And although her old logo looked superb, it just didn't fit the business anymore. Karen ended up having to pay for a second logo design that would better convey the essence of her service. "If I had taken a little more time to do market research, I could have avoided this costly change," she says.

Experts cannot stress enough how important your graphic identity is to your marketing strategy. It can be just as critical as buying your inventory or making sales calls.

So when you're budgeting out your start-up capital, don't overlook this all-important consideration. If you do it right in the beginning, your logo will grow with your company. It will save you thousands of dollars in advertising and promotion expenses, help create a strong image, and compel customers to buy your products or services— huge benefits from a little glyph.

8

SETTING UP AN OFFICE

TURNING YOUR HOME INTO A FINE PLACE TO WORK

I f you were to start out in a spanking-new office building, chances are good that your office would be ready to go. The phone lines are in, the bookshelves are in place, and the name's on the door. All you have to do is turn on the coffee machine and get to work.

If you are starting a business at home, however, you're up against an entirely different task. Homes are not designed with business in mind. You have to mold your home into a satisfactory office, and this means furnishing it with the right furniture and giving it a professional office image.

The fact is, today's home office can be a paragon of advanced design and technology thanks to office furnishings that are inexpensive yet comfortable, attractive, and (most of all) space efficient.

As home-based business continues to get a vast amount of media attention, it has also captured the interest of the office-furniture industry. Manufacturers are eager to capture their share of the home-office furniture market, which amounted to about $7.9 billion in 1988, according to the National Office Products Association, and will be worth an estimated $9.2 billion in 1990. Retailers who traditionally have stayed away from office furniture are now changing their minds. Retail sales of home-office products have increased from $1.9 billion in 1987 to approximately $2.6 billion in 1988 (this figure includes both furniture and equipment such as computers, telephones, etc.), and 25 percent of home and small businesses prefer to buy their office products from retail outlets. All of this means that furniture is more accessible, more varied, and more reasonably priced.

The type of business you run will dictate the kind of furniture you'll need. For example, if you are an artist, designer, or architect, you will need a special type of desk and work area; this is also true if you sew, knit, or use special machinery to run your business. Our intent here is not to launch a detailed analysis of every kind of office setup. Rather, we want to point out the main points to look for in choosing your office furniture and decor. The finer points are up to you.

THE DESK

Your desk is by all means the most important piece of office furniture you will have. If you are like most people, you will spend as much as 75 percent of your day sitting at your desk. Therefore, it makes sense to invest in the best and most comfortable desk you can find.

Desks come in every shape and size, from massive nineteenth-century pigeonhole rolltops to metal portable computer tables. You might prefer a particular style, such as an antique rolltop with a swivel stool. It may look very stylish, but remember that ergonomics (the relationship between technology and man) and human comfort hadn't even occurred to our ancestors when they made "serious" furniture. These old-fashioned desks are often short on storage and elbow room, and they can also be hard on the back, the rear end, and the neck.

Therefore, your first consideration should be comfort. A desk should be the proper height, for one thing. If it's too high or too low, it will put strain on your neck, shoulders, arms, and wrists. Over time, a slight discomfort can turn into real fatigue and affect your ability to concentrate and be productive. In general, writing-desk surfaces are about thirty inches from the ground, while computer desks are about twenty-six inches high. Some desks will offer bilevel or adjustable work surfaces, so that you can have both a computer and a writing level.

Figure out in advance where your desk will be so you can measure the available space; width and length (and height, if necessary). If the room is only ten feet long, the desk should only be four or five feet long; if it's any larger, it will overpower the room. A table-style desk, which has four legs and is open underneath, makes a room feel less cramped than if you had a cube desk of the same size. However, you will probably have less drawer space.

The width of your desk should be adequate to give you ample work space yet not interfere with the room's traffic flow. Try to fit the desk into an alcove or recessed corner to save space and give a further sense of privacy.

YOUR CHAIR

Next to a desk, your chair is the most important piece of office furniture you'll have. You will spend hundreds of hours in it, entrusting your physical well-being to its padded seats, contoured armrests, and adjustable angles. You should spend some time shopping and testing a variety of office chairs to find the one you feel most comfortable in.

Here are some features to look for:

- *General sturdiness:* Sit down in the chair and examine the base, armrests, backrest, and seat. Does anything seem fragile or flimsy? What is the seat fabric like? Is the frame plastic, wood, or metal? All of these materials are sturdy if the chair is put together properly.
- *The backrest:* Some backrests are short, reaching to

about your middle back; others extend to the bottom of your shoulder blades. They are designed to support the natural S-curve of your spine. Look for adjustability in a forward and backward tilt and an up-and-down movement.

■ *The seat:* The seat should be padded enough for comfort but not too soft. Over time, a soft seat won't support your weight and posture. It should also be rounded so that your leg circulation isn't restricted. A leather or vinyl seat is comfortable and nice-looking; however, a textured fabric may breathe better.

■ *The base:* Some chairs have a lever for raising and lowering the height by several inches. This is useful if you have several different work-surface heights. Many office chairs are now made with five points, or legs, to help prevent your chair from falling over if you lean back. Also, if you prefer a rolling chair over a stationary chair, look for dual-wheel casters, which give a smoother ride and are easier on your floor than ball casters.

■ *The armrests:* Actually, armrests are not necessary, but they can help alleviate wrist and arm fatigue if you do a lot of computer work. Flexible plastic is comfortable; if the arms are metal, look for a plastic or fabric-covered surface (metal is cold and clammy).

FILING CABINETS AND STORAGE

You should start good habits right away by investing in a good storage system. At the office, file cabinets were the usual choice. At home, you can have either file cabinets or bookshelves or even convert a couple of your built-in cupboards into storage units.

If you choose a file cabinet, you have two basic sizes to choose from: letter-size or legal-size. Unless you're a lawyer, the letter-size file is the most appropriate.

For a home office, a two-drawer file cabinet will probably be adequate. Look for one with racks for hanging file folders. They make it easier to move your files around and to see the headings. For easy access, you can put your materials in manila folders within these hanging files.

Look for strong locks (if you need them), decorator colors such as black, white, red, or even wood finishes, and a good, solid construction. (Tip: Cheap file cabinets are likely to fall apart faster then well-known, more expensive brands. If you will be using your file cabinet a lot, invest in a good one.)

If you don't want to use a file cabinet, consider a bookshelf. Make sure the shelves are deep enough to hold your folders so that they don't stick out; use color-coded side labels to organize your categories. Keep the folders upright with bookends until the shelf is full enough for the folders to stand on their own.

Your own cupboards are probably the least convenient storage area, but they will do in a pinch—or until you've been in business long enough to require more space. A linen closet can be converted into a system much like the bookshelf system, with upright folders and side labels. Or a shallow cardboard box placed inside the cupboard will work.

Remember, no matter which filing system you choose, the secret is to keep yourself organized. Label each file carefully, make copies of everything, and be sure to put your files back in the right place after you've used them. The most sophisticated file cabinet with tons of drawers isn't worth anything if your filing methods are poor.

LIGHTING

Because of an increasing use of computers in almost every work environment, lighting has become one of the biggest concerns to big and small businesses alike. Staring at a computer screen all day, with small glowing letters and numbers, is known to be tough on the eyes. Business newspapers and magazines have run dozens of reports on how poor lighting in the workplace has caused all kinds of problems such as eye strain, dizziness, headaches, even vision loss. Many companies have responded by bringing in lighting experts to redesign their lighting and placing glare filters over video monitors.

Your home lighting system is designed for living, not for working. You probably have some overhead lights, with lamps in the corners, as well as natural light during the day from the windows. But achieving good light for reading and writing, and for working with a computer, will require some rearranging.

The best light for working is natural indirect daylight. If your home gets light from the north or the south, you'll notice that it is a softer light with less glare than from a direct eastern or western exposure. Skylights are also good sources of natural light.

Of course, not all of us are fortunate enough to have well-lighted rooms with big bay windows and a northern exposure. Furthermore, there are times when you won't have any daylight at all, either because of the weather or because it's nighttime. That's when you will need good artificial light.

Incandescent

An incandescent lamp gives off an intense light when a filament within the lamp (or light bulb) is heated by an electric current. This is the kind of light you most likely have in your home. Since the lamps are small, they give off more of a "spotlight" effect, illuminating a relatively small area with an intense light. Incandescent light gives off a yellowish glow, which tends to be easier on the eyes than fluorescent light. It works well for giving direct, intense light to a work surface, such as your desk.

Fluorescent

Fluorescent light occurs when a tube coated with a fluorescent material and containing mercury vapor is hit with electrons from a cathode, emitting ultraviolet light, which is seen through the fluorescent tube as visible light. In layman's terms, it's a bluish soft light that's used in office buildings.

Fluorescent light requires less electricity and lasts longer than incandescent light. However, it will require expensive rewiring and new fixtures if you were to install it in your home. There is such a thing as a fluorescent light bulb that can be inserted into an incandescent socket. However, the resulting light may be an unhappy medium between the two.

Lighting the Way

Probably the best solution would be a combination of incandescent and fluorescent lighting. Use a flexible study lamp for the area where you read and write. Your computer screen should not have any direct light on it. Instead, you should place it so that you have a soft, diffuse light around you, either from a fluorescent fixture or a muted overhead incandescent light. (A light with a dimmer switch is ideal.) Invest in a glare screen or hood; it fits over your monitor to further shade the screen.

Several small lamps will give off a better, more even light than one big lamp. You can have too much light, so you should experiment with different levels to see which is the most comfortable on your eyes. Check to see that your wall hangings and mirrors do not reflect any glare; close the shades at night so that your windows don't reflect any glare either. Light paint on the walls and ceiling will also help illuminate a room.

GUEST FURNITURE

If the nature of your business requires you to have visitors—clients, vendors, customers, etc.—you'll need to have some kind of reception area. For some, the living room is fine; it's comfortable yet more formal than the kitchen or den. Look at your living room and picture you and your clients discussing business. Do you know where everyone will sit? Will you have somewhere to put your papers and something to write on? Is the lighting adequate? Is it private and quiet enough for a business conversation? If the answer to any of these questions is no, figure out a way to rearrange the furniture. Make one corner a business center with two comfortable chairs side by side, a table in the middle, and lighting behind you.

Another possibility is the dining room. If you have a formal dining room with a nice, large table, you and your clients may be most comfortable there. Again, make sure that you have privacy and that all personal items (clothing, dishes, toys, etc.) are cleared away.

No matter where you decide to have your reception

area, the basic furniture required are two or three comfortable armchairs, a table, and good lighting.

DECOR

Just because you're at home, don't think you can pass up on the touches that will make your office "homey." In fact, decorating your office will help make it seem more like an office instead of a room at home where you work.

First of all, keep your work area clear of personal clutter. Decorate it almost as you would an office in a commercial building—a few plants, some framed photographs, and a bulletin board above your desk for calendars, business cards, schedules, etc. But because you're in your own home, have a little fun with your office, too. Put up a small neon sign, for example, or decorate the walls with colorful posters. If music helps you concentrate, get a small desktop stereo.

Wall decor is very important both for you and for any visitors. It makes an office feel complete, it gives you visual stimulation, and it provides a good combination of a professional and a homey touch to your visitors. You probably already have a nice array of wall hangings in your home or apartment, but take a look at the area around your desk. Do the walls look bare? Does it look as if you just shoved the desk against any old wall, without any thought to the placement of the pictures around it?

Try to look at your work area with fresh eyes. How would it look to visitors? Organized or unfinished? Tasteful or tacky? If you aren't good at hanging up pictures, enlist the help of an artistic friend or family member.

THE PROFESSIONAL TOUCH

To illustrate the importance of a professional image, consider the story of Andrew, an aspiring advertising-agency owner. Andrew had worked as a creative director for a large advertising agency for fifteen years before he thought about going into business for himself. Over the years, he had built up a number of clients who he handled on a free-lance basis, and he decided that he would have enough business from them to keep him going for quite a while.

So one day, Andrew left his high-rise office with its panoramic view of the city, polished oak beams, and plush gray carpeting and cleared the spare bedroom of his bachelor apartment for his new home-based office/ studio. Despite his creative genius, Andrew had no talent or inclination for interior design. His office consisted of a battered old drafting table, an electric typewriter, and a couple of cast-off kitchen chairs. The walls were covered with a bedraggled mix of old movie posters, Mexican sombreros, and a shelf full of old sports trophies. He never bothered to clean out the closets, which were stuffed with athletic equipment and boxes of assorted junk. His filing system consisted of a cardboard box sitting on the floor next to his desk.

Everything worked okay for a while. Andrew was comfortable in his surroundings. And even if he lazed around a little more than usual, he got his projects done.

Then one day a prospective client came by unexpectedly to talk about a project he wanted Andrew to do. After watching the client gaze around in surprise at the shabby, unorganized office, Andrew nervously took the client into the living room, which wasn't much cleaner. Andrew offered him a drink, but he had no clean glasses or ice cubes. The dog kept running in and out of the room. The last straw was when the dog jumped up on the client and knocked some papers out of his hand. The client took his business to more professional surroundings.

Andrew's background was impeccable, he had plenty of time and money to invest in his new office, and he had some projects lined up in advance. But the crucial part of setting up shop he had overlooked was making himself look professional. This means much more than having the right furniture or a new coat of paint. It means paying attention to the small details that will impress a client— good lighting, room to move around in, plenty of writing pads and pens handy, matching glassware, and a good array of sodas, juices, and ice—all of these things will convince your visitors of your dedication to running a reputable business. And as we've said, this is twice as important when you are working from home.

You don't have to make your home office a clone of your old office. Part of the appeal of a home office is that it is warm and personal. The people who visit you can get more of a sense of who you are by looking around your home. But you must have a good balance of homeyness and professionalism, and show that you take pride in your business. Borrow some of the things you liked about your old office—a functional desk set, the gray-and-blue color scheme, a big black chalkboard—and build on it with your own style.

If you can't seem to get the right look and feel on your own, consider hiring an interior designer or decorator who has experience in designing home offices. They can often squeeze more space out of a small room, and have ingenious (and often inexpensive) ways to create a professional yet casual atmosphere.

THE BIG PICTURE

Setting up a home office can be a simple matter of buying a few extra lamps and moving the couch across the room, or it can be a long, involved process of redecorating your entire house or apartment. It all depends on the type of business you will run, how many visitors you expect to have, and how much of the furniture and accessories you already own. The three rules to remember are: Set up your office so that you can work comfortably and efficiently; get the most out of the space and furniture you have; and give your office an air of serenity and professionalism. If you can achieve all of these things, your home office will serve you well for many years to come.

9

GETTING EQUIPPED

ALL THE EQUIPMENT YOU NEED TO OPEN YOUR DOORS

One of the biggest reasons for the boom in home-based business is today's business equipment. Never before have machines that make your life easier been so small, affordable, and flexible. Many of today's successful home-based businesses would not exist if it weren't for this wave of high technology. Using the right equipment can make a small business more efficient and thus competitive with larger companies. It also allows one person to complete the tasks of several people in as much or less time.

With equipment like modems, fax machines, and cellular telephones, the home-based business is no longer the "desert isle" it used to be. Russ, a home-based graphic designer, used to spend hours running back and forth between his clients and his office. "Every time I finished an illustration, I would drive over to the client's office and show it to him," says Russ. "If there were any changes—

and there always were—I would drive back to my office and it would start all over again."

Now, Russ uses a fax machine to send illustrations back and forth. The time savings has enabled him to take on several more projects, which have more than paid for the machine.

The simple telephone-answering machine has also made a tremendous impact on the home office. For less than a hundred dollars, you can have a machine that answers your phone, "talks" to the caller in your own voice, and stores messages to review when you return. The answering machine has been on the consumer market for at least fifteen years, but now it serves an entirely new function as a business answering machine.

The right equipment will help the professional image of your home-based business as well. Here are just a few of the machines that make a big difference, and why:

- Today's full-featured word processors and electronic typewriters produce crisp, typeset-quality documents and correct spelling and typographical errors automatically. Your clients are more likely to trust your business abilities if you present yourself well on paper. In fact, a nicely printed letter may be the first impression they will get from you.
- Being able to tell your customers/prospects that they can fax you an order or that you can fax them a bid makes a good impression, too. Investing money in state-of-the-art equipment shows that you are serious about your business and plan to stay in it for the long haul.
- Having a telephone with call waiting or two lines allows you to service your clients better and faster. A cellular phone makes you available to your clients at all times, even if you're on the road. They will have a sense of security in knowing they can reach you whenever they need to.

KNOW WHAT YOU WANT

Sounds great, right? But before you invest your life savings in home-based business equpment, there are a few important caveats to consider. For one thing, you may be confused by the vast array of manufacturers, models, and available features. Unless you have some idea of how the equipment works and what it does, you will not be able to make a wise buying decision. The idea is to buy only what you need.

What equipment do you need? We hope this question is answered in the following pages as we take you through some of the basic equipment available for the home-based business. We'll explain how each machine works, its standard and optional features, and average price range.

Each business is different and has its own needs. So ultimately, you will have to be familiar with your own business to be able to decide what you need. Take the time to shop around and test a variety of products. Don't be afraid to ask about discounts, warranties, and service agreements.

POWERHOUSE PROBLEMS

Another point to consider is the electrical wiring in your home or apartment. Using a lot of extra equipment may put a burden on your household electrical outlets. The equipment could become damaged by uneven electrical "surges" caused by power outages, appliances going on and off, and radio or television interference. It could also become overheated or damaged by static electricity.

To check the adequacy of your electrical outlets, the best thing to do is check with an electrician or discuss it with your landlord. Either one should be able to tell you whether your home can support equipment with high voltage requirements.

The best way to prevent electrical surges is to invest in a surge protector. A surge protector is a unit containing several outlets. The surge protector will smooth out a bumpy electrical flow before it reaches your machine. These lifesavers are available at most retail computer stores and cost around $50.

To prevent equipment overheating, make sure your computer, copier, or any other machine that generates a lot of heat is kept at a moderate room temperature (between 50 and 80 degrees Fahrenheit). Also, keep machines away from direct sunlight, and make sure that each piece of equipment has plenty of air circulation around it. Stacking components on top of each other is *not* a good idea!

SERVICE REQUIREMENTS

Buying an expensive piece of equipment doesn't stop at the store. Remember, machines break down and they need to be serviced from time to time. You need to know what kind of warranty your equipment has—what does it cover and how long does it last? Sometimes you can purchase a service contract over and above a warranty. Service contract costs run about 10 to 20 percent of the hardware cost per year. This is expensive, but if the standard warranties are short or you plan to use your equipment extensively, then a service contract may be worth the money.

Here's another hidden cost: refills and replacement parts. Printers and facsimiles need paper, copiers need toner, and typewriters need ribbons. You have to factor in the cost of these accessories to the total price of the equipment.

You will probably be able to install some home-based equipment yourself; however, some pieces will require a professional. Facsimile machines, telephones, modems, and cellular phones are a few examples of machines that require professional installation because they involve complicated cabling. Be sure that you get thorough instructions on how to use the equipment from the place that sells it to you. Check to see that the product includes a user's manual.

LEASING VERSUS BUYING

If you think your equipment investment will be large, compare potential tax savings available through leasing. See your accountant for current rulings and to determine if your potential leases would be suitable for write-offs.

If your start-up capital is limited, then equipment leasing may be a viable alternative to buying. Through leasing, your initial cash outlay can be significantly less than when you buy on an installment contract. The disadvantage, if you have a legitimate tax-deductible lease, is that you do not acquire equity in your equipment and therefore do not build up your balance sheet.

A financial statement showing a strong net worth is important to any business. In addition, the total cost of leasing over a period of years is higher than if the same items were purchased. On the other hand, leasing needed equipment may be better than doing without. Consult your accountant as to the wiser choice for you.

Tax laws generally make the purchase of equipment, whether new or used, more attractive than leasing. Some financing sources offer no-money-down options for equipment purchases or leases. No-money-down leases enable you to own the equipment when the term of the lease is completed.

ANSWERING MACHINES

Your credibility as a home businessperson hinges on whether or not your phones are answered during normal business hours. If a client calls when you've stepped out of the office and is greeted by continual phone ringing, you will quickly lose your credibility. For this reason, consider investing in an answering machine.

Answering machines were once deemed the scourge of the eighties. As they've become more common, resistance to them has decreased. Now, many people are annoyed if you don't have an answering machine.

Answering machines differ by the types of features they have and whether or not they contain microchips. Some machines have one tape for an outgoing message and another for incoming messages; newer models will store a digitized vocal message and receive messages on a microcassette. The latter are more compact and lightweight, but the messages are not as clear.

Some features to consider include:

■ Message length: Callers are allotted either an unlimited amount of time, or ten to thirty seconds.

■ Beeperless remote: allows you to call from any touch-tone phone to retrieve your messages or change your outgoing message.
■ Message indicator: Some machines will flash a series of red lights to show how many messages there are; some have a digital display showing the number of messages.
■ Built-in handset: a phone and an answering machine in one unit.

The more features you want, the more expensive the machine will be. A good answering machine will run anywhere between $60 and $200.

AUTOMOBILE

If you use your own vehicle in the operation of your business, you will reduce the amount of up-front capital needed to begin your home-based business. If your employees also need to use a vehicle, you can have them use their own. Pass along the straight automobile expense to them as compensation, or have them deduct it from their taxes. Under this system, most people are willing to use their own car.

If your car isn't appropriate to use for your business or you have limited access to it (i.e., you share it with your spouse), then you will have to consider either leasing or buying another car.

Car dealers can set up lease packages for you. The advantage of leasing over buying is that no initial down payment is required in order to set up a financing plan. Most dealers require only two months' lease payments to begin the contract. You'll be responsible for periodic installments after that, a percentage of which is tax deductible.

The other option is buying a new car. This is initially the most expensive way to go since it will require a down payment of several thousand dollars. However, if you are able to buy the vehicle outright, you'll have a valuable asset on your financial statement, which may help you borrow money in the future. If you can't afford a new car, don't despair. Few fledgling home-based businesses can afford this option. If this describes you, using your own car or leasing one will do the trick. A used vehicle that's in top condition is also an option. Just make certain it's in good running order. An unreliable car can be worse than no car at all.

CALCULATORS

For quick and easy mathematical calculation, electronic calculators are still the most widely used piece of business equipment around. Today's calculators can double as adding machines, with their large digital displays and oversize keys. But calculators perform many mathematical functions that adding machines don't, such as sine, cosine, tangent, logarithms, square root, present value, feature value, etc. Some calculators include built-in alarms, telephone directories, and foreign-currency conversions for the traveling entrepreneur. For others, features like an easy-to-read display, red and black print (for negative and positive cash flow, get it?), and adjustable keypads are important. Calculators run anywhere from $20 to $200.

COPIERS

You may be able to get around purchasing a copier by using your facsimile machine to make quick copies or by using a public copier in the library or instant-print shop. However, buying your own copier may not be as extravagant as it sounds. To determine the cost-effectiveness of owning or leasing your own copier, try tracking your copying volume for one month. Count the number of copies you make, how much you are charged per copy, the number of trips you make to the copy shop—including how much time, gas, and mileage it takes per trip. The total volume and cost (in both time and money) may surprise you.

If you generate about a thousand copies per month, then you may want to consider a minicopier. Minicopiers are small, compact machines that can fit on top of a desk or table. They can handle up to a thousand copies per month and will produce between five and ten copies per minute.

The next largest copier would be considered a low-volume copier. These copiers can handle from three thousand to eight thousand copies per month, at speeds of around fifteen copies per minute.

Other features to consider include dual-side copying, reduction/enlargment, automatic document feeding, and automatic sorting. Again, review the kinds of copying you most frequently do—letters? orders? reports? bound proposals? If the majority of your work is straightforward one-page, one-sided documents, don't invest in fancy features you won't use.

Copiers aren't cheap. They'll cost you anywhere from $1,500 to $4,000. That's why many dealers offer leasing arrangements (see the Leasing section in this chapter).

FACSIMILE MACHINES

Without a doubt, the premier business machine of the eighties and nineties is the facsimile machine. The fax is causing a minirevolution all over the world. Facsimile transmissions allow someone in Tokyo to receive a memo from London in a matter of minutes. This is possible thanks to a scanner that distinguishes between light and dark shadings on paper. The scanner then converts the information into electronic signals, which are in turn transmitted over a telephone wire to the destination facsimile machine. These signals are converted back into an exact replica (or "facsimile") of the original document.

Facsimile machines have evolved significantly over the last ten to twelve years in terms of how fast they can transmit documents. The first group, or generation, could transmit one page in about six minutes. The second generation transmits one page in about three minutes, and the third generation (current models) in about twenty to thirty seconds. There is a fourth generation, but it hasn't caught on in great numbers in this country yet. Speed is important, because you are charged for the facsimile transmission as if you were making toll calls— by the minute.

Besides speed, consider resolution. Different facsimiles print at different resolutions, depending on whether they have "fine" or "superfine" modes. These two modes can pick up significantly more details because they use a finer "grid" to scan the paper to find subtle lines and shadings. Half-tone modes, which pick up shades of gray as well as black-and-white images, produce better photograph facsimiles.

Another important feature to consider is whether you need a facsimile that can transmit more than one page at a time. Will you be sending one-page order forms or multipage reports? Arm yourself with a "wish list" before shopping for a facsimile machine. Again, if you don't need extra features, don't buy them. Instead, invest in a facsimile machine with a respected name, sold by a dealer or rep who will stand behind the product.

For a home-based business, compactness is essential in order to fit all of your equipment and furniture into a small space. Fortunately, facsimile machines are getting smaller and smaller; some of them are lightweight enough to carry around like a briefcase. You will have to give up some features, though, in exchange for space efficiency.

Facsimile machines range in price from $900 to $2,000, depending on brand and the number of features they have.

HOME SECURITY

As a homeowner, you may already have some kind of home security—a burglar alarm, window locks, or a neighborhood that has its own community-watch system. But if you invest in expensive equipment, you may want to reevaluate how much protection you have. Office equipment and cash attract burglars; the threat of fire damage is also real. Therefore, as a home-based-business owner, you should be aware of home-security systems such as burglar alarms and smoke detectors.

Burglar alarms can be as elaborate as professionally installed perimeter systems (alarms that are attached to all points of entry) or as simple as proximity devices, which protect a certain piece of equipment by going off only when someone is within inches of it. You can also turn a computer into an alarm by connecting it to magnetic switches on doors and windows. If the switches are disturbed, the computer can sound an alarm or even dial the local police.

You probably already have smoke detectors in your home, but you should check them periodically to make sure they work. If they aren't already installed, you can purchase simple smoke detectors at any hardware store.

Depending on their complexity, home-security systems will cost anywhere from $500 to $2,000.

MODEMS

No doubt you've heard of "telecommuters," people who work for companies without ever leaving their home. They are able to do this thanks to one piece of equipment: the modem.

A modem links your computer with your telephone, allowing you to send or receive data instantly between computers. It translates the electronic impulses from the computer into audio signals. The audio signals are carried over normal telephone wires and then translated back into electronic signals by the modem at the other end. So, a journalist can write his or her stories at home and transmit them to the copy desk just as quickly as if his office were down the hall.

For those who run a business out of their home, the modem is just as helpful. It gives you access to hundreds of on-line services. Through electronic billboards, you can access investment information, research, AP and UPI newswires, newsletters, patent checks, yellow-pages directories, travel reservations, and much, much more.

Modems are either external or internal. An external unit is connected by a cable to the computer and by a wire to the telephone. An internal modem is a card that fits into a slot within the CPU [Central Processing Unit].

Your decision will be based on both speed and price. The speed at which a page of text is transmitted is measured in bauds. A 1200-baud modem, for instance, will transmit a page in a few seconds. Some modems can transmit as fast as 19,200 bauds, but they are only as fast as the receiving modem. Either a 1200- or 2400-baud modem should be adequate for your business. Expect to pay between $150 and $800; some functions (such as electronic mail) will require special software.

TELEPHONES

The vast majority of home-based businesses start off with home telephones. However, a day will come when you will need to move beyond the one-line, one-phone arrangement. Think not in terms of a telephone but of a communications system.

Thanks to deregulation of the phone companies and new technology such as fiber optics, telephone systems provide many time-saving and toll-saving features they've never had before. From the basic telephone with one line, you can move on to a telephone with call waiting and then a telephone with two to three lines and a hold button, and so on. An intercom system is useful if you have a partner and conduct business in two distant areas.

Here are some other available features:

- *Speed dialing:* The telephone can be programmed with anywhere from ten to a hundred frequently called numbers. The caller then presses just one button to get a full ten-digit number. Some telephones have display screens that indicate the time, date, and last number dialed.
- *Automatic redial:* If a number is busy or doesn't connect, pushing one button automatically redials it.
- *Call transfer:* This feature allows you to transfer a call to another telephone in the office. As a home-based business, this feature is usually irrelevant.
- *Speaker:* Speakerphones have microphones built in, allowing the caller to speak without lifting up the handset. It also allows on-hook dialing and group conversations. *One-way speakers* allow on-hook dialing and group listening but not two-way conversations.
- *Call forwarding:* Allows you to program your phone to

send calls to any desired number. This is a function of both your phone and the telephone company.

Besides telephone hardware, you need to consider telephone services. Long-distance carriers offer two important business-oriented services: Wide Area Telephone Service (WATS) lines and 800 numbers. WATS lines provide subscribers with unlimited access to certain geographical areas at a discounted price, and an 800 number enables your clients and customers to call you free of charge. Ask your long-distance carrier (AT&T, MCI, US Sprint, etc.) for services like these that are designed for small businesses. They will tell you about any call volume or installation requirements.

Cellular Phones

Since 1983, cellular technology has brought full-featured car telephones to 1.6 million subscribers, and that number continues to grow. By 1995, it is estimated that 4 percent of all automobiles in the United States will be equipped with cellular telephones. Cellular phones have dropped the reputation of being a rich man's plaything and are looked on as an important business tool.

Cellular technology divides a geographical area into small "cells" served by a low-powered radio transmitter. Each cell contains an antenna, which receives telephone signals and transmits them to cellular telephones in the area. When a phone moves out of one cell's range, the signal is handed off to the next cell within a fraction of a second.

There are three kinds of hardware: *car phones, transportables,* and *hand held.* Car phones are installed permanently in the vehicle and cannot be carried around. Transportable cellular phones can be carried around with a battery pack and weigh about ten pounds. Hand-held (or portable) phones weigh about two pounds, with limited battery and receiving power. They range in price from $700 to $1,500.

Cellular service is available through two carriers in your area (the FCC allows only two carriers per Metropolitan Statistical Area). Each service company has a map showing its area of coverage. Compare this to areas where you are most likely to use your cellular phone, and remember that there's an additional charge if you need to access service from another company. Average monthly fees range from $20 to $50; average per-minute charges range from 15 cents to 50 cents.

Note: There are still a few areas in the country not yet covered by cellular-service companies. Check with your local telephone company, or call the Cellular Telecommunications Industry Association at (202) 785-0081.

TYPEWRITERS AND WORD PROCESSORS

Typewriters revolutionized business over a hundred years ago. Today, electronic typewriters and word processors are bringing in the twenty-first century.

What sets these two products apart from their predecessors is their internal memory. Electronic typewriters can store anywhere from 1,200 to 12,000 characters; dedicated word processors can store at least 64,000 characters, or about 25 pages of text. Just about every home-based business relies heavily on one of these two systems.

Electronic Typewriters

For basic usage—business letters, invoices, and checks—electronic typewriters are excellent. For anywhere from $400 to $1,000, you can get a brand new electronic typewriter with a one-line, 40-character liquid crystal display (LCD) that allows you to edit and correct text before printing; an 80,000-word spelling checker; a built-in glossary, which stores abbreviations for commonly used words or phrases and prints them out automatically; and page and line storage. You still have the ease of entering a piece of paper or envelope directly into the carriage and typing away.

Some electronic typewriters resemble word processors. They are screen-based and use special word-processing software. Some can even hook up to your computer and be used as a printer. If your needs are simple, however, opt for a simple electronic typewriter with an established name. You will get better service and will have no trouble finding supplies like typewriter ribbon if you go with a reputable brand.

Word Processors

The newest thing in dedicated word processors are those with built-in printers. These systems contain a much larger storage capacity than electronic typewriters, yet they can switch to a typewriter mode if you need a quick letter or envelope printed.

The main disadvantage with word processors is that you are paying at least $500 for a machine that has only one function. If you have a personal computer, word-processing software, and a printer, you can do exactly the same thing in addition to all the other functions a computer can accomplish. Nevertheless, word processors are still popular for home-based businesses, especially for writers.

DON'T UNDERESTIMATE THE POWER OF GOOD EQUIPMENT

Being a one-man or one-woman show is hard enough without denying yourself the amazing capabilities of today's office equipment. Manufacturers are paying more and more attention to the home-based market, designing equipment that's compact, easy to use, and inexpensive.

The right equipment will enable you to reach new levels of efficiency and productivity—and help you compete with much larger firms. Investing in equipment now could mean years of additional profits in the future.

10

COMPUTER EASE

HARDWARE AND SOFTWARE SOLUTIONS FOR YOUR HOME-BASED BUSINESS

Thanks to computers, a single entrepreneur can accomplish the tasks of several employees. This is a particular boon to home-based businesspeople, since most don't want a team of typists, bookkeepers, administrative assistants, and graphic artists roaming their home hallways. Today's computer systems are not only powerful and versatile but are also relatively simple to use.

What can a computer do for your company? Its four main strengths are:

1. Speeding clerical tasks by eliminating redundancy.
2. Monitoring and controlling income, expenses, and taxes.
3. Reducing out-of-pocket costs.
4. Providing better customer care.

Of course, not every business needs a computer. Your decision to buy (or not to buy) will depend on the type of business you're starting, the amount of outside help you plan to enlist, and the money you have to invest. Basic computer systems cost anywhere from $1,200 to $10,000 and more, so arming yourself with information before you buy is a smart idea.

HARDWARE

When people discuss computer systems, they usually make a distinction between hardware (the nuts and bolts of computing) and software (the machine-readable instructions that control the hardware).

The usual hardware complement includes a keyboard, display, processor, disk-storage device(s), and printer. Popular accessories include alternate input devices such as a mouse or graphics pad and options like modems, hard disks, power line conditioners, and tape-backup systems.

The Processing Unit

At the center of today's computers is a box containing the microprocessor chip (the CPU, or central-processing-unit chip) and related electronics. More than anything else, your choice of processing units will affect the performance and expandability of your system. It will also determine which operating system and application software you can run.

You may have heard about the 8088, 80286, and 80386 chips used in IBM-compatible systems and the 6800 Series microprocessor chips used in many non-IBM compatibles. These chips are the "brains" of the computer. In the IBM-compatible world, obsolescence-conscious buyers are opting for computers containing 80286 and 80386 chips, since much of tomorrow's software will require them. On the other hand, bargain hunters are scooping up systems with older 8088 chips. This money-saving strategy is recommended only if you are on a very strict budget or don't think you'll want advanced software in the future.

Different microprocessors operate at different speeds, and this can affect overall system productivity. That's why you'll see ads boasting MHz (megahertz) ratings of 10, 12, 16, 20, and higher.

A processor unit also contains random access memory (RAM), a collection of chips used to store data and programs while the power is turned on. Think of it as a scratch pad the microprocessor uses. When the computer's power is turned off, the contents of RAM are lost. The amount of RAM and the speed at which it operates affects system performance.

Memory size is commonly measured in bytes, and today's popular systems contain thousands or even millions of bytes of RAM. Memory usually comes in standard increments of 1024 bytes, and memory size is expressed in a kind of abbreviated slang. When people talk about having 640K of RAM, they really have 655,360 bytes (640 × 1024).

Many software programs require at least 640K of RAM. However, MS-DOS, PC-DOS, and many IBM-compatible systems can't handle more memory than 640K gracefully, so several schemes have evolved to "work around" that barrier.

"Extended" or "expanded" memory is memory over and above a computer's "conventional memory" of 640K or less. Not all software needs this extra RAM. It is most useful if you do large spreadsheets, word-processing documents, or graphics-intensive applications using software that can take advantage of the extra memory. It probably doesn't pay to purchase more than 640K in the IBM world or 2MB (2 million bytes or megabytes) in the Macintosh world to start, unless you know you're going to need it for a specific purpose.

The processor unit also contains storage devices that hold information even when the power is turned off. The most common of these are floppy-disk drives and the floppy disk, or diskettes, they use. Usually, the drives themselves are built into the processor housing, although "external" drives are also available.

Floppy disks store anywhere from 360K to more than a megabyte of information. Many newer machines use smaller, 3 ½-inch, minidiskettes. Some diskette formats are incompatible. If you plan to have more than one computer in your company or to pass diskettes back and forth with clients or vendors, you all need to have compatible disk formats.

Most computer users end up with a hard-disk drive or two in addition to floppy drives. Hard disks hold anywhere from ten to hundreds of megabytes of information. The good ones give you lightning-fast access to data. Cheap ones are almost as slow as floppy drives and can be quite unreliable. Don't cut corners when shopping for a hard disk. The length of the drive's warranty is usually a good indication of the seller's confidence in the product.

Hard disks operate at a variety of "access" speeds, measured in milliseconds (abbreviated *ms*). Access speed can tell you a lot about a drive's potential performance. Typical drives range from as fast as 24 ms to a lumbering 65 ms or slower. Expensive drives usually run the fastest.

Hard-disk packages usually consist of the disk drive, a controller board, and cables to connect the two. Some hard-disk makers offer one-piece drives and controller boards that slip into a single expansion slot in your processing unit.

Before moving on to other components of your hardware system, let's consider two things: expansion slots and power supplies.

People usually buy a less powerful computer than they need when they're just starting out. In addition, computer makers are fond of the modular concept that permits them to manufacture a family of products by starting with a stripped-down basic "platform" and adding options, Detroit style. That's why most computers have empty connectors or "expansion slots," which accept additional memory boards, internal modems, and controller boards for tape drives, disk drives, and displays. Chances are, your computer will come with boards already in several of the expansion slots. Consider how many additional slots you'll need down the road.

Most processing units also have small expansion connectors on the back. These input/output connectors (I/O ports) play an important role in connecting your computer to external accessories. Many computers come with one or more serial and/or parallel ports. Frequently, however, you'll need to purchase additional ports as options if you plan to use a variety of external devices. There are limits to the number of serial and parallel ports that most MS-DOS computers can service. If you need a lot of external accessories, consider other external expansion schemes such as local area networks (LANs), device switching, or approaches like Apple's Appletalk and Small Computer System Interface (SCSI).

Features like SCSI simplify expansion and take much of the worry out of planning for the future—you'll never run out of space inside the computer. Many computers now offer both slots and external expansion.

Finally, consider the power supply built into the computer's processor unit. The power supply converts AC voltage from wall outlets into DC voltage for the computer. Not all power supplies are created equal. Older and cheaper ones do not always have the necessary capacity to power a boxful of today's fancier add-ons. You can usually upgrade power supplies, but it's easiest to start out with one that's big enough for anything.

Displays

Talk about choices! There are big displays, little ones, square ones, tall ones, wide ones, displays with orange letters or black ones . . . it all boils down to this: Will the display that you like work with your computer and software, and can you afford it?

If you buy a Macintosh Plus, Macintosh SE, or one of many portable MS-DOS computers, you really don't have a choice of displays. If you buy a Macintosh II, or most desktop PCs, however, there is a mind-boggling set of alternatives.

Today, most monochrome (single color) display systems, including low-cost clones, handle graphics. If you want multiple colors and sharp displays, turn to IBM's Enhanced Graphics Adapter (EGA). For most purposes, EGA is good enough.

You may also consider PGA and VGA monitors. Since these are relatively new offerings, the MS-DOS software support is still a little thin and the price, steep. If you want graphics in the IBM world, VGA is probably the better bet. When buying a name-brand VGA adapter board, be ready for some software compatibility problems.

If you like high-resolution color graphics but can't find the software you need in MS-DOS land—or if you want more colors—look at Apple's Mac II, Atari, and Commodore systems.

Bigger displays don't always display more data than smaller ones. The software you use and your display controller board play a major role in how much data you can fit on the screen. There are "projection displays" that can reproduce your data on a large screen. These are great for training rooms, sales presentations, and other group gatherings.

Shop around before you decide on a display. Stare at full color, single color, and LCD displays from the operator's position. Look at the amount of glare and the sharpness of the images, particularly in text modes. Popular display name brands include NEC, Phillips (Magnavox), Zenith, Samsung, Princeton Graphics, Electrohome, SuperMac, Sony, Wyse, and Tandy.

Input Devices

Input devices let you enter data and instructions to "control" your computer. You can choose from keyboards, mice, graphics tablets, graphics scanners, optical character recognition (OCR) systems, video input devices, and more. As with any accessory, make sure the device is compatible with the software you plan to buy.

■ *Keyboards.* Some computer makers offer a choice of keyboards; others ship only one style. There are a variety of factors to consider when buying a keyboard. Older IBM-style keyboards have only ten special function keys, labeled F1 through F10. Newer IBM-style keyboards provide twelve such keys. Others, such as Apple's, have fifteen or more special function keys. If you will be using software that can take advantage of keys F11 and up, it's worth a few extra dollars for this feature.

Check the keyboard layout. Can you reach everything easily? Is it too cramped? Keyboards take a serious pounding in the business environment, so get something rugged. Is the cable long and strong enough? Are extension cords available?

■ *Mice and trackballs.* More and more computers, including IBM's next generation of products, have mice, and much of the newest software requires the little rodents. Better software products give you the choice of using mouse or keyboard commands. With some systems, like Macs and Ataris, mice are standard equipment. Other computer makers like IBM and Compaq offer them as accessories. Optional mice usually require a serial port or an expansion slot. Popular mice breeders include Microsoft, Logitech, and Mouse Systems, to name a few.

Trackballs accomplish the same thing as mice but use less desk space. Instead of moving a mouse over a square foot of desk space, you spin a Ping-Pong-size ball mounted in a small box. Try it.

■ *Grapics tablets.* Graphics tablets are becoming popular and affordable general business tools. Use them to capture hand-drawn illustrations, signatures, and even text in your computer. Once the images are captured, you can use paint and drawing programs to modify them, and desktop publishing, advanced word processing, and presentation software packages to display and print them.

■ *Scanners.* Graphics tablets capture things as you draw them; scanners capture images that have already been created, such as clip art, drawings, and photographs. Most people spend between $1,000 and $2,000 on a scanner.

Generally, you cannot edit scanned text with word-processing software. However, the better word-processing packages let you electronically "paste" scanned pictures into documents for printing. Some scanners have flat beds that let you copy from books. Models that don't have flat beds scan only sheets of paper that can be fed into

the scanner. A few scanners offer optical-character-rec-
ognition capabilities.

- *Optical character recognition.* Optical character recognition (OCR) systems are scanners that can recognize
  text on paper and turn it into ASCII characters, which
  are stored as data or text files. OCR systems usually
  "know" how to read a finite variety of typefaces and
  styles. Most expect to see typewritten copy, not hand-
  written text. The better, more expensive units can learn
  new typestyles, and a few can recognize handwriting.
  See the machine work before you buy it. If you need
  OCR only occasionally, consider using local service
  bureaus instead.
- *Video input.* Now that computers have high-resolution
  color capabilities, people are using them as video-pro-
  duction tools. Video-input devices let you grab images
  from video cameras or still frames from videotape for
  modification.

Printers

People frequently spend too little money on printers
and too little time shopping for them. Although printers
look pretty simple, they are almost as complex as the
computers they serve.

For our purposes, let's divide printers into four broad
categories: impact dot matrix, laser, formed-character,
and specialty.

The most popular choice is the impact dot matrix
printer, which comes in a staggering variety of models
and makes. Pins strike the printer ribbon and the paper,
making dots, which create the illusion of fully formed
characters. Generally, printers with 24 or more pins print
better-looking characters but run slower. Expect to pay
no less than $300 for a reliable dot-matrix printer.

Laser printers also print dots, but they print many
more of them per inch than impact dot matrix printers.
Common laser printers print about 300 dots per inch
(DPI). High-end lasers print 600 to 1200 or more DPI.
People love laser printers because of their speed, quality,
flexibility, and quiet operation. Prices range from under

$1,500 to more than $15,000. Most people spend between $2,500 and $4,000 on a full-featured, fast laser printer.

Until laser printers became affordable, people wanting true letter quality used formed-character printers like NEC's Spinwriter printer and Diablo's family of daisy-wheel products. While many of these printers are still in use, it is becoming more difficult to justify their relatively high cost. They are almost always slower than dot matrix and laser printers, don't print high-resolution graphics, and require an additional investment in print wheels or thimbles. However, they are useful for printing envelopes and multipart forms, things that are difficult or impossible to do with many dot-matrix or laser products. While formed-character printers can be had for less than $400, the better ones still cost over $1,000.

Finally, take a look at specialty printers. Some print in color. Others offer noiseless, near-letter-quality dot-matrix printing. The most popular ones use ink-jet technology. See them demonstrated with the software you plan to use.

When shopping for a printer, print the same document on a variety of printers to judge quality and speed. Consider the noise the printer makes. Look into sound-reduction covers. Watch how the printer handles paper. Find out about necessary printer stands, trays, and maximum cable lengths. Does the printer you like have an appropriate interface for your computer? Find out how much supplies cost and whether they are readily available.

Be sure that the software you'll use supports the printer features you like. Pay particular attention to special fonts, font sizes, bold, italic, underscored, or graphic printing. Just because a printer has a special feature doesn't guarantee that your software can use it. The reverse is also true: Ask about your printer's ability to support page description languages like Postscript if your software uses them. Finally, ask about the warranty and service costs.

Communications

Take a look at modems, which connect your computer and phone lines and let you exchange data with other computers. They sell for $100 to $600. Some modems slip inside your computer and occupy an expansion slot. Others need an external I/O port.

Hayes, Robotics, and Apple make a few of the many name-brand modems. Hayes makes the best-known modems for micros and has truly set the standards. Expect to pay an additional $100, $200, or more for a Hayes modem.

While 1200-baud modems were the standard a few years ago, 2400-baud units appear to be winning the popularity race these days. You may find their higher cost worthwhile if you'll be transmitting lengthy files.

SOFTWARE

Shopping for hardware is only half the battle. The software programs you choose will determine what your computer can do. Do you plan to use your computer for accounting? Word processing? Graphics? There are programs available to help you accomplish these tasks and more. The difficult part is determining what you need.

Before you buy, remember that most people buy the wrong software (and hardware, for that matter) the first time around. Typically, people spend too little money on their system and too little time exploring their options before purchasing. They get frustrated by all of the available choices and buy something popular or something a friend uses "just to get started." Do your best to avoid this temptation. Take a computer class or two in a computer-equipped classroom. Try out some word-processing, spreadsheet, accounting, and maybe even desktop-publishing and graphics software before you decide.

Soon you will know which product features you like and which you don't like. You'll better understand how long it takes to do things on a computer. You'll know if you have the artistic ability to do your own artwork and desktop publishing. You'll know whether you want to do your own bookkeeping or farm it out. But best of all, you'll be a better consumer. Nothing is worse than spending weeks learning how to use a software package only to find out later that it's the wrong one for your business. It wastes valuable time and drains you of the energy you need for business survival.

Plan for the future. Make certain that the software you buy can grow with your company. For instance, if you think that someday you'll want to have more than one employee access the same database at the same time, buy software that will work with a network. Saving money on inadequate equipment now will only cost you money down the road.

Putting Thought into Words

Word-processing programs can help you create error-free, professional-looking correspondence. And today's better packages do much more, particularly when teamed with laser printers, databases, and graphics packages. You can create your own letterhead, mailing labels, forms, and logos, given the right combination of capabilities. Today's word processors let you create multiple, personalized form letters using names and addresses from your computerized customer or prospect databases.

There are hundreds of word-processing packages on the market today. The knee-jerk reaction in the MS-DOS world is to buy WordPerfect, MultiMate, WordStar, or Microsoft Word. Look at these popular programs, of course, but don't stop there. You should also consider products like PFS: Professional Write from the Software Publishing Company, or Volkswriter Deluxe Plus Spelling. You may find these alternatives easier to use and powerful enough for your work both now and in the future. Macintosh users will want to explore word-processing programs like WriteNow from T/Maker and MacWrite from Claris.

Remember, though, that output from word-processing software is only as good as the hardware you use it with. Be sure you see how graphics and type styles will actually look on your planned computer and printer configuration before making the investment. Remember, too, that things that are easy to do on one system configuration can be difficult or impossible on another.

Buying the right word-processing software isn't enough. Organize your disk files and create libraries of stock paragraphs, form letters, and so on. Make certain that you can find them when you need them. Remember, computers should eliminate redundant tasks.

Database Decisions

Many people resort to computers when they become overwhelmed by their manual filing systems, or lack thereof. If your Rolodex is a mess and file folders litter your floor, database software can help—but it's not a cure-all. People usually fail to realize that computerized databases take a long time to set up and must be maintained once established. Moreover, that transitional period when you have half of what you need in the computer and the other half in file folders can be hell.

That said, there are plenty of good reasons to create computerized customer databases, inventory systems, vendor databases—you name it.

Basically, there are two kinds of databases—flat files and relational databases. Flat files are electronic replacements for Rolodex files or three-by-five cards. They let you store, sort, search, and report with amazing ease. Many flat-file systems can interface with compatible word-processing packages so that you can create personalized form letters, invoices, catalogs, price lists, and so on.

Popular MS-DOS flat-file managers include PFS: Professional File and Jim Button's low-cost PC-File family. Macintosh users frequently turn to the Claris FileMaker II.

Relational database packages take things a step further. They let you connect (or relate) multiple, separate databases using a field common to the databases you want to connect. For instance, you could have one database containing a list of customers' names, addresses, phone numbers, and their customer numbers. You might have a different database containing descriptions and quantities of items purchased and the customer numbers of the clients who purchased them. Suppose you wanted to telephone all of the people who purchased a particular product. You could use a relational database to create a report containing the names and phone numbers from one database and the product numbers from the other.

The common customer number would tie the two databases together for reporting purposes.

Popular MS-DOS relational databases include dBASE IV from Ashton Tate, R:Base from Microrim, and Paradox from Ansa. Macintosh relational databases include 4th Dimension, marketed by ACIS, Inc., Ashton Tate's dBASE IV for the Macintosh, the Omnis family from Blyth Software, and Apple's own HyperCard.

The more powerful database programs like dBASE, Omnis, and 4th Dimension include procedural languages and other programming tools that let skilled users automate and personalize database entry, rearrangement, and reporting tasks. Many entrepreneurs find these features addicting and end up ignoring their real job while they master the computer. Know when to quit. Instead of getting bogged down in such details, explore predefined databases and procedural templates that already know how to do the things you need to get done. You can get templates for most popular databases and applications. Your dealer and/or the manuals that come with your database software will tell you how to find template sources.

Spreadsheets to Start With

No software category is more frequently used and abused. In the right hands, spreadsheets can help a business grow to star results. All too often, they have the opposite effect. Simply put, spreadsheets like Lotus 1-2-3 and Excel are the electronic equivalent of blank accountants' worksheets. You enter assumptions or facts about things like income, expenses, or inventory quantities into rows or columns on the screen, then show the spreadsheet software how to perform math on the entered data. You end up with official-looking computer output. Today, this means charts and graphs as well as rows and columns of printed numbers. Whether the numbers and charts reflect reality or not depends on your skill and attention to detail.

Everybody will tell you to buy Lotus 1-2-3 for your PC, but our resident computer consultant's personal favorites for the MS-DOS environment or the Macintosh is Microsoft's Excel. A new product called Wingz is worth considering for the Mac.

There are lots of spreadsheet templates available and some spreadsheet add-ons worth exploring like Lotus's HAL, a wonderful "English-language front end" for 1-2-3. Check out Lotus's small-business template packages, too.

One more spreadsheet observation is in order. Any banker with enough experience and authority to approve your loan has seen unrealistic spreadsheet projections before. Do yourself a favor. Don't expect that the bank or the IRS or even your rich mother-in-law will believe whatever you present simply because it came from a computer. Those days are over.

Basic Bookkeeping

Should you buy accounting software and keep the books yourself, or turn the task over to a pro? With accounting software, you can do the job yourself first, if only to fully understand where your money comes from and where it goes. When things get bigger, you may want to delegate these tasks. But for starters, set up simple spreadsheets and databases or use a personal money manager or small-business bookkeeping system.

Managing Your Money is a possible solution. Consider also the Peachtree Back to Basics accounting series or Monogram's Dollars and Sense. They are all available in both MS-DOS and Macintosh versions. Migent's In-House Accountant is another excellent option for Mac users. Most of these products print checks, manage receivables and payables, project cash flow, help you spot deadbeats, and assist in countless other ways. If you do anything requiring time billing, take a look at Timeslips III for either MS-DOS or Macintosh computers. It's sold by North Edge Software Corporation.

You may need help setting up fancier accounting systems unless you have an accounting background. Read the manuals before buying, to see what you think. None of these programs is a replacement for a good tax adviser. You may find several of the programs too limiting for your business, particularly if you are involved in something tricky like a partnership, import/export activities, or a temporary help service with payrolls, time billing, and the like.

Ask your accountant for advice about the best programs. One advantage of computerized accounting: It's possible that you can reduce your accounting fees at tax time if you come in with a disk or properly organized computer report rather than a shoe box filled with receipts.

Integrated Solutions

What if you need word processing, database, spreadsheet, and accounting software? Take a look at integrated packages. They combine many of the important features of separate programs, and the best of the bunch let you move information easily from one place to another. For example, you could create a check register database containing both personal and business checks, then move copies of the business-check data into a spreadsheet for analysis, then copy the results into a word-processing document.

While integrated packages usually require compromises, they may be compromises you are willing to make. Many of today's better packages sell for $200 to $300. Consider Q and A, the MS-DOS word-processing-and-database combo from Symantec. It outperforms databases costing twice as much and has a great little word processor, too. Many people swear by PFS: First Choice, a combination word-processing, database, spreadsheet, and data-communications package for the MS-DOS user. Or take a look at Microsoft Works for either Macintosh or MS-DOS requirements.

Another possibility is to purchase separate programs that you like and integrate them yourself. You'll get the ideal combination of no-compromise features. If you do, though, be prepared to buy plenty of RAM and a hard disk to accommodate all your work.

11

THE ABCs OF INSURANCE

COVERING YOUR BETS WITHOUT PAYING THROUGH THE NOSE

As a home-based entrepreneur, you can avoid many of the hassles of setting up a new business. You don't need to negotiate a lease, furnish a bare office, or calculate commute times. However, you cannot avoid the reality of managing your risks. And that means insurance.

Though no one likes to sort through the maze of jargon, technical information, and visions of disaster that the subject of insurance conjures, managing your risks properly is one of the most critical elements in running your business. Insurance can save your company from unforeseen bankruptcy. And unpleasant as paying your premiums can be, this relatively small investment is well worth the price. Imagine your relief if a disaster should occur in your business. Insurance isn't fun, but it is valuable.

What Are Your Risks?

Most home-based companies are small. And because they're small, their insurance needs are far less complex than those of large corporations. Many large companies hire professional risk managers to help them determine their insurance needs. You, on the other hand, will probably find enough help through your local insurance representative. In choosing a broker or agent, look for someone who's thorough, experienced, and knowledgeable. Don't buy blindly everything he or she pitches to you. Consider your individual needs carefully before you make a decision.

The risks you face as a new entrepreneur run the gamut from consumer liability to fire. If you have employees, you must insure against the possibility of injuries or accidents that involve them. Additionally, you may want to take out life and health insurance on yourself and your employees.

Depending on your particular field, you may also need auto insurance, errors and omissions insurance, or special coverage for toxic chemicals, etc. For more information on your particular needs, consult your trade association and your insurance representative.

The Risk List

Starting any business is a risk. Recognizing the exposures of your home-based business to potential hazards is the first step. You, as the entrepreneur, must be keenly aware of all phases of your business—management, marketing, contractors, personnel, maintenance, and your service or product itself—as well as their attendant risks.

Strategic planning is critical. First, consider liability. Spell out your possible areas of liability before you contact your insurance representative. For instance, chart your customers' path as they enter your business, step by step. Imagine a client walking across the sidewalk, through the door, under the ceiling fan, and into your living room. Or if you perform services on site, envision the various steps of your service. Are there any potential hazards? Is there any possibility of property damage?

After identifying the risks, estimate the probability of

financial loss from the various sources of danger. Develop a worst-case scenario: shop damage, employee injuries, customer problems with your product or service.

Then decide what the best and most economical method of handling each risk might be. Your four basic options are assumption, avoidance, reduction of hazards, and transfer of risk to an insurance company.

Dealing with Risks

When you assume a risk, you take responsibility for any financial damage that occurs. Sometimes, absorbing a risk is a good idea. For instance, if you are a one-person operator and have a wallpapering service, there is little chance of anything expensive going wrong. If you put up the wrong paper or do a sloppy job, you can simply do the job over again or refund the customer's money. This type of setback, while annoying, won't put you out of business. By clearing the room of furniture and covering valuable carpets before you start work, you should be able to avoid any damage to the household. Since the probability of financial disaster is low in this case, you might decide to assume the risk instead of insuring.

Avoidance, or removing the cause of a risk, is the most obvious solution—yet it is often overlooked. If, for example, you work with a caustic material that has you and your employees hesitant and fearful, look for another, nonhazardous, substance to use in its place.

Similarly, you may be able to reduce risks by modifying your operations and your workplace. Ask for suggestions from your employees and the insurance firm's safety representatives. Installing safety guards around machinery, replacing faulty wiring, and keeping transportation vehicles in tiptop shape with regular maintenance checks—these steps all help to reduce your liability.

You may even transfer risks to another party altogether by subcontracting certain services. Instead of offering your own deliveries, consider contracting a delivery service to take all the headaches away. You can also contract for maintenance, electrical, plumbing, carpentry, landscaping, and security services. Yes, this is a form of insurance. You have shifted the risk and responsibility to another party for a negotiated fee.

Be warned, however, that shifting this risk does not necessarily shift liability. If a little old man falls into the cactus plant in front of your home office and injures himself, you may still be liable for having it planted there. Get a written contractual agreement concerning those shared and mutually exclusive areas of liability.

Review your overall liability—especially product liability, if it applies. You will need property and casualty insurance—including auto insurance—in the course of everyday work. In addition, you may need special coverage for specific circumstances. A common insurance package should be complemented by special coverage for the risks involved in your entrepreneurial enterprise.

A final hint: Cover your largest loss exposure first— the lives and health of you and your workers. Take a long, hard look at your employees, keeping in mind just how long it took them to reach the high standards you have set. They are your most valuable asset.

LIFE AND HEALTH

Health Insurance

When you quit your job to start your own company, you leave behind your company benefits—and that includes health insurance. Unless you're covered by your spouse's health plan, you'll need to find your own. Fortunately, there's a wide range of choices available to you: HMOs, PPOs, hospital service associations, and traditional indemnity plans. A professional insurance representative can help you sort through the particular benefits of each type of plan.

Don't skimp on health insurance: You can't run a successful company if you're critically ill or injured. A good medical plan will ensure that you have the resources to recover from health problems and get back to running your business.

The same applies to your employees. Providing them with health benefits makes good business sense: You need them to be healthy and working. Moreover, workers have come to expect medical benefits from their employers. Failing to provide basic insurance could cripple you in terms of attracting quality people. In addition to medical coverage, you may also want to explore the possibility of optical and dental plans.

Group Life

Though life-insurance benefits are somewhat less common than health insurance, they are the kind of benefits that attract and keep good, solid workers. These policies are generally figured on some multiple or fraction of the worker's yearly salary. An employee making $20,000 a year typically is insured for $20,000.

If you're a sole proprietor—or you have fewer than ten employees—you may not be eligible for group life insurance. Consider purchasing individual term life insurance instead. Employers who aren't prepared to shoulder the whole financial burden of employee life benefits might consider making copayments with their employees. Remember, the more benefits you can offer potential employees, the higher the caliber of people you attract to the firm.

Key-employee insurance indemnifies you against losses resulting from the death or total disability of a key employee in your firm—including yourself, other owners, or partners. If your sole employee is irreplaceable, then insure him or her adequately. Naming your firm as the beneficiary may have negative tax consequences. Consider a partner or family member as the beneficiary. By taking out an insurance policy on his or her life, you will have ample funds to recruit and train a successor.

For Partners Only

Many partners don't realize this, but unless you have provided otherwise, a partnership dissolves when one partner dies. This means that for all practical purposes, the business is finished. The surviving partners become personally liable for any losses incurred if assets do not cover losses. The only business that is allowed to continue is the winding down of the firm.

To avoid this confusion, arrange for an adequately financed buy-and-sell agreement with your partner(s). This agreement provides for the purchase of your deceased partner's interest at a prearranged price. Under a general partnership agreement for two or more persons, a buy-and-sell agreement should be arranged in the event of death, disability, divorce, or retirement.

This contractual agreement is the first step. The second is to take out a partnership-insurance plan. This plan will ensure that should your partnership dissolve for any of the reasons listed above, the remaining partner will have the funds needed to buy the other partner's interest.

With two partners, each purchases a partnership plan on the other partner. Each partner, in return, pays his or her own premiums. Where there are three or more partners, it is common practice to have the firm buy a policy on the life of each partner.

Setting up a formula under which the full value of a partner's interest can be paid at an unknown time in the future can be tricky. Determine equitable distribution via an arbitrator, independent appraisal, or fair market value well in advance.

The importance of a buy-and-sell agreement, backed by an insurance plan to ensure proper funding, cannot be stressed enough. It will determine in advance what will be done in the event of a death and make funds immediately available for accomplishing the objectives of the plan. In other words, you will have the power and the capital to keep your business afloat even in the absence of your partner.

Cobra

Government legislation requires that you offer continued health insurance benefits even after an employee has been released. COBRA, the Consolidated Omnibus Budget Reconciliation Act, calls for this privilege to be extended to any worker in a firm with twenty or more full-time employees. Though this may not affect your current business (few home-based firms employ twenty or more people), you should be aware of this as your business grows.

Signed into law in 1986, COBRA affects both union and nonunion plans.

Under COBRA, the employer must offer continued coverage—but does not have to pay for it. Any employee who elects to continue coverage must pay the full cost of that coverage. This includes both the employer's and employee's share. Employees may elect to remain covered under the firm's plan for up to eighteen months; dependents can maintain coverage up to thirty-six months.

Failing to comply with COBRA procedures can result in stiff financial penalties, including loss of tax deductions. In a small firm, the owner may be subject to a personal fine of $100 per day for failing to notify an employee of his or her COBRA rights.

LIABILITY

General Liability

The standard homeowner's or apartment dweller's policy does protect from personal liability if a house guest is injured while visiting. However, it doesn't protect if the visitor is coming to your home for business purposes.

Customers, employees, repair people, delivery people, and anyone else who comes in contact with your business or property can hold you liable for your failure to take the proper degree of care to ensure their safety. This can be as simple as keeping your sidewalk swept or shoveling the snow. If someone is injured as a result of your negligence, the court will generally find in favor of the injured party, even if your negligence was only slight.

Most homeowners' policies can be upgraded to protect you for business purposes. General liability insurance will protect you for about $200 a year.

A comprehensive general liability policy covers:

- payments due to injuries or damage accidentally caused on your property or by your employees;
- any immediate medical expenses necessary at the time of the accident;

- the attorney fees and expenses for investigation and settlement; and
- the cost of court bonds or other judgments during appeal.

The limits of liability are determined on a per-accident and per-person basis. Additional limitations may include a total on bodily injury or property damage. Additional liability-insurance policies can take up where general comprehensive leaves off.

Deciding how much liability insurance to buy is a complicated matter. Use your own best judgment, and be sure to consult your insurance representative. While you don't want to overbuy insurance, you don't want to underbuy, either. Even a small case in court can set your business back substantially.

Automotive Liability

Business policies for auto liability are basically the same as those of regular consumers—only, if you use many vehicles in a variety of situations in your business, the details may be more complex. The amount of collision and comprehensive coverage you choose will depend on your business budget. Be certain that all of your employees are listed on the policy and have an active driver's license in your state. Beware of coverage gaps between owned, nonowned, and hired vehicles. Do not cut corners on coverage.

Product Liability

In manufacturing, and in certain sectors of retail trade, you may have an assumed product liability as a result of selling a product you knew or should have known was defective. In a service business, product liability may be a factor if you are in the repair business, for example, and inadvertently cause an accident or injury.

As a result of strict judicial interpretations, companies have been held accountable for injuries to people using their product fifteen or twenty years after its manufacture or sale. Even if the product met all known standards of safety at the time of production, the company may still be held liable if it is deemed unsafe by later standards.

Consult an insurance representative who is well versed in this area of specialization, as premiums vary widely depending on the accompanying risks. If you manufacture ski-lift parts, your premiums will be considerably higher than those of a firm that makes lenses for snow goggles.

Worker's Compensation

Worker's compensation provides for unlimited medical coverage during the course of employment. This covers all job-related injuries that take place on company property or in the pursuit of an employee's livelihood. An injured delivery person, for instance, would receive compensation if he or she were hurt while unloading your goods at another site.

You may be able to lower your rates by making your workplace safer. Asking employees for their suggestions on doing just that may not only lead to money-saving improvements, but may also further your rapport with your workers—a valuable safeguard against lawsuits should an accident occur.

In some states, worker's compensation insurance must be purchased from a designated provider. In other states, you may have a choice of companies, though either way your rates aren't likely to be very competitive. When figuring out your worker's compensation needs, don't forget to include yourself in the policy.

PROPERTY INSURANCE

In addition to protecting your business in the event of death, illness, injury, or liability, you will also want to protect your business property. Fire, theft, and flooding are just a few of the calamities you need to consider.

There are two types of compensation you can receive from your property plan: actual cash value or replacement. If your policy provides for actual cash value, you will receive the replacement cost of the item, minus depreciation. Replacement, on the other hand, provides you with the actual cost of replacing the item.

An all-risk policy will cover you for virtually anything under the sun—except for anything that's specifically omitted from the policy. This type of policy may help you to:

- eliminate duplication and overlap of coverage;
- avoid gaps in covering your liabilities through a number of specialized policies;
- encourage quicker settlements by working with one attorney and one agent instead of many; and
- reduce expense of carrying many different policies.

If your local or regional location has a propensity toward earthquakes, tornadoes, or other specific calamities, you may consider additional coverage. A professional insurance representative can help you evaluate your needs. He or she may suggest a business owner's policy, or BOP. This is a ready-made package for small-business owners that should cover most of your basic needs.

SPECIAL COVERAGES

A gamut of risks fall under the heading of "special named perils." Some of them may never have occurred to you. Following are a few types of specialized coverage you might want to consider. If you operate a specialized enterprise that might involve other particular risks, consult your insurance representative for further advice.

Care, Custody, and Control

This coverage is a must for a service business, particularly if you have customer goods in your control at any time during the business transaction. Should some unforeseen accident happen, the insurance company will reimburse you (and the customer). This applies to the service/repair sector: framing pictures, furniture repair, and bicycle assembly. Basically, if you have the customers' goods within your grasp at any time in the business transaction, you are liable for the full value if the goods are damaged or destroyed.

Business Interruption

If your business were destroyed in a fire, how would you and your family survive while you rebuilt the company? How about your employees and their families? Business-interruption insurance provides for limited compensation while your business is "closed for rebuilding."

Business-interruption insurance will reimburse the business owner for future profits and fixed charges that are the result of damages due to named perils. These perils must be specifically accounted for in the policy: Weather damage is the most common. Thus, other causes, like a strike or material shortages, will not be applicable. Depending upon your geographical location, the inclusions (i.e., tornado, hurricane, or flood) and exclusions (earthquake, mudslide, or tidal wave) may get technical. The period of loss is typically defined as the period necessary to return to normal business operations. Otherwise, the payments are only made until the business can physically reopen (even if in a makeshift pattern).

Profit

What, you may ask, is the difference between profit and business-interruption insurance? Interruption covers future profits, while profit insurance covers the loss of goods already manufactured but destroyed before they could be sold. This specialized coverage is aimed at manufacturers, not the service sector.

Electronic Equipment

Like many home-based-business owners, you probably use a personal computer for business purposes. You may want to get a special "floater" policy covering electronic equipment—that is, computers, copiers, and electronic typewriters. These can be insured against fire, theft, malicious damage, accidental damage, mechanical breakdown, or electrical breakdown.

A separate electronic data processing (EDP) policy can cover hardware as well as software. Should a fire occur, the standard property-insurance policy might pay you the price of replacing a blank, black roll of computer tape; an EDP policy could compensate you for the cost of reconstructing the data.

Other Specialized Packages

Errors-and-omissions rider clauses are available for owners and managers who are in the business of giving professional advice. A garage owner's policy covers any damage to vehicles while within your care if you are customizing or repairing automobiles. Companies that use or produce chemicals, drugs, or industrial pollutants are wise to carry specific endorsements for these hazards.

How much is too much? Only you can decide. Ask yourself what you stand to lose and how much you can afford in premiums. There is a happy medium between overinsuring and inadequate coverage.

BUYING INSURANCE

Regardless of whether you deal with an independent agent or insurance broker or work directly with an insurance company, be certain that you've done some comparison shopping before you sign up.

Just as you cannot always buy products from a single supplier, neither can you expect to one-stop shop with insurance. Think of buying insurance as a backpacking trip. Your goal is to outfit yourself with adequate provisions, seamless protection—coverage that has no gaps, other than deductibles and unnecessary extras. You can go without if you're prepared to brave the consequences. Or you can prepare yourself for any circumstance—but you must be willing to shoulder the extra burden.

Agents, Brokers, and Direct Writers

Direct writers are employed by specific firms and may have special focuses in the field of insurance. Though tied to one firm, the insurance representative can still handle any number of insurance lines: auto, home, health, and life. The commission paid to a direct writer should be somewhat lower since you're purchasing the insurance factory-direct, so to speak.

An agent is an independent businessperson who usually deals with a variety of coverages and insurers. The independent agent may have gathered a greater breadth of knowledge across different fields of insurance. His or her interaction with many firms and policies increases the scope and awareness of cost-effective coverage. Though the commission for an independent agent is generally higher, as an entrepreneur and his own boss, he may strive to give you the best service possible.

An insurance broker negotiates with different insurers for different types of policies. The broker represents you, the insurance buyer, not the insurance company. Brokers are particularly adept in business dealings, and thus their costs may be higher.

An advanced agent should have the designation C.L.U. after his or her name. This stands for Certified Life Underwriter and is the industry's oldest and most recognized official sign of excellence. An even more advanced seal of approval has been initiated in the field, Ch.F.C., Chartered Financial Consultant.

Evaluating Insurers

The general axiom of insurance is that the lower the premium, the higher the deductible and vice versa. The difficulty lies in comparing apples with apples. Aside from cost, how are different insurance companies different? Some firms have better track records in paying dividends. The most difficult matter to evaluate, yet the most important, is their record of paying out claims. One way to find out is to ask another policyholder. Word of mouth is often the most reliable.

Convenience may be a factor. If the firm specializes in your industry—say, light manufacturing—it may behoove you to stick with it for other insurance needs so that you can deal with one agent.

The bible of the insurance trade is *Best's Insurance Reports.* This publication rates the reliability of property and liability insurers (at least four years' operating experience) in terms of dealing with policyholders, quality of underwriting, economy of management, adequacy of reserves, adequacy of resources to absorb unusual shock, and soundness of investments. Nearly all firms fall in the top ratings: A+, A, B+; if not, look closely at the firm.

Deciding on a Deductible

Take the highest deductible your budget can afford without overextending your business. Insurance experts are unanimous that businesses should try to hold down premiums by maintaining reasonable deductibles. Researching the average claim in your industry group can give you a thumbnail sketch of what to expect. Be bold, ask a friendly competitor for a ballpark figure. Buying first-dollar coverage against accidents that may never occur is unreasonable. At a minimum, accepting a moderate deductible to reduce your premium is the way to go.

Tax Tips

Insurance premiums for fire-, casualty-, and burglary-insurance coverage on business property are all deductible for tax purposes as trade or business expenses.

Insurance premiums paid by a business on life-insurance coverage provided to employees are also tax deductible, but premiums paid on a life-insurance policy covering the life of an officer, employee, or other key person are not deductible if the business is a direct or indirect beneficiary under the policy.

Also Consider . . .

Before speaking with an insurance representative, write down a clear statement of expectations. Do not withhold any important information from your insurance representative about your business and its exposure to loss. Treat your insurance representative as a professional helper.

Get at least three competitive bids using brokers, direct writers, and independent agents. Note the interest that the representative takes in loss prevention and suggestions for specialty coverage.

Avoid duplication and overlap in policies; you will be paying for insurance you do not need. Entire insurance packages for small businesses do exist in certain sectors.

Ask your insurance firm if it is an "admitted insurance company." If so, it has a solvency fund should a catastrophe put the insurance company in danger of going under. An unadmitted carrier has no such solvency fund.

Mutual employer trusts are another form of insurance. Though rates may be attractive, check the backing of funds and note the lack of legislation or guarantees in some arenas.

Get your insurance coverage reassessed on an annual basis. As your firm grows, so do your needs and potential liabilities. Underinsurance is a major problem with expanding firms. Get an independent appraiser to value your property. If it has been over five years since you last did an evaluation, you will be surprised.

Keep complete records of your insurance policies, premiums paid, itemized losses, and loss recoveries. This information will help you get better coverage at lower costs in the future.

DEALING WITH A LOSS

Virtually all policies require prompt notification of an accident within twenty-four, forty-eight, or seventy-two hours of the incident. The claim itself does not necessarily have to be filed at this time; however, the loss must be reported. Failure to do so may nullify your right to recovery. There must be some proof of loss, though you will have a reasonable period to provide documentation if need be.

The insurer usually has three options to fulfill the terms of a replacement policy: paying cash, repairing the insured item, or replacing the insured item with one of similar quality. Don't hesitate to ask if you prefer a specific reimbursement method.

Disputes in the amount of the settlement are put to arbitration. An independent appraiser acts as judge in the conflict. Don't hesitate to utilize this system of resolving differences in claim amounts or processing. Only if no compromise is met can a lawsuit be initiated.

III

RUNNING YOUR BUSINESS

12

Suppliers in Demand

ESTABLISHING GOOD VENDOR RELATIONSHIPS

Even if you're launching a one-person business, you aren't in this alone. Other people will have a serious impact on the success of your business. And among the most important of these people are your vendors.

The best way to illustrate the value of a good vendor is to point out the pitfalls of a bad one. Suppose a customer calls to say he needs 250 black-and-white-balloon bouquets delivered to various clients next Wednesday—your largest order yet. You call your supplier immediately to order 1,500 black and 1,500 white balloons. Though the supplier says it's no problem, by Monday the shipment hasn't arrived. You call to make a fuss, and the shipment arrives Tuesday—only it's not what you asked for. You got 300 balloons in hot pink and yellow.

By then, your choices are few. The supplier has agreed to take the order back and refund your money, but what about your client? You dash from shop to shop buying up inventories of black and white balloons—at full retail price. You stay up all night inflating balloons and tying bouquets and by morning you've only completed 200. Thanks to an unreliable supplier, you've alienated a big client, exhausted your energy, and wasted a large chunk of your profits.

A good vendor can't make a business succeed, but a bad one can put you on the road to failure. As a home-based businessperson, your need for good vendors is acute. You don't have unlimited space to stockpile goods, so you don't have an inventory cushion to fall back on if suppliers don't come through on time. Your staff is small (perhaps consisting only of you), so making up for late deliveries with faster production is difficult. And because your operation is modest, you probably will rely on outside services for a number of things—from delivery to printing, advertising, and shipping.

THE BUCK STARTS HERE

The best supplier is no substitute for good management. You can do your part in cementing good supplier relations by anticipating your needs, ordering promptly, minimizing rush jobs, and paying on time.

It's also your job to let vendors know what you need. If one-day turnaround is going to be important to you, tell your suppliers that up front. As a home-based business, you may encounter suppliers who don't take you seriously. This problem can be partly remedied by maintaining a professional image (for more on image consciousness, see chapter 23). But you must also be willing to assert yourself. Suppliers who don't value your business should be replaced by ones who do.

Cultivating a good working relationship with your suppliers will take some effort. Strive for mutual respect, trust, and concern. Be clear in your directions and firm in your demands, but be reasonable as well. Treating a supplier like dirt is no way to put him in a cooperative mood. Remember that your attitude and competence are key factors in your relationship as well.

FINDING THE RIGHT SOURCE

List everything you need to get your business off the ground. In addition to inventory, your list might include office supplies, business cards, signs, paper goods, packaging materials, computers, equipment, or machinery. Now you're ready to start shopping.

There are three basic factors to consider when choosing a supplier: quality, service, and price—in that order. In many beginning businesses, price gets first consideration. After all, you don't have billions of dollars in the bank. How bad can bad be?

Bob became a home-based marketing consultant when he was fired from his regular position in a direct-mail firm. With a tiny investment, he put together a makeshift office, splurged on a computer, and had just a little left over for supplies. Through a catalog, he spotted computer paper selling for less than half of what local stores were charging. Delighted with his find, he bought three cases of it—only to discover that it was unusable. The coarse grain was little better than newsprint. It jammed his printer and fell to pieces with the slightest use.

Bob's bad experience proves that buying cheap products doesn't always save money. This doesn't mean you shouldn't shop for bargains—especially on goods that do not directly affect the quality of your end product or service (like office supplies). But price should not be the primary consideration. Above all else, make sure the goods you buy are usable. Otherwise, they aren't worth a cent.

After quality, consider service. Will the supplier be able to fill your orders on time? What are the terms of payment? How will the orders be shipped? Will rush orders present a problem? How eager does the supplier seem to secure your business? Is he helpful? Standoffish? Rude? Remember that your supplier can spell the difference between a completed job and an unmet deadline. Look for a supplier you can work with, now and in the future.

Your final consideration is price—and it's an important one. Ask potential suppliers if any discounts are available. Many companies offer incentives for prompt payment. One example is the fairly standard 2/10 net 30 provision, which allows you to take a 2 percent discount if you pay within ten days; otherwise you pay within 30 days. If you've already received a lower quote for the same merchandise, mention this to the supplier and ask if he can match or better that price. Don't be afraid to make a supplier work for your business. His eagerness to win your account could be an indication of future service.

PUT IT IN QUOTES

Linking up with the first supplier you find is like buying a car from the first dealer you visit. It simply doesn't make sense. In today's competitive market, you can't afford to pay more for goods and services than you have to. That's why it's essential for you to get as many competitive quotes from suppliers as possible. You must consider all sources and prices before you buy if you are to make an informed decision.

This applies to any business-related expense, whether a major purchase like office equipment or simply an overnight courier. By comparison shopping, you'll get the best value for the least money. The result will be lower operating expenses and a higher profit margin.

Check the availability of reliable used equipment wherever possible. Gary, a public-relations consultant, built his million-dollar company with the help of a used Xerox machine and used phones. "If it works when you buy it, it isn't going to break," he contends. Thanks to his frugality, he was able to move his home-based firm into beautiful downtown offices. Often, you can find used or distressed merchandise at auctions.

Shopping around for competitive quotes on goods, supplies, or services doesn't mean calling one or two distributors from the local phone book. Though this is a good place to start, don't stop here. Remember that you rarely get the best prices over the phone: Ask to see a sales representative in person. And don't rule out suppliers from nearby metropolitan areas or even across the

country. Saving money or securing better service is worth
the cost of delivery.

IT'S NEGOTIABLE

In an ideal world, your vendors would provide you with
excellent quality, supreme service, and rock-bottom
prices. They would extend unlimited credit, overlook late
payments, and deliver early every time. But in the real
world, you aren't likely to get exactly what you want
unless you negotiate for it.

One of the axioms of business is that everything is
negotiable, and this is true in your relationships with
vendors. In some situations, you may want to meet with
vendors to iron out the particulars of delivery, payment,
and other apsects of your relationship. You stand a much
better chance of coming to a mutually beneficial agreement on just about any issue by dealing with vendors
face-to-face.

In any negotiation, both sides should be flexible.
Otherwise, negotiating is pointless. To that end, enter
into your discussions with the understanding that you
will make some concessions. Remember, too, that not
every vendor can meet all of your needs, just as you will
not be able to meet every vendor's requirements. If the
terms presented are unacceptable, shop around. One of
the benefits of negotiating is the opportunity to learn
more about suppliers—for better or worse.

Sharpen Your Negotiation Skills

Like any skill, negotiation is learned. And ultimately,
practice makes perfect. You can, however, hold your own
in a negotiation by remembering a few basics:

- *Do your homework.* What are your key objectives in
  this negotiation? What about the other party's? What
  information will you be asked to provide? What do you
  need to find out? The first step is to prepare yourself—
  mentally and emotionally—for the negotiation process.
- *Consider motivation.* Why has the other party agreed
  to this negotiation? Is he in a hurry to close a deal?

Does he want to uncover more information about you and your company? Is he anxious to improve customer relations? Target your arguments toward your adversary's motivations. For instance, if he is feeling guilty about a recent glitch, point out that he can start fresh with your company by agreeing to a particular demand.

- *Use and identify straw issues.* Introducing irrelevant issues into the negotiation process is a common tactic. Be alert to this possibility. If your discussion takes an unexpected turn, ask yourself if the new topic is really important to the other party or if it might be a straw issue. Conversely, don't be afraid to throw less important demands into the process yourself. They give you something to bargain with so you don't have to sacrifice important demands.

- *Be persuasive.* Ultimately, you must convince your negotiating adversaries to meet your demands. Use your best salesmanship. Answer any questions they might have. Point out the advantages they will enjoy if they do things your way (your continued association, increased business). As a rule, it's best to ask for more than you expect: They're more likely to counter with acceptable proposals. If you ask only for what you want, you'll probably end up getting less.

- *Make concessions.* In an effective negotiation, compromise is the key. That means you'll probably make some concessions, and in turn so will your adversary. Before you agree to anything, though, know your limits. Which issues are negligible? Which are critical? How flexible are you willing to be?

SATISFACTION

Negotiating with your vendors is hard work. Why should you bother? With some vendors, you shouldn't. If you plan to buy five hundred business cards every ten years from your printer—and nothing more—just shop for the best price and be done with it.

Some suppliers will play a bigger role in your success, however, and with these people it's critical to establish a mutually agreeable relationship. You must each understand your responsibilities, and you must both be satisfied with the terms you set. With the right mix of assertiveness, flexibility, and cooperation, you and your vendors can establish a partnership that benefits both of you for years to come.

13

ADVERTISING, PUBLIC RELATIONS, AND PROMOTION

GETTING THE WORD OUT ABOUT YOUR HOME-BASED BUSINESS

I f you've done your homework, your new business already has potential customers just waiting to discover your product or service. But how will they find you? Somehow you have to reach all those unsuspecting consumers out there who are dying to try your gourmet-food-delivery or love-letter-writing service. And since you can't reach them all by going door to door, you'll probably rely on advertising, public relations, and promotion.

Fortunately, there are many options available to new entrepreneurs. You don't have to hire a Madison Avenue ad agency and a $100,000-a-year publicist to get results. With some know-how and planning on your part—and a little help from professionals—you can get the word out about your new business without bankrupting it.

ADVERTISING

Advertising is the most basic way to promote your new business. Whether through direct mail, television, radio, trade magazines, or the local paper, advertising can reach your potential customers and alert them to your products or services. Advertising has only one major drawback: It costs money.

In many cases, advertising costs a lot of money. Display ads in major magazines, for example, cost thousands of dollars. Similar ads in major metropolitan newspapers cost as much or more. A direct mailing to five thousand households can easily set you back $3,000—and five thousand addresses is considered a paltry mailing.

With costs like these, blind experimentation is out of the question for most small operators. Since you probably won't have many advertising dollars to spend (compared to the average multinational conglomerate), you'll have to make every dollar count. And that means careful targeting, planning, and budgeting.

Who Will Buy?

Aiming your advertising efforts at as many buyers as possible is not the way to maximize your budget. Focus on your best prospects. This requires a clear, well-defined understanding of your market. The more specific you can be, the better. Here are some questions to consider:

1. Who are my potential clients? Are they men or women? Are they affluent? Single or married? Old or young? What attributes do they have in common (they own cars; they're overweight; they like to ski; they enjoy music)?

2. How many potential clients are there? Do you need millions and millions of small accounts or just a few large ones?

3. Where are they located? If you're starting a microwave-oven-repair service, your potential customers are located within a ten-mile radius. If you're starting a mail-order firm, they may be located across the country. You may also break geographical areas down into types of communities. You may decide, for example, that you want to draw customers from an upscale suburb nearby, or target your direct mailings to affluent communities around the U.S.

4. Where do they now buy the products/services I want to sell them?

5. Can I offer them anything they are not getting now?

6. How can I persuade them to do business with me?

The more you know about your target market, the more effective you'll be at choosing the right media. Your demographics may not be as straightforward as you think. A few years ago, Bill decided to launch a home-based business producing sports broadcast spoofs in which clients are the star athletes. He was targeting kids but found that only a small percentage of his inquiries came from parents. Most recipients were grown men. So Bill changed his advertising focus. Instead of zeroing in on kids' catalogs, he took out classifieds in upscale men's magazines. The switch worked, and now his business is a hit.

Working Out a Budget

How much advertising can your new company afford? Most companies base their advertising budgets on a percentage of projected gross sales—usually, anywhere from 2 to 5 percent. So if your projected gross sales for the first year are $250,000 based on your business plan, then your ad budget might be $12,500 ($1,042 per month), or 5 percent of your projected sales. You probably would budget extra funds to announce your new business— twice the usual monthly amount is standard.

Calculating how much you can afford to spend on advertising is only half the picture. The other half is finding out how much the advertising you want costs. Sometimes budgeting 2 to 5 percent of projected sales doesn't get the job done. Your product or service may require more advertising and promotion—especially at first. You can also base your ad budget on the amount of advertising you need. How much is that? Without past experience to guide you, the best way to find out is through trial and error. Try various methods and media, monitor results closely, and base your future buying on careful evaluation.

A Wealth of Options

You won't find the right campaign for your budget if you don't know what's available to you. Small-business advertising goes far beyond blurbs in the yellow pages. Here's a short list of affordable advertising options you shouldn't overlook:

- *Weekly community newspapers:* Display ads are often cheaper than in major metro dailies. Even less expensive classifieds are often available.
- *Flyers:* Hire teenagers to distribute them in high-traffic areas, in office buildings, or on car windshields.
- *Transit ads:* You can have your business touted both inside and outside public-transportation vehicles. And don't forget ads on bus-stop benches.
- *Coupon mailing:* In many communities, direct-mail advertising is available through coupon-mailing services. Your coupon can be included in a packet sent to area residents by a central service. This is usually cheaper than coordinating and mailing announcements yourself.
- *Radio ads:* Radio may not be as expensive as you think. The typical price for a 30-second spot nationwide is only $29. Remember, though, that you'll have to factor in production costs. Contact local radio stations for details.
- *Brochures:* Not only can you give informative brochures to inquiring clients, but you can mail them to prospective customers you haven't met yet.
- *Newsletters:* Once you've established a clientele, keep in touch through a quarterly newsletter. You can target people who have a proven interest in your business and keep them posted on your latest offerings.
- *Trade magazines:* If you're in the business of serving other businesspeople, trade magazines may be an excellent choice for you. For instance, if you make and sell pizza cutters, a regular ad in *Pizza Today* magazine is just the thing—probably far more effective than concentrating on local ads.
- *Television:* While you probably won't be able to book 60-second spots during the Super Bowl, you can get 10-second spots and off-hours time relatively cheap. For some entrepreneurs, off-hours advertising is a real bargain. Mike, who owns a satellite-TV-installation ser-

vice, reaches the real TV addicts through his late-night ads.

- *Direct mail:* Through direct mail, you can target people in your community or around the country. In addition to thousands of lists available commercially, many may be available informally through other businesses. For instance, if you're a wedding photographer, you may be able to secure the names and addresses of clients at local wedding sites.
- *Specialty ad items:* From customized pens to imprinted sunglasses, specialty ads keep your name in front of potential customers longer. They're affordable, fun, and effective for many home-based businesspeople.

Of course, this list is not comprehensive. For every option we've named here there are dozens more we haven't mentioned. Keep your eyes open for good advertising media. Which ads do you notice? Which do you respond to? Which best fit your clients' needs and life-styles? All varieties of advertising exist: Your job is to find the right type for your business and budget.

Choosing the Right Media

Selecting the right type of advertising is especially difficult for small firms. Large-market television and newspapers are often too expensive for a firm that services only a small area (though local newspapers can be used). Magazines, unless local, usually cover too much territory for a small firm to use them cost efficiently. Metropolitan radio stations present the same problems as TV and metro newspapers. Conversely, you may find that your market is scattered across the country, making community papers, flyers, and other local advertising virtually meaningless.

How can you determine which media are right for you? Consider the following factors:

- *Cost per thousand:* How much will it cost to reach a thousand of your prospective customers? This method is used in comparing the print media. To determine a publication's cost per thousand (CPM), divide the cost of the advertising by the publication's circulation in thousands.

■ *Cost per point:* How much will it cost to buy one rating point against your target audience? One rating point equals 1 percent of your target audience. This method is used in comparing the broadcast media. To determine a broadcast medium's cost per point (CPP), divide the cost of the schedule being considered by the number of rating points it delivers.

■ *Impact:* How will the medium convey the appeal of your product or service? Is color important? Sound? Motion?

■ *Selectivity:* To what degree can the message be restricted to those people who are known to be the most logical prospects? Paying good money to reach unlikely prospects isn't an efficient use of your funds.

■ *Reach:* In using specific media, how many individuals (or homes) will be exposed to your media schedule within a given period of time? Reach is expressed as a percentage. For example, let's assume we aired one commercial in each of four television programs (A, B, C, D), and each program has a 20 rating. These four programs combined deliver 80 gross rating points (20 × 4). It is probable that many viewers will see more than one announcement. Some of the viewers of Program A might also view Program B, C, or D, or any combination of these.

Once you've calculated the costs and potential effectiveness of each medium, you can make an educated choice about which media to pursue. Your responsibilities don't end there, however. Find out which ads are most effective, and don't dismiss the possibility of trying new venues as they present themselves. You won't be able to experiment indiscriminately with a limited budget, but you should be able to try new ideas from time to time.

Cutting Corners
You don't have to hire the most expensive advertising agency in town to get good results. Chances are, your

needs are modest. Hire free lances to do creative and production work wherever possible. Use people who moonlight. Use the smallest advertising agency you can find so that you're an important client—if you use an advertising agency at all.

If you can, deal directly with the media yourself. You won't have to deal with the ad agency's commission. Often, media that deal with small-business advertisers have production people who can put together an effective ad for you. Some media will allow trade-outs: Trading your products or services in exchange for media space or time. This is particularly common with small radio stations, smaller television stations, and community weekly newspapers.

Advertising sporadically is not a good way to cut corners. Advertising has a cumulative effect. Occasional splurges rarely pay off: It is much better to advertise regularly and continuously on a small scale than to plan large campaigns infrequently. If you can't afford large display ads on a frequent basis, use smaller ads instead. Cutting back on frequency is more harmful than cutting back on size.

The Creative Process

Your creative needs will depend on the medium you choose. If you opt to run a classified ad in the local weekly, you won't need professional help to proceed. But if you're planning to run a series of cable-television commercials, you may want to enlist the help of a production company, scriptwriter, actors, or any of a number of other professionals. The choice is yours: You know your abilities and limitations. If you feel you need outside help, get it. The success of your ad campaign depends partly on how good your ad is.

But whether you get help or go it alone, you'll need to know a few basics of ad composition. Generally speaking, the best ads have the following characteristics:

- They're easy to understand.
- They're truthful.
- They're informative.

- They're sincere.
- They're customer-oriented.
- They tell who, what, where, when, why, and how.

Take note of other companies' ads. Look through magazines, newspapers, and the phone book. Watch television; listen to the radio. Which ads grab you? Which do you remember? Clip ads you find particularly effective. Keep notes on commercials you especially like. You can use these to help evaluate your own ideas.

PUBLIC RELATIONS

Advertising is the surest way to get the word out about your business. As an advertiser, you control when and where your ads appear. You dictate what they say and how they say it. But you also pay—and often you pay dearly.

Public relations, on the other hand, costs you virtually nothing. Loosely defined, public relations is the process of getting your product or company visibility without the benefit of paid ads. This might be through a feature story in the local paper, an interview on a television talk show, or a guest spot on a radio show.

But wait! Do you really have what it takes to attract coverage in the newspapers or on television? After all, you're just a humble businessperson. The answer is yes—most businesspeople can get some kind of publicity if they play their cards right. Look for yourself—the media is full of gardeners discussing the latest bug infestations, marketing consultants predicting the newest trends, restaurateurs offering cooking advice, entrepreneurs rising above poverty to become successful. Where did the media find these folks? Often, by companies' contacting them. A businessperson or publicist sold the features editor or talent coordinator on an idea.

Less Control, More Credibility

Again, public relations does not give you the control that advertising does. Since you don't pay for the media space or time, you don't dictate the final outcome. When you try to get stories written about you and your company, you are dealing with reporters, writers, editors, and producers who decide what goes into their publication or show. They don't have to accept your material or put it where you want it to go. They don't have to be entirely complimentary, either. Remember, you're a subject, not a client.

On the up side, though, editorial coverage has advantages all its own. If you become the subject of a feature newspaper story, you have the chance to say more than you could ever say in an ad. Potential clients are reading with rapt attention. Customers may get the chance to see you as an instant expert—someone who knows everything about organizing an office, clearing away dead shrubs, or keeping accurate books. Or they may get a glimpse of your personal side, so you're more than just the decorator next door.

Editorial coverage also has credibility that ads don't. We all read ads with a certain measure of skepticism. When your ads tell customers that your office-organizing service is the most efficient in the city, do they really believe you? Only partially. But if a reporter says the same thing, they give it almost full credence. What's more, they figure you must be competent if the media contacted you. This adds up to some pretty positive exposure—all for a lot less than you'd pay for a major ad.

Finding Your Angle

In general, a small business cannot afford, nor does it need, a full-blown $100,000 public relations campaign designed by a big agency. Can you duplicate the efforts of a team of PR professionals yourself? Probably not. But you can use some of their techniques to gain yourself publicity. You may not land your face on the cover of *People* magazine, but you may score a piece in the local paper or an interview in a trade magazine. And who knows? Many a small-time entrepreneur has landed on nationwide television as the result of his own efforts. It could happen to you.

The first step toward getting publicity is finding an angle. As a self-styled publicist, you must figure out how your business constitutes news. Publicists divide news stories into three classifications: *spot news*, which is not planned or developed by the publicity; *feature news*, which has broader interest and less-critical timing than spot news; and *created news*, or news you control or helped create. Here are seven effective ways to create news for yourself:

1. *Tie in with news events of the day.* A local day-care center is accused of being negligent in caring for its fifteen juvenile clients. Parents are in an uproar. You also provide day care in the area. As a local expert on day care, you issue a statement to the local press defending the integrity of local child-care providers. How can you do this without linking yourself to the accused center? Display your own competence and back it up with facts. Point out that many parents have no choice but to use day care and that the solution is to be selective. Give the media ten things to look for in a qualified day-care center. The local news media will gladly cover your side of the story. And you'll be established as a local expert.

2. *Stage a special event.* Perhaps you can team up with a local pediatrician and offer low-cost inoculations at your center. This extra service builds goodwill and makes your center more visible in the community.

3. *Release information that is useful to the general public.* Parents need all kinds of help these days. Make a list of fun, inexpensive places to visit with young children. Offer tips on throwing a low-cost, low-effort birthday party. Suggest strategies for dealing with difficult children. Name disciplinary mistakes parents often make.

4. *Start a committee.* The committee's purpose can range from dealing with a problem in your industry to dealing with a civic or community issue. For instance, the committee may wish to study the life-styles of single parents and then make recommendations on how single parents can deal with the demands of work and parenting. A free copy of the committee's report should be available to the public by contacting you or by sending a stamped, self-addressed envelope to the paper or TV station.

5. *Give out an award.* It can be given to one of your employees for outstanding achievement or extraordinary

service to a customer. Or award one of your students. Study the newspapers and see what kinds of awards they most frequently publicize.

6. *As a local expert, you should be on the lookout for problems to analyze, surveys to report, and predictions to forecast.* Look for statistics on the number of working mothers, reports on the long-term impact of day care, even reports on poor conditions at other centers. Then provide your own analysis. You might note that as many as 75 percent of the parents you deal with are ill informed about what to look for in a day-care center. Make predictions based on facts. For example, as more and more parents need child-care services, the opportunities for poor facilities to open up increase.

7. *Celebrate your anniversary.* It may be your first month, first year, or twentieth year in business. If possible, try to tie in your anniversary with a major news story of the day. For example, a major story breaks about a local chapter of the Muscular Dystrophy Association sponsoring a concert in the park to raise funds for its cause. To celebrate your anniversary, you volunteer to coordinate activities for young children at the event. Your efforts will aid a worthy cause. Your donation and anniversary will be of interest to the local news media.

Establishing Good Relations

If you have contacts in the media, use them. Of course, asking your cousin Albert to run a story about your business when you have nothing newsworthy to offer isn't much better than asking a stranger. But if you've done your homework—you've developed an interesting story, assembled fascinating facts, made provocative predictions—contacting someone you know simply makes sense. A foot in the door always helps. Even if your acquaintance is casual, don't be afraid to call.

For that matter, don't be afraid to contact strangers, either. The news media is constantly looking for newsworthy information. Write a one-page pitch letter describing yourself and your business, what you want from the media, and how they can contact you. Remember to stress your best angle, be that news ("Local Day Care Providers

Unite Against Deteriorating Standards") or human interest ("Ex-Corporate Employee Finds New Rewards Working at Home"). Your pitch letter should be concise and to the point—heavy on facts and light on everything else.

Address your pitch letter—in full name and title—to the media person who is responsible for the type of story you are pitching. Pitch letters with solid news angles should be sent to the city editor of a local paper, the news director of a local radio station, and usually the person in charge of the assignment desk for a local television news show. If you're pitching a story with a less timely human interest or a feature angle, send it to a newspaper's features editor or the talent coordinator of an afternoon TV talk show. If you aren't sure who these people are, call the newspapers and stations yourself and get the correct name, title, address, and telephone extension of the person to contact. Mind your spelling. Jumbling a person's name and title is a good way to show him or her how careless you are.

A Complement to Advertising

Publicity is a powerful tool for promoting your business. But public-relations experts agree that publicity is no substitute for advertising. Rather, the two complement each other. Publicity can get you into publications you couldn't afford as an advertiser. It can lend your business credibility and, if the story is complimentary, endear you to readers. But it is not the basis for an entire marketing program. In the big marketing picture, public relations is just a small slice of the pie, along with advertising, merchandising, and sales promotions.

PROMOTION

For a small business, promotion is a vital part of a public-relations plan. When you promote your business, you are essentially putting your business forward in the best possible light. You can promote yourself, your company, your staff, your product, or all of the above—in millions of different ways.

Often, publicity and promotional efforts overlap each

other. What one person calls a sales promotion another might define as an attempt to get publicity. It doesn't really matter what you call it as long as you understand what the goal is, who you're trying to reach, and how you are going to conduct the promotion.

Most people who read the Sunday comics have seen headlines at the top that say, "Win a Sitmar Cruise for Two Through the Panama Canal!" Sitmar has been given the top portion of the Sunday comics, and it's not costing them anything. How did they do that? Through promotion. Sitmar runs cruises through the Panama Canal, and two tickets are worth $2,500. They go to the sales-promotion department of the paper and say, "We'll give you two free tickets if you give us $2,500 worth of space." The sales-promotion department figures it's not a bad deal since the cruise can be given away in a contest sponsored by the paper. The paper will sell more copies, resulting in more advertising revenue. Discussions are held, and the paper makes a deal with Sitmar. The cost to either party is not really $2,500, yet they both get something of equal value.

You can work out a similar concept for your business—perhaps on a smaller scale, but using the same principles. You can run promotions such as giveaways, contests, or special discounts. The key to making them pay off is knowing how to run them.

The Small Promotion

When you have two tickets on a luxury cruise to give away, the appeal is obvious. But what if your business isn't glamorous? And what if you can't afford a major prize? A little innovation and resourcefulness go a long way. If people are willing to pay money for your products or services, chances are they'll be happy to receive them free. You just have to find the right presentation.

Elaine is a home-based marketing consultant in a growing Midwestern city. To promote her business, she contacted a local networking group for businesswomen. She offered to speak at its annual awards dinner and to sponsor an award for the most innovative business. The prize? A free month of consultation. The presentation gave Elaine the chance to show off her expertise. The local paper printed a short story about the award winner, mentioning that Elaine's firm was sponsoring the award. Elaine got favorable coverage and built goodwill in the business community. Down the road, when networkers needed marketing advice, they called Elaine.

You don't have to sponsor a contest on your own, either. Teaming up with entrepreneurs in related fields could help you make a bigger splash. For instance, suppose you run a calligraphy service. You're willing to give away custom-designed invitations and hand-addressed envelopes as a promotion. But the media isn't enthused. How would they promote such a thing? On the other hand, if you got together with a bridal shop, a limousine service, a caterer, and a mobile DJ and offered a complete wedding package to the "Bride of the Year," then your local paper could get involved. It would get a fun event to promote, and you would get some excellent exposure— more than any individual business could get on its own.

Don't be afraid to be offbeat. One East Coast baker had an art student paint his delivery van to look like a giant loaf of bread. The ensuing media coverage brought a definite rise in business. One shoe-repair store in Los Angeles brings in clients and curiosity seekers alike with a company car shaped like a giant boot.

Getting Television Coverage

Television stations will send out camera crews to cover promotional events, but they have to be interesting and visual. Presenting a plaque to a local resident may be a nice promotion, but it's not especially visual. Releasing five thousand multicolored balloons to celebrate the anniversary of your event-planning service is. If TV coverage is important to you, build visual elements into your promotion from the start.

A couple of weeks before the event, send a press release to the assignment editor announcing that you are sponsoring X event, with the date, time, place, etc. Then, the day before the event (or the morning of), send a hand-delivered media alert or telegram briefly reiterating the day's event. This will probably be posted on the newsroom's bulletin board. A few hours later, call the station to make sure it was received. The editor may sound abrupt on the phone, but don't let that bother you. Editors are always on a deadline.

Ask the assignment editor if there's any chance of having a camera crew come out for your event. You will never get a definite answer. The assignment editor will say something like, "If we have the manpower and time, we'll try to be there." Newspeople can't commit themselves in concrete: What if a plane crashed right before your event? They have to remain flexible. However, if your event is well constructed and well organized, you have a good chance of getting television coverage. Good visual material is hard to find, and yours may offer the viewing audience a good mix.

The ideal promo day is Friday, because it's usually a slow news day. All the politicians have taken off for a three-day weekend, but the camera crews are still on duty. Many PR veterans also recommend holding a promotion in the early afternoon—at one or two P.M. That gives the camera crew time to get there and back in time for the evening news feature.

It's All in the Package

Whatever promotional event you devise, it too is just a portion of your push to make yourself and your business known. Take the time to map out a general marketing strategy for your business before you get started. Look for ways to take advantage of the advertising, public relations, and promotional opportunities that are available to you. The first step toward increasing sales is letting people know you exist.

14

SALES SAVVY

THE BEST SALESPEOPLE ARE BORN—
AND MADE

Advertising, public relations, and promotions will tell potential customers about your business. But simply alerting them to your existence isn't enough. All of your good intentions in starting your own business won't mean a thing without sales. Everything you do in your business boils down to one pursuit: Getting and keeping customers. Without customers, you have a fine but useless operation. And without sales, you aren't likely to have many customers.

For many new entrepreneurs, the notion of selling inspires terror and loathing. One reason is that most people view selling as an inborn trait. Most of us know people who were born to sell. They approach strangers undaunted. They are unabashed about pitching their businesses, even in social situations. They're affable, unflappable, and they shrug off rejection. Only someone with bizarre natural talents could be that *cool*—right?

Wrong.

While some people do have a knack for sales, selling is a learned skill. Effective sales techniques depend as much on knowing your product, identifying your market, and listening to clients' needs as they do on personality and pizzazz. With a little practice and effort, you can become a crack salesperson.

WHAT ARE YOU SELLING?

This may sound like a foolish question, but if you are going to pitch your product or service to professional buyers and purchasing agents, you'd better have a pretty good answer. What does your product do? Why does your client need it? What separates you from the competition?

Once you know what you're selling, find out who your customers are. The old joke about selling air conditioners to Eskimos holds a grain of truth. If you don't know who is likely to buy your product or service, you'll waste plenty of time trying to sell to people who aren't interested.

Also, find out who has the authority to buy within a given company or household. Pinpointing the right target person at a given company may be time-consuming. But pitching to the wrong person is even worse. Statistics show that the average sales call costs more than $200. Before you invest that kind of money, make sure you're talking to the right person.

REACHING YOUR TARGET MARKET

Once you've found the companies, households, and individuals you want to sell to, you must decide the most effective way to reach them. One commonly used method is mail order. Through the mail, you can reach a large, geographically diverse base of potential customers. In some cases, a direct mailing will bring in a flood of orders with little or no further prompting.

Often, however, direct-mail solicitations are followed up with a sales call. Your call will be most effective if you follow a few simple steps. As mentioned earlier, make sure you're prepared. Also, take some time to polish your image—are you dressed properly? Are you sitting up straight and speaking clearly?

If you have no prior sales experience, consult a book, audiocassette, or video on sales. Several are available at your local bookstore or library. Boning up on sales basics will not only teach you a few tricks of the trade but will also give you confidence in your abilities. You'll be a more effective salesperson if you feel like you're in control.

After all the preparation is said and done, don't despair if you're still nervous or rough around the edges. According to Bob Hishrich of the Enterprise Development Center at the University of Tulsa, inexperience can be an advantage. "Entrepreneurs are not as polished, not as slick [as the average salesperson]," he says. "I think they have a little advantage as a breath of fresh air to a buyer." Your excitement about the sale (after all, nervousness is excitement) may work to impress the buyer. You're inadvertently showing him or her that you care about his business.

FOCUS ON THE CUSTOMER

Several years ago, Brian quit his job to start a janitorial service. He had no problem approaching building managers to pitch his services but found that most already had janitorial help. Then one building manager told Brian he was having a "heck of a time" finding someone to do parking-lot maintenance. Brian volunteered for the job and ended up securing similar contracts with the same manager. This was the start of his highly successful outdoor-maintenance company.

Of course, you can't always change your product or shift your focus to accommodate customers. But the more attuned to their needs you are, the better your chance of making a sale.

Beginning salespeople often don't give their customers' needs ample consideration. They're so concerned about getting their points across that they forget the real focus of the meeting: the customer. Before you even meet with a potential client, find out as much about him or his company as possible. You may uncover a specific need for the product or service you're selling. Not only will your research provide you with a strong argument for his buying your product or service, but your initiative will impress the client.

Once you're in the meeting, ask questions. Are the clients currently using a product or service like yours? Do they have any complaints about it? If they aren't using a similar product or service, what objections have they had? Through careful questioning, you'll be able to discover their greatest concerns. Suppose your client says she tried a secretarial service and found it couldn't provide a fast enough turnaround. You can counter by asking, "If I could promise you a twenty-four-hour turnaround on most projects, would that be acceptable?"

In describing your product or service, speak in terms of benefits, not features. Pointing out that your gourmet-food-delivery service saves customers time and stress is more effective than saying your service is fast and simple.

A HANDFUL OF TIPS

Though it's impossible to tell you everything you need to know about sales in a single chapter, here are a few tips on effective selling. With these, and some practice, you could become an excellent salesperson:

1. *Create a selling mood.* Come across as knowledgeable, friendly, helpful, and trustworthy. Speak firmly and clearly, and amplify your voice so you don't lose the person (don't yell, of course).

2. *Be specific.* Don't tell customers you're better than the competition: Tell them you're faster, cheaper, shinier, friendlier, brighter, more thorough, larger, smaller, more qualified, less complacent, closer, neater, or kindlier. Being vague is a good way to make your listener lose interest or become distrustful. If you're not clear, you must have something to hide.

3. *Control the time.* Don't tell chatty stories. And don't try to top a story that the listener tells. This is not a contest. If a prospect wants to show off, let him. You'll reap your rewards when you make a sale.

4. *Control the pace.* Slow down when making impor-

tant comments so that you can emphasize these points. This will get the listener's attention at just the right moments.

5. *Take the "ums" and "ahs" out of your speech.* If you can't think of anything to say, say nothing. Moments of silence can be used to your advantage. Filling them up with meaningless sounds eliminates this advantage and is annoying to the listener.

6. *Ask questions.* Phrase them so they cannot be readily answered in the negative: "Do you like to see results?" "Do you want this to be your best year ever?" By getting the prospect to keep saying yes, you're making him think positively about you and your product or service. What this accomplishes is a series of closes—points where the prospective customer has to make a decision, however small or seemingly insignificant. These closes build to the most important one—that of the sale, when the final agreement is pinned down. Once the deal has been struck, compliment the prospect on his good decision. Make him feel positive about himself—and you.

7. *Don't run your mouth.* One of the worst things you can do in a sales situation is to monopolize the conversation. If you don't let the prospect get a word in, he'll be convinced that you're not really listening. If that's the case, the prospect won't listen to you. And if the prospect is not listening, it's unlikely that there will be any sale. You are not the center of attention. Your prospect is, so steer the conversation toward him.

8. *Don't use unnecessary humor.* You can tell a joke, but be smart about it. Jokes that fall flat or make you sound silly will not project the image you want. The best way of avoiding the problem is not to crack jokes in the first place.

9. *Don't interrupt.* Barging in when your prospect is speaking is a good way to show him that you're not listening. Nor do you care about his feelings. Would you want to do business with someone like that?

10. *Don't rush the customer.* If the prospect is slow to speak or act, be patient. Speeding a potential client along will make him feel inconsequential.

11. *Meet objections.* When your prospect speaks, lis-

ten between the lines. Listen for clues to his real objections, then offer suggestions for getting around them. He can't afford your product this month? What if you defer billing until next? He already has a vendor for your service? Would he be willing to try your company for a short trial period, just to see if he likes your service better?

12. *Decide on a sales pitch.* Anticipate likely questions, and write out answers in advance. Putting this information on paper is essential. You can work out the kinks in your arguments, then commit them to memory. The clearer you are on your company's selling points, the more effective you'll be at defusing objections.

13. *Don't take rejection hard.* At no time are you more likely to be rejected than when you're selling something—especially if you're making cold calls. Don't take this personally. Some people are going to want what you're selling and some people aren't. When a prospect turns you down, just move on to the next.

CLOSING THE SALE

When everything is said and done—when you've gone through all the benefits of your product or service, answered a plethora of questions, addressed your client's concerns, and generally made the best impression possible—it's time to close the sale.

According to sales experts, knowing how and when to close a sale is the novice's greatest challenge. Only 30 percent of all salespeople actually ask for the close. Yet it's your responsibility to initiate the sales transaction. Don't wait for the buyer to act—that's not his job.

Does the prospect of asking a buyer to commit to a sale scare you? You aren't alone. For a professional salesperson, who deals with it every day, rejection is a necessary, if frustrating, part of doing the job. For the entrepreneur, whose involvement with his business is so much more intense, the possibility that the buyer will say no is terrifying. Recognize that this part of making the sale will be a little frightening for you, but don't let your fear immobilize you. Ask for the sale anyway, remembering that any rejection is not necessarily a reflection on you and your business. You're going to win some and lose some. Every lost sale brings you closer to your next win.

HIRING HELP

Most small-business owners end up doing at least some of their own sales—especially in the early stages of their business. Without substantial resources, hiring a sales force may be difficult or out of the question.

But in some cases, getting outside help may be desirable. If you're trying to market a new product to retailers, for example, you may decide to hire manufacturers' representatives to get your products into stores. Their skill and contacts can make your entrée easier.

You may also enlist the help of an outside telemarketing firm. With the cost of sales calls on the rise, more and more small companies are turning to telemarketing firms for help. Telemarketing is a good way to reach a large, targeted audience on a one-to-one basis.

Before you hire reps or salespeople, however, bear in mind that even the most dedicated outsider won't have your enthusiasm, determination, and drive. The sales rep you hire may also represent dozens of other products.

15

BALANCING THE BOOKS

THE NUTS AND BOLTS OF
MANAGING MONEY

Running a successful business requires more than a good concept and a knack for marketing—it also takes sound financial management. For many new entrepreneurs, this is the most difficult aspect of starting a business. They undercapitalize, then come up short during the first lean period. Or they spend on unnecessary extras and end up eating their profits. In between, they find themselves fending off angry vendors or going without a paycheck for months on end. Don't let this happen to you.

As a home-based entrepreneur, you've already made a sound financial decision. You can start your business without paying out huge leasing costs, utility deposits, furniture bills. But this is only a first step. Good financial management involves the following:

1. Managing old and new assets so that every dollar

provides the maximum benefit to the profitability of your business.

2. Managing your current assets to ensure the maximum return possible on all money invested in your business.

3. Generating additional capital to acquire additional assets.

4. Evaluating the requirements for new assets in the future.

5. Servicing debt from current operating capital.

These tenets are easier said than adhered to. Yet if your business is going to succeed, you will need to master these objectives early on—and continue managing your finances throughout the life of your business.

In the following pages, we'll discuss some of the basics of financial management. While this is anything but a comprehensive guide, it should provide you with a rudimentary understanding of your own capital requirements. From here, experience, research, and outside help will keep you on the right track.

WORKING OUT THE BASICS

The best place to start is at the beginning. How much money will you need to start your new venture? Don't answer too quickly. Many new business owners underestimate their capital requirements—especially if they're going to work from home. They figure they won't need much, maybe just a telephone and a typewriter. For that, $500 is probably more than adequate.

But what about your salary? You have to pay rent, feed yourself, buy clothing, go out for an occasional lunch— how will you cover these expenses? Are you prepared to support yourself on your savings for as long as a year? And what about that direct-mail campaign you've been planning? When everything is said and done, your modest little mailing will cost you $5,000. Then there are the incidentals: business cards, car expenses, medical bills. All this, and then your best client weasels out of paying you. He declares bankruptcy. Now, that $500 is looking pretty paltry. Where did you go wrong?

Don't leave your finances to guesswork. Make a detailed list of everything you'll need to get your business going. Some of these expenses will be one-time deals: phone installation, equipment purchases, furniture. Others will be continuous—like rent, utilities, and your salary. Estimate your start-up costs and monthly expenses. Then, try to estimate your sales for the first year or so. Be realistic. The first year of business is typically slow, so don't overestimate your capacity to sell.

If you don't think your sales will be adequate to cover expenses, consider your options. Do you have a personal line of credit? Is your bank likely to extend credit to you? Is a loan possible? How many credit cards do you have? Even if you do have adequate capital, it's wise to make contingency plans now. In the event of a temporary shortfall, you should be able to keep your business—and your personal finances—afloat. Meet with your banker and discuss the possibility of establishing a credit line. Having access to even a little extra money could spell the difference between continuing your business and folding.

No doubt, your estimates won't be accurate. You will incur unexpected expenses, but you may also find bargains you didn't foresee. You may encounter slow periods—or you may hit a surprise windfall. Your estimates don't have to be exact to be useful. Even if you have to make adjustments later on—and you will—having some kind of realistic guideline from the start will make your planning a lot easier.

MONITOR YOUR WORKING CAPITAL

Once your business is up and running, pay careful attention to your working capital. By studying your working capital on a regular basis, you will know where your business stands financially. Are you experiencing a downturn? Are you richer than you thought? You won't know unless you track your working capital closely.

Many small-business people misinterpret the term *working capital.* Most think that working capital is the same as sales revenues. It's not. Working capital is the difference between a company's current assets and current liabilities. There are six components that make up your working capital:

1. *Cash and liquid assets.* This is the capital most readily available to your company. It includes all incoming cash from sales or other sources and all marketable securities and short-term certificates of deposits.

2. *Accounts receivable.* If you extend credit to your customers, your receivables are the amount your customers owe and intend to pay based on predetermined terms. Receivables can be positive or negative. If you have credit accounts on which no one is paying, you are rich on paper but poor in fact.

3. *Inventory.* In most retail, manufacturing, and wholesaling operations, the amount invested in inventory may total more than 60 percent of your current assets.

4. *Trade credit.* Your suppliers may be willing to extend credit to you on very favorable terms. The amount you owe suppliers through these arrangements is your trade credit.

5. *Debts.* The payments you make to lenders subtracted from your working capital.

6. *Operating expenses and taxes.* Items such as utilities, payroll, marketing, insurance, professional fees, and so on represent operating costs that must be met from month to month.

One of the most critical financial duties you have is monitoring your working capital from month to month. By maintaining complete and accurate records, you'll be able to react more quickly to any financial change your business experiences.

ACCOUNTING AND RECORD KEEPING

Keeping complete, accurate records will help you manage your cash flow—and comply with federal, state, and local tax laws. When you start your business, make it a priority to establish a bookkeeping system. People who have no talent for this type of work should seek help from an accountant. Setting up a record-keeping system need be done only once. Do it right from the start, and avoid problems in the future.

Keeping Your Records Straight

There are dozens of methods for keeping business records, ranging from complex computer programs to single-entry manual systems. The method you choose for your business will depend on the complexity of your needs. A midsize firm with a large inventory, complex financing, customer-credit programs, and a hundred employees needs a more sophisticated system than a home-based sales consultant working alone.

Opening a separate bank account for your business is a must—regardless of its size or complexity. Though maintaining a separate bank account is no guarantee that you'll stay on top of your cash flow, combining your business and personal accounts will ensure that you don't. Set up a business checking account, as well as a petty-cash fund for incidental expenses. If you use petty cash to buy business supplies or equipment, remember to retain a receipt or memorandum so your expense will be documented at tax time.

Businesses with few bookkeeping requirements might consider using a one-write system. In a one-write system, every check you enter is automatically recorded in the cash-disbursements journal, thus saving you the time of recording expenses twice. This type of system works well with personal-service businesses. An accountant, for example, pays the rent and some miscellaneous bills—adding up to less than twenty checks per month. Though CPAs use computers to handle their clients' finances, they often do their own books manually because their businesses require few checks.

If your needs are more complex, or if even a simple system confuses you, consult your accountant. He or she will be able to put you on the right track with a system that's both simple and adequate.

What to Save

Though your accountant may play a vital role in your record keeping, he or she cannot follow your every move. You are responsible for retaining certain papers and records for documentation on your taxes. The following should be retained in a safe place for tax and/or legal purposes:

- canceled checks
- paid bills
- duplicate deposit slips
- purchase invoices
- receiving reports
- copies of sales slips
- invoices sent to customers
- receipts for cash paid out
- cash register tapes
- any other documents that substantiate entries in your business records

Payroll Requirements

Even if you have only one lone employee, you are required to maintain all records pertaining to payroll taxes for at least four years after the tax becomes due or is paid, whichever is later. There are twenty kinds of employment records that must be retained. They are:

1. Name, address, and Social Security number.
2. Amount and date of each payment of compensation.
3. Amount of wages subject to withholding in each payment.
4. Amount of withholding tax collected from each payment.
5. Reason that the taxable amount is less than the total payment.
6. Statements relating to the employee's nonresident alien status.
7. Market value and date of noncash compensation.
8. Information about payments made under sick-pay plans.
9. Withholding exemption certificates.
10. Agreements regarding the voluntary withholding of extra cash.
11. Dates and payments to employees for nonbusiness services.
12. Statements of tips received by employees.

13. Requests for difference computation of withholding taxes.

14. Amount of each payment subject to Social Security (FICA) tax.

15. Amount and date of FICA tax collected from each payment.

16. Explanation for the difference, if any.

17. Total amount of Federal Unemployment Tax (FUTA) paid during the calendar year.

18. Amount subject to FUTA tax.

19. Amount of contributions paid to the state unemployment fund.

20. Any other information requested on the unemployment tax return.

BEYOND ACCURATE RECORDS: ANALYSIS

Once you've established a good system for recording income and expenditures, you're ready to examine your financial situation. This means reading and interpreting financial statements. Anyone can find the bottom line on a financial report. But what about what happens before the bottom line? What's working and what isn't in your business? What changes can you make to improve your profits? An intelligent, informed analysis of your financial statements will help you answer these questions. Here, then, is a short explanation of these statements.

The Balance Sheet

A balance sheet tells you what your business is worth to you at any given time. It takes into account your assets, liabilities, and equity. You may generate a balance sheet when books are closed after a specific period of time— monthly, quarterly, or annually.

Anything that contributes to the total value of your business is an asset. Current assets include cash or any item that will be converted to cash or used by the business in one year or less (i.e., receivables, inventory, or supplies). Long-term or fixed assets are durable and will last longer than a year (your building, fixtures, furniture, equipment). Your business may also have intangible assets like patents, copyrights, or trademarks.

Anything you owe is a liability. Like assets, liabilities may be divided into current and long-term. If a debt is due in one year or less, it is current—for example, your payables, salaries, utilities, and taxes. If a debt is due over a period longer than a year, it's long-term (i.e., bonds, mortgage payments, or payable notes).

Capital is your claim on the assets of your business. It does not refer to money in an accounting sense. Rather, it's the total value of assets minus liabilities. For instance, if you have a car worth $5,000 (your asset) and you owe the bank $3,000 (your liability), then your capital claim is $2,000 ($5,000 minus $3,000). Your $2,000 in capital is not cash. It is the monetary value of your equity in the car.

Your balance sheet is based on the following equation:

$$\text{assets} = \text{liabilities} + \text{capital}$$

For example, if you start a business on a $10,000 investment, the business has $10,000 in assets and you have a capital claim of $10,000. Suppose you decide to borrow an additional $20,000. Now the business has $30,000 in assets and $20,000 in liabilities. The equation would look like this:

$$\text{assets} = \text{liabilities} + \quad \text{capital}$$
$$\$30{,}000 = \$20{,}000 \ + \$10{,}000$$

From this equation, you learn what your business has and what it's worth (its assets) and how the assets were financed (liabilities) and to whom they belong (capital claim).

Statement of Earnings

The statement of earnings, or profit-and-loss statement, measures the economic performance of your business over time. As we all know, fabulous sales don't always indicate a fabulous profit. Your statement of earnings will tell you how profitable your business is after subtracting the cost of sales, operating expenses, and other costs of doing business.

Your statement of earnings centers around a string of several equations. They are:

1. sales − cost of sales = gross profit
2. gross profit − operating expenses = net operating profit
3. net operating profit − other expenses = net income before taxes
4. net income before taxes − taxes = net income after taxes.

The cost of sales is the value of merchandise or services at your cost. Suppose the merchandise you sell for $5,000 costs you $3,000 to buy. Your cost of sales on that $5,000 is $3,000, and your gross profit is $2,000.

When you look at your cost of sales, also remember that it costs you money to hold inventory. How much money? Look at the costs involved in holding $1 worth of inventory: financing at 20 percent, insurance at 2 percent, obsolescence/shrinkage/theft at 3 to 10 percent. Given these figures, your cost of holding inventory would be 35 cents. If your business has a $100,000 inventory, you are spending $35,000 a year to hold it. If your business is goods-oriented, take a close look at the cost of holding inventory. Most businesses can stand some improvement in this area.

Where Does Your Money Come From?

What does a business owner mean when he says he brings in $100,000 a year and nets $30,000? Often, he's including his salary in that $30,000. He may not account for "free" services—the overtime he puts in, his wife's help with bookkeeping, his daughter's help with deliveries. He may think the business is netting $30,000 a year, but what is it really making?

In this case, the business owner makes $18,000 a year as store manager. His wife makes $6,000 a year as bookkeeper. And his daughter makes $5,000 as a delivery person. The business itself makes $3,000 a year—that's quite a drop in profits!

Of course, this new information doesn't affect the

owner's style of living: He still took home $30,000. But it does shed some light on his profit margin. He's not making a 30 percent profit—he's making a 3 percent profit. And that means he doesn't have much room for error. When you're calculating your business's profit-ability, don't forget to deduct a reasonable salary for yourself. That's not part of your profit—it's a cost of doing business. If you include your salary in the profit picture, you're not getting an accurate reading of your company's financial standing.

CHOOSING THE RIGHT PROFESSIONAL

The best news about monitoring your finances is that you don't have to do it alone. Unless you have vast experience in accounting, you'll probably want to hire an accountant to help you.

A good accountant is the single most important out-side adviser a business owner has. He or she can save you money on your taxes, help you comply with changing laws and regulations, and even offer tips on keeping your business in the black. But how do you find a qualified accountant?

There are several factors to consider in hiring an accountant. The first step is finding prospective accoun-tants to contact. Going to the phone book is not the best way. Ask fellow business owners or your lawyer for refer-rals. Then, look for the following:

- *Credentials.* Is this person a CPA? If not, what back-ground and training does he or she have in accounting and finance?
- *Experience.* Has this person worked with businesses in your field before? Has he or she worked with home-based companies?
- *Services.* All accountants are not created equal. What services can this person provide? Does he do all the work himself, or does he use assistants?
- *Rapport.* How comfortable do you feel with this person? You're going to be working closely with this person for years to come. Does he use a lot of jargon? Is he pushy?

Inattentive? Dense? Or does he take the time to explain complicated matters to you in terms you understand?

Shop around for an accountant who inspires your confidence and trust. With the right guidance, careful planning, and constant attention, you can manage your finances ably and help make your business the success you want it to be.

16

CONSULTATION TIME

THE HOWS AND WHYS OF CHOOSING A CONSULTANT

Home-based businesses epitomize the lean-and-mean ideal. Chances are, you will be your new firm's only employee. And even if you hire help, your staff will probably be minimal. After all, a home-based business can't accommodate dozens of workers—unless your home is Warwick Castle.

Having a small staff will be an advantage in many ways. Your overhead will be low. And your control over all aspects of your new business will be high. However, even the most ingenious entrepreneur can't do it all alone. When you need help in a specialized area of expertise—kicking off a new marketing program, setting up a database system, or sorting through various tax laws—consider hiring a consultant.

Consultants are experts who hire their services out on a temporary basis. They exist in any number of fields—from franchising to security, production, finance, and marketing. They usually work out of their own facility (which means they won't be invading your home office), and they can give you the luxury of working with a top-flight expert without the expense of hiring someone full-time.

WHEN DO YOU NEED A CONSULTANT?

Howard Shenson, author of a monthly newsletter, *The Professional Consultant & Seminar Business Report,* offers eight situations that typically signal the need for a consultant.

1. You need expertise, talent, or skill that you simply do not have in-house. In this case, it's more cost-effective to hire a consultant than a full-time employee. And it's better to have the expertise than to do without.

2. You want an independent, unbiased, outside opinion. People inside the company may not be completely candid, or they may lack the experience to help.

3. You need temporary technical assistance. You have an impossible deadline or an immediate problem and need temporary expertise to solve it.

4. You are having cash-flow problems. An inexperienced business owner does not want to deal with this confusion. A consultant can determine what the problem is, take corrective action, raise revenues, and cut expenses.

5. You need resources for acquisitions. For instance, you might hire an executive-search consultant to help you hire a key employee. You may also want to acquire other resources—additional dealerships, capital, or raw materials. Specialists are available to solve these dilemmas, too.

6. You are facing political problems. This tends to be the case in larger firms, though on occasion even small companies get involved in legislative or organizational tangles. If you feel you're in over your head, call in a consultant.

7. You have to meet complex regulations. Government regulations are plentiful—and often baffling. The Federal Trade Commission and the Environmental Protection

Agency alone enforce enough regulations to keep a consultant hopping.

8. You need training, either for yourself or your employees. The money is well spent if you do not have an internal training program.

There are many more reasons to hire a consultant, but don't run out and enlist help on a whim. Consultants may be well worth the expense, but they are expensive. Paying a professional consultant $75 to $100 per hour is common. A more specialized consultant charges more than $1,000 per day. Cheaper consultants exist, but be cautious about whom you hire. A consultant isn't worth a dime if he or she can't solve your problem.

DO YOUR HOMEWORK

Ask business peers, friends, lawyers, or accountants for referrals. Running a reference check on a consultant should be a fundamental part of the search. Ask the consultant for several names of previous clients. Call the references personally, talk to the individual that the consultant worked with, and determine whether the consultant produced the desired results.

Scrutinize experience and educational background. Investigate industry certification programs—not all are legitimate. Nearly seven hundred certification programs exist in the business community. For instance, there are certification programs for business-forms consultants, personnel consultants, and insurance specialists. Although the vast majority of certification programs are legitimate, some organizations are little more than diploma mills that sell books on the side. Approach certification letters with caution.

Prepare a statement outlining the scope and purpose of the assignment before you contact any consultant. This will help you determine the kind of consultant you need. As an astute client, you should analyze the problem at hand, check out the consultant's background, and specify how much time the consultant should spend on the project. Remember, with solid preliminary research, you can get very efficient and cost-effective results.

THE SHOPPING PROCESS

Ask three consultants to submit proposals describing their course of action. Be certain that they spell out the objective to be accomplished. You should have a clear understanding of the fee, who is going to be responsible for various expenses, and the total project cost.

Billing methods vary. The consulting firm may charge per-diem or hourly rates for each consultant assigned. In this case, a total-fee estimate usually will be included. A bracket quotation gives a minimum and maximum fee, with the understanding that the work will be finished within this range. This fee arrangement is often used in conjunction with the per-diem fee. A lump sum or fixed amount usually includes both per-diem fees and out-of-pocket expenses. A contingency fee is conditional on the achievement of certain goals or benefits.

Establish milestones, particularly for a lengthy consultation. Achievements need to be benchmarked so you are in a position to evaluate how the consultant's services benefit you.

Once the objectives, fees, and benchmarks are agreed upon, develop a formal written accord that succinctly describes the agreement's conditions. Include all pertinent information: the fee, each party's responsibilities, time and travel constraints. Spell out the services to be rendered: staffing and equipment needs, final-report format, and measurable results—for instance, a cost/benefit assessment. Also, both parties must be given a right to terminate the agreement for extenuating circumstances.

Right from the beginning, you must communicate to the consultant that you are willing [to hear the bad news]. Consultants may fear that if they are too critical, the business relationship will be terminated. Both you and your consultant must be open, honest, and frank.

Hiring a consultant for the wrong reasons can be a waste of time and money. Establish a firm idea of the benefits that consulting will bring your business. Don't hire a consultant unless you are willing to make a solid financial commitment to implementing his or her recommendations. And don't hire a consultant expecting him or her to implement new plans. Consultants make recommendations; you must decide how to enforce them. Don't hire a consultant unless you are ready to deliver ongoing support during and after the project.

Stress three criteria in choosing a consultant: experience, references, and rapport. The first two can be readily researched. However, the third—rapport—is more subtle. As qualified as a person may be to do a job, if he or she is abrasive or does not fit into the general atmosphere, look elsewhere. You can gain without pain.

Choose your consultant carefully. Ideally, he or she should be someone who understands your goals and is willing to work toward them—not someone who tries to force your company into a preconceived mold. The right consultant won't drive you to greater success but can provide a road map.

17

PAYING YOUR TAXES

FACING THE NEW RESPONSIBILITIES
OF BUSINESS OWNERSHIP

Now that you're starting a home-based business, your taxes are going to get more complicated. Entrepreneurs in general have more to consider at tax time—profits and losses, self-employment taxes, business write-offs, and payroll requirements. In addition, home-based-business owners have the option of deducting certain business-related expenses that they incur at home. This could mean tax savings for you—but it will also mean keeping up with records and regulations.

In this chapter, we'll outline some basic tax requirements for the home-based business. We do not offer this information in lieu of your seeing a qualified accountant. Your taxes require individual attention—the kind only your accountant can provide. Furthermore, tax laws are constantly changing. While the information in this section is correct at the time of this writing, you should keep abreast of new regulations that may have come into effect since.

Even with an accountant's help, though, the more you know about tax requirements, the better. Your accountant can't watch your every move. You must be aware of your responsibilities and make sure your records are accurately maintained on a day-to-day basis.

HOME, SWEET DEDUCTION

If you hope to deduct various expenses related to your home office, you must first establish an area in your home that's devoted exclusively to business. You may consider your dining-room table a legitimate office, but the IRS does not. If you type there by day and eat there by night, it's not an exclusive office area. This doesn't mean you can't set up shop this way. You'll just be more limited in your deductions.

Direct Expenses

Any expenses that are directly related to your setting up an exclusive and separate home office are deductible. For instance, if you've taken over a spare bedroom and need to recarpet, that carpet is deductible. Paint, furniture, or equipment used for business purposes are also direct expenses and therefore deductible. As long as the improvements apply only to your home office, the expenses related to them are deductible.

Indirect Expenses

But what if you recarpet the whole house? Can you write that off, too? No. You may only deduct the portion of that cost that went toward carpeting the office.

You can determine this portion by measuring the square footage of the space you use as an office and dividing it by the total square footage of your house. For instance, if your office is 100 square feet and your total square footage is 1,000, you may deduct one tenth of the total cost—or 10 percent—as an indirect expense.

You may also calculate the deductible percentage based on the number of rooms in your home. If you use one room exclusively for business and you have five rooms total, you can deduct one fifth, or 20 percent, of your indirect expenses.

What are indirect expenses? They're expenses that benefit your entire house, not just your office. Central air conditioning, for example, is an indirect expense. Utility bills, insurance, home repairs, new plumbing, cleaning services—these are all indirect expenses.

Using this formula, you can deduct a portion of your rent. If your business occupies one tenth of your apartment and you pay $1,000 a month in rent, you can deduct $100 monthly. Homeowners can deduct a portion of the depreciation on their home.

Meeting the Requirements

Not all home offices qualify as deductions. As we mentioned before, workspaces that aren't used exclusively for work are not deductible. Your home office must be your sole and primary place of doing business. If you maintain another office somewhere or if you perform most of your work somewhere else, your home office is probably not deductible. Check with your accountant for specifics.

BUSINESS EXPENSES

In addition to any write-offs your home office may supply, you are also entitled to standard business deductions. These include:

- advertising
- salaries
- office supplies
- legal and professional services
- shipping, postage, and delivery charges
- auto expenses
- furniture
- office equipment
- uniforms and protective gear
- professional and business publications
- business and liability insurance premiums

Of course, to claim these deductions, you must have proper documentation. Keep careful records and save your receipts, canceled checks, and other documents.

AUTOMOBILE EXPENSES

Most business owners use their car to conduct business in some capacity—whether to pick up supplies, deliver goods, or travel to and from clients' offices. At this writing, business related automobile mileage is deductible at 22.5 cents per mile for the first 15,000 miles; over 15,000 miles, the deduction is 11 cents a mile.

Here's how to calculate your straight mileage deduction: Suppose you put 20,000 miles on your car this year. Of those, 12,000 were for business purposes. Your deduction would be 22.5 cents × 12,000 miles, or $2,700. Now take three-fifths of that to represent the percentage used for business: 60 percent × $2,700, or $1,620. Under the straight-mileage approach, you would get a deduction of this amount.

When is a mile a business mile? You cannot deduct commuting expenses—especially since home-based-business owners don't have a commute. However, any distance that you travel from your place of business to a client's office, supplier's location, or on a business errand counts. Remember, though, that you must document these miles. Maintain a log of your business miles for tax purposes. You can do this by logging the miles on your appointment calendar every day.

If you don't deduct for straight mileage, you may deduct actual operating expenses. The normal deductions in this area are gasoline, maintenance, insurance, and depreciation. Using the same example we made earlier, suppose you made the following operating deductions instead:

$2,800 for depreciation
$ 400 for insurance
$ 500 for maintenance
$1,600 for gasoline

Your total would be $5,300. Take this figure and multiply it by the fraction of business miles over total miles driven

(12,000 business miles divided by 20,000 total miles, or 60 percent). Sixty percent of $5,300 is $3,180. In this case, deducting for actual operating expenses yields a higher deduction: $3,180, versus $1,620 for straight mileage.

If you use the second method of calculating your deductions, you must continue to use it for the life of your car. If you sell the car for a profit, you have to take the depreciation off its cost to determine its tax basis. If you sell it for more than its base, you'll have a taxable gain.

ENTERTAINMENT AND TRAVEL

When entertainment and travel relate to business, their expenses are partly deductible. Currently, 80 percent of entertainment expenses are deductible, provided you have recorded the following information in your log:

1. The amount of the expenditure.
2. The date of the expenditure.
3. The name, address, and type of entertainment.
4. The reason for entertainment and the nature of the business discussion that took place. General goodwill is not acceptable to the IRS.
5. The occupation of the person being entertained.

A deduction is no longer permitted for travel, food, and lodging expenses incurred while attending a conference, convention, or seminar related to investment activities like real estate, stock investments, etc. However, the cost of the actual seminar is still deductible.

Whatever you do to expand your awareness of your field is tax-deductible. For instance, you can deduct convention expenses. The cost of getting to and from the convention and the cost of your stay are also deductible. There are restrictions, however. If you're attending a convention in a foreign country or on a cruise ship, for instance, check with your accountant for the latest rules. Also, if you stay for three days after the convention ends, these expenses are not deductible. Nor are expenses incurred by your spouse, unless he or she is active in the business.

THE IMPORTANCE OF BOOKKEEPING

You won't be able to take any deductions without proper records. The IRS does not look favorably on haphazard documentation. If you take deductions without records to back them up, you run the risk of facing an audit, paying back taxes (with interest), and being slapped with penalties.

For more information on maintaining accurate books, consult Chapter 15. In addition to keeping a journal of cash receipts, general journal, payroll record, and general ledger, you should also maintain a log book. Here you can record entertainment, travel, and auto expenses as well as any incidental cash expenditures you've made.

WHEN YOU'RE THE TAX COLLECTOR

As a business owner, you don't just pay taxes—sometimes you collect them. Here's a brief rundown of taxes that business owners are commonly required to collect and turn over to the government. Again, check with your accountant for specifics on your business.

Employer Tax Identification Number

Every employer must withhold income tax and Social Security tax from each employee's paycheck and remit these amounts to the proper tax-collecting agency. Obtain an employer tax number from the federal government using IRS form SS-4. If your state has an income tax, get an ID number from the state as well. The IRS and any relevant state agencies will be happy to send you forms and information regarding your responsibilities.

Independent Contractors

If you hire independent contractors, you must file an annual information return (form 1099) reporting payments totaling $600 or more during the calendar year. Independent contractors should submit invoices to you with their names, addresses, and Social Security numbers, as well as the relevant dates and amounts paid.

Don't try to pass off employees as independent con-

tractors. The IRS has strict guidelines on what constitutes an independent contractor. Some of their considerations include:

1. Does he have his own business license?
2. Does he have cards, stationery, and a real business
address?
3. Does he have a business bank account?
4. Does he sell his services regularly to various customers?

Personal Income Tax

If you don't pay yourself a formal salary, no income tax
is withheld from your earnings. You must estimate your
tax liability each year and pay it in quarterly installments
on form 1040ES. At the end of the year, you must file an
income-tax return as an individual and compute your
total liability on the profits earned in your business for
that year. Your local IRS office will supply the forms and
instructions for filing estimated-tax returns.

Corporate Income Tax

If your business is organized as a corporation, you will
be paid a salary like other employees. Any profit the
business makes will accrue to the corporation, not to you
personally. At the end of the year, you must file a corporate tax return no later than March 15, unless you operate
on a fiscal-year schedule.

Sales Taxes

Businesses that sell merchandise to end users are
required to collect and remit sales taxes to the appropriate
state and local agencies. Contact the relevant agencies in
your state, county, or city to find out which items are
subject to tax and how often you must file sales-tax returns.

Advance Deposits

Many states require advance deposits against future
taxes to be collected. For example, in California, if you
project $10,000 in taxable sales for the first three months
of operation, you must deposit 6.5 percent ($650) with

the state-tax bureau when applying for your sales-tax permit number. Check with your state-tax board for more information. If your state requires a deposit or bond, keep the amount low by estimating sales on the low side.

IV

LIVING WITH YOUR BUSINESS

18

IMPOSING STRUCTURE

FINDING A ROUTINE YOU
CAN LIVE WITH

Now that you've decided to work at home, you can leave the regimentation of the nine-to-five workday behind. No more six A.M. alarms, no more eating breakfast on the run. As a home-based entrepreneur, you're free, free, free.

Or are you?

Melissa has a steady nine-to-five job as an investment banker. She wakes up at seven-thirty; devotes a full half-hour to exercise; showers and dresses until approximately eight-fifteen; grabs something quick to eat; and then commutes to work. This young executive's two-and-a-half-hour routine is adhered to closely on a daily basis in order to keep her organized and on time.

Melissa's former coworker and friend Heather, on the other hand, recently launched her own home-based business. From a study in her two-bedroom apartment, Heather operates a small accounting company. Unlike

Melissa, Heather is free to set her own schedule—to wake up when she wants and to quit for the day whenever suits her fancy. Right?

Unfortunately, this young entrepreneur doesn't have as much freedom as she may have anticipated. Initially, she thought, I won't have to commute. I can go to aerobics classes in the middle of the day if I want. I can take three-day weekends—it'll be fantastic.

If you're dreaming about sleeping in, quitting early, and taking long lunches, it's time to wake up. While working at home may seem more ideal than working under the reins of a regimented corporate schedule, being home-based isn't as free as all that. In fact, Heather has had to set up an even more regimented daily schedule than her corporate friend in order to accomplish everything she needs to get done.

CLASSIC PITFALLS

Although it may take you a while to become accustomed to the singular demands of a home-based business, it is important to outline a schedule as soon as possible.

There are some pitfalls that are easy to encounter if you fail to incorporate a schedule into your daily life—whether you plan to work weekdays or weekends. Initially, your biggest variance will be an apparent lack of work to fill your day. As a new home-based-businessperson, many of your hours will be free due to your lack of steady clientele. However, you should not look upon these empty hours as an excuse to while away the time on personal phone calls and television. It may be the most natural and comfortable way to pass the time, but it's certainly not the most productive. Business won't just come to you. And if you're not careful, the first few months of lethargy can set a continuing pattern. You'll become comfortable participating in activities that should be saved for personal time when you should be marketing and promoting your company.

So when you're in the infant stages of your business's growth, take advantage of slack time to plan your marketing strategy and put it into practice. Organize an open house, schedule appointments with potential clients, and blanket the neighborhood with brochures and flyers. This time could prove to be very valuable in the end.

Once you have survived the first lean months of your business, there is another major pitfall to watch out for: going to the opposite extreme. Once your business gets off the ground, you may find yourself working an excessive amount of overtime. And while it's normal to want to devote extra time to the success of your business, it's unhealthy for you to become so ensconced in work that you have no personal life.

Home-based entrepreneurs are especially prone to burnout. The same forces that may tempt you to shirk (after all, you can work later . . .) may also provide unrelenting pressure. People who work in offices or plants leave their work behind when they go home. You, however, do not. A set schedule may be the only division you have between home and office. Making those boundaries distinct is vital to your personal—and entrepreneurial—well-being.

Getting yourself on an even keel in an effort to balance your business and personal lives and avoiding these pitfalls is one of the most basic ways to put your new business on the right track.

GET OUT OF BED!

Dragging yourself out of bed in the morning may be the most difficult thing you'll have to do as a home-based entrepreneur. There's no red-faced boss standing under the time clock in anticipation of your arrival—a fact that's both a blessing and a curse. You have to roll out from under those covers sooner or later. And some say the sooner you do it, the better.

Home-based authorities often tout the benefits of waking up early to reap the most from the day's work. This is fine for early risers. For them, getting up with the birds is the most productive way to start the day. For others, though, rising too early is the start of a long, unproductive day. Some people simply don't function at full steam in the morning.

If you fit into the first category, follow your instincts and get a jump on the workday. But if you're a classic example of the second group, don't feel that you're a failure if you sleep until nine or ten A.M. One of the biggest advantages to running a business from your home is being free to set your own hours. Do exactly that. As a small-business owner, you no longer have to do what other people say is best for you. Forcing an unnatural behavior will slow down your creativity and productivity. Reach a happy medium with yourself and be flexible. Just don't become so flexible that your business suffers.

GET DRESSED

Being a home-based entrepreneur requires a lot of discipline, and getting out of bed is only the first step. Once you've handled that challenge, it's time to get dressed!

Another common pitfall for home-based businesspeople is the tendency to stay in bedclothes for half the day. This is a big mistake! While it's not absolutely necessary to dress in Armani suits every day just to sit in your home office, it is important to get out of your pajamas. The experts say that the way you look has an instrumental impact on the way you feel and perform.

Be comfortable but professional. Although your business may not require that you meet with clients regularly, you never know when one might come knocking on your door with a question or comment. Getting caught in your pajamas won't give you that competitive edge.

ARRANGING YOUR SCHEDULE

Now that you're dressed and ready to go, it's time to face your day head-on with the discipline of an office executive. And the best way to do that is to have a schedule sitting on your desk from the day before.

Many home-based entrepreneurs swear by the benefits of taking time out at the end of a day to map out a tentative schedule for the following day. Patrick, a home-based graphic designer, says, "I never leave my home office without establishing some sort of a schedule for the ensuing day. I usually work from my yearly calendar and my personal notes to determine what appointments I need to fit into the day, and I detail them on a single piece of paper. That paper serves as a schedule, which I adhere to fairly closely—I don't often sway from that itinerary."

Patrick is somewhat rigid in his approach to scheduling, and this method works well for him. However, in general, experts don't recommend an extreme adherence to a daily agenda. It's important to remain flexible and willing to vacillate from the schedules you set for yourself. Inevitably, events will arise unexpectedly and calls will need to be placed that cannot be anticipated a day in advance. Having an itinerary doesn't mean you can't make adjustments.

Although it's difficult to be prepared for the unexpected, a good way to plan ahead for these events and calls is to have a loose weekly itinerary in mind. Keep it in a daily-planning calendar book. If you have an all-day seminar scheduled for Friday, you can call the client who indicated she might want to meet with you on Friday and schedule an appointment for Thursday.

PRIORITIZE

Prioritizing, or determining what's most important, is the most effective means of determining how to arrange your schedule to accommodate both planned and unplanned activities. Of course, when setting up appointments with associates and clients, you should work to coordinate times that are most appropriate for each party. This, in itself, is prioritizing. However, such things as lengthy phone calls, budgeting, administration, and the actual work that defines your business can be manipulated into your agenda based upon their importance.

Ask yourself these questions: When is the paperwork due on the Harris account? What materials must be prepared for the ten o'clock meeting with Jonathan Ross? Which telephone call has the most bearing on the day's activities? And, which meeting can I postpone in order to complete the finishing touches on the Harris report?

Once you have answered these questions, you are in a better position to arrange your schedule effectively.

BE REALISTIC

One of the most common downfalls of the home-based entrepreneur is trying to do too much. Deborah, a California-based interior designer, says that cramming more than she can do into her schedule is a major problem.

"It never fails," she laments. "I get on the phone and promise a sketch to one client and private consultations to three more. I guess it's because I think I'll lose their business if I don't accommodate them right away. But as soon as I hang up, I'm scrambling to fit everything in."

Deborah's dilemma is typical. But the problem can be rectified through the understanding of two things: her own limitations and her client's expectations. She must realize that not only do her clients understand that she can't always provide such prompt service, but they would also be more satisfied with her service if it were undertaken at a more reasonable pace. Be honest and accommodating with your clients and associates, and they will appreciate your frankness.

You should know after several weeks of operation how long a personal consultation will take and how long you can expect to spend typing a report, etc. Once you have a general idea of the time commitment entailed for certain business tasks, allow some leeway time between appointments. Give yourself approximately fifteen minutes extra for late arrivals or extended meetings. Even if your appointment ends exactly when you had planned, it's better to have a few minutes to relax and prepare for the next activity than to be frazzled and rushing to the next one. Although you may not be able to fit in as much work during the day, you will appear far more professional to your clients and your work will benefit, too.

On the other hand, don't be too lax. Not scheduling enough meetings and concentrated work time into your day can also cause some significant conflicts with clients and your bottom line. Again, it will take some time before you can gauge what can be accomplished during certain time allotments. However, squandering the time you have can result in a loss in profits and clientele.

During the first few months of operation, determine how much you can realistically accomplish without getting burned out and without being lazy. Remember, your profits are completely dependent upon the product or service you—and you alone—provide.

INTERRUPTIONS

Spending more time with your family may be one of your primary motives for starting a home-based company. That's why Shelley, a Boston native, left her full-time job as a hospital administrator to establish a home pet-care service. Until she changed careers, Shelley's infant girls were carted off to day care Monday through Friday. Today, the thirty-two-year-old businesswoman spends her days in the house with the kids while still contributing to the household income.

But even this arrangement had problems. Her children and her husband—not to mention her friends—all knew that she was home during the day. Her friends and husband called her "just to talk." And her children, despite the fact that they were being cared for by a sitter, constantly knocked on her door to visit. Quite simply, Shelley had too many interruptions.

You cannot indulge interruptions. After all, an effectively orchestrated day, complete with appointments and concentrated work time, can be thwarted by too many distractions. Shelley solved her problem by being straight with her husband, kids, and friends: During work hours, she cannot be interrupted. You may face an entirely different set of distractions—from busybody neighbors to the good old refrigerator. Don't let them get the best of you. Controlling your work time is critical if you're going to succeed. (For more on dealing with interruptions, see chapter 20.)

PRIVATE TIME

If all this sounds like a lot of structure to you, it is. You are not a free spirit when you work at home. In fact, maintaining guidelines may be more important to home-based entrepreneurs than it is to office workers. Offices are professional environments. Everyone in an office is there to work. You have to work hard to create the same effect at home. Regulating your time, avoiding personal calls, and maintaining a regular schedule are all important to the effort.

However, that doesn't mean you have to cast aside the flexibility that prompted you to "go home" in the first place. You can be flexible without being loose. Heather, who left her investment-banking position to start an accounting company, wanted more time for aerobics and the chance to sleep later during the work week. Now that she owns her own company, the flexibility she wanted has become a reality. She can sleep later and she can participate in aerobics classes during her free time. If she wants to meet with friends, she can do this too.

But this doesn't mean that Heather is undisciplined. For example, if she is going to sleep late on the weekdays, she must make up for that time after five o'clock, when she would normally be quitting. Stretching out the work day is an excellent way to build in some time for sleep or play. Heather takes aerobics whenever she wants during the day, then makes up the time in the evening.

The key is manipulating your agenda to accommodate all of your business needs and responsibilities. With proper organization, you can do everything you want to do—including making your business a success.

19

COPING WITH ISOLATION

WORKING ALONE DOESN'T HAVE TO BE LONELY

Michaela is a home-based day-care consultant in Denver. She's twenty-eight, single, and lives alone in an attractive two-bedroom apartment in the heart of the city. She loves working from her home. She doesn't have to shovel her car out early in the morning after snowstorms, she can set her own hours, and she's her own boss. Being home based has been a welcome relief from her job as an elementary-school teacher. But she'll be the first to admit that there are drawbacks, too.

Along with the obvious advantages of working from a home office there are also some significant detractions—and loneliness is the most apparent. You may not have considered the loneliness factor in anticipating your home-based business, but it's there. In a standard business environment, you have coworkers and associates around you constantly. Even if you work in your own office behind a closed door, you always have the coffee room, lunch hour, and quick strolls down the hall to look forward to. At home, none of the socialization that exists in an office is built in. In effect, you are isolated.

The side effects of isolation—above and beyond loneliness—are also troublesome. Being isolated leaves your social life in a state of disarray, and networking for supplementary work and potential clients is difficult. You don't have built-in motivators and incentives (thanks from your boss, appreciation from coworkers) to keep you going. At your regular job, you probably took these things for granted. As a home-based entrepreneur, you will probably miss them.

However, you can turn the tables. With a little planning, you can enjoy the input and camaraderie of others and make working alone more productive.

PREPARE YOURSELF

Start by anticipating the change. Michaela, like most home-based entrepreneurs, found shifting gears a little jarring. "When I decided to start working from my apartment, I was totally unprepared for the quiet and the loneliness day after day," she says. "After working around kids and teachers every day, I had grown accustomed to the companionship and conversation. I really enjoyed the silence at first, and I accomplished a lot in my business. But after a while, I became genuinely lonely. If someone had warned me about what to expect from a home-based business, I think I would have been better equipped to deal with it."

Face up to the reality that your afternoon chats with coworkers and regular meetings with the boss will no longer be. Once you come to grips with the potential problem, you can take steps to avoid it.

PEACE AND QUIET

Experts report that one of the most effective means for beating entrepreneurial loneliness is to look at isolation in a positive—rather than negative—light. Derek, a home-based copywriter in New York, agrees. "For me, quiet is especially important because I need silence to complete my work," he explains. "That reality has helped me to look at isolation as stimulating rather than boring or stifling. I take advantage of the isolation and make it work for me. I get so much more work done than I used to when I worked at the agency with a myriad of interruptions."

While a new perspective is the first step to conquering feelings of isolation, don't stop there. Another important technique is active socialization, both during your workday and in your personal life. Being alone in your home—or with your family during the evenings—may be comfortable, but it's also important to get out and see other people.

BUSINESS MEALS

Start interacting through business breakfasts, lunches, or dinners. No matter what kind of business you own—whether you're a tax consultant or a wedding planner—your company probably requires you to meet with clients during the workday. If this is the case, plan luncheon or breakfast meetings. Lunching with a client is a great way to break up your concentrated work hours.

Michaela reports that the benefits of business lunches are twofold. "I like meeting with my clients over lunch or dinner because it creates a relaxing atmosphere for us to discuss business," she says. "In comparison to meeting in either my office or the client's office, a restaurant is far more casual—with welcome diversions. In addition, the less businesslike approach puts us on a different level, and we build a personal rapport that helps in the negotiations and dealings that occur later on."

If your business is one that doesn't entail client appointments—perhaps you own a landscaping service—you can still benefit from the relaxation of a luncheon date. Call a friend and plan to meet for an hour or so. It will get you out of the house and into the social atmosphere of a restaurant. Here, you can talk to your heart's content and get that tendency to chat out of your system for the better part of the day.

TAKE A MEETING

Another way to boost your activity is to arrange for your business to take you out of the home. Schedule in-person meetings with your clients and associates. Think about your workday. Evaluate how many times per day you talk with clients over the phone and how many meetings you arrange in your office per week. Could any of those conversations be held in person at your client's office? Not only will communicating face-to-face help you socialize, it will demonstrate a few important qualities to your clients. First, it will show that your clients' business means enough to you to leave your home to meet them. And second, it demonstrates that you are willing to make meetings convenient for your clients, even at the expense of your own convenience.

If you own a real-estate business, meet at the house you're trying to sell. And if you are an accountant, go to your client's home or office for a meeting. However, be careful not to let your meetings get out of hand. It's one thing to "escape" from the solitude, but it's another to spend hours on inconsequential matters. By keeping your meetings relatively brief you'll be able to fit more of them into your schedule without interfering with your regular work.

JOIN A CLUB

When you were in high school and you wanted to meet new people or socialize, what did you do? Chances are, you joined a club, a team, or an organization. Perhaps you were a cheerleader or a member of the debating team. Although your cheerleading or varsity-football days may be over, the value of joining a club or an organization is very much alive.

Consider joining a business-related organization. The National Association of Home-based Businesses is one. This association has chapters all over the country, and its members regularly get together for dinner meetings and special events related to owning a home-based business. Of course, this is only one option. There are thousands of other organizations that you can join to meet people with common interests.

There are several ways to learn about the groups and clubs in your vicinity. The *Encyclopedia of Associations*, published by Gale Research, Inc., is a great source of information. This book provides a comprehensive listing of organizations and their locations around the country—from the Shipbuilders Council of America to the Educational Foundation for Foreign Study. You will find this book at your local library, in the reference section.

At your local library, you will also find trade publications. These are magazines or newsletters targeted directly toward your needs as a member of your industry. Trade publications contain helpful information on your field, and they also serve as a connection between people in the field and the organizations established by them. If you're a home-based advertising copywriter, for example, *Writer's Digest* and *AdWeek* are applicable publications for your use. *AdWeek* is particularly helpful because it's directed at regional areas and will provide specialized calendars of upcoming meetings and functions, as well as newly established clubs. If you find a trade publication you like, subscribe. Your subscription will put you on the mailing list for further information on organizations and groups.

When seeking new clubs and organizations, don't overlook your local newspapers, television, and radio. All of these media are excellent sources for activities happening in your area. Look in the events section of your paper, and listen for public-service announcements on radio and television.

Finally, don't hesitate to talk to your friends, clients, and business associates about the clubs they belong to. They know firsthand how useful—or fun—an organization is. People are more than happy to provide recommendations if they're enthusiastic about their involvement.

START YOUR OWN CLUB

If the kind of club you want to be a part of doesn't exist in your area, start your own! Entrepreneurial support groups are one outlet for meeting other businesspeople. Starting one from scratch may be easier than you think.

Your club may take a while to get off the ground, but don't be discouraged. Remember, your club doesn't have to be formal or large to be successful. In fact, your new club doesn't even have to be a club. Start by calling your organization a peer group and make it casual and convenient for members.

You can start a group like this easily—all it takes is a few phone calls to associates and friends. Set a date and a meeting place. Your home will suffice initially, then you can trade meeting locales with your regular members. At first, attendance might be low, but don't be alarmed. Even if you only have three people at your first few meetings, chances are the ensuing meetings will fill out. And even a small group can be productive and enjoyable.

NETWORK!

One of the most substantial disadvantages of working at home is the lack of networking opportunities. Unless you make a concerted effort, there is little networking to be done. Yet for a small company, there are few aspects of business that are more important than networking.

Fortunately for you, you can use some effective techniques to increase your networking capacity. One of those tools is the business lunch. Whenever you meet for lunch with an associate or a client, look at that meeting as a potential contact for future business. That's not to say that you must talk about business and business alone. In fact, strong selling is counterproductive. Be subtle but not sly. Put yourself in the position of your associate. Sincerity and concern are more likely to impress than the old hard sell.

Business appointments are another excellent environment for developing business contacts, particularly when you meet in your client's office. There, you are likely to meet new people who could benefit from your services in the future. Keeping this in mind, always project a professional image and carry an ample supply of business cards when you visit clients—or even friends. The written materials you hand out, the clothes you wear, and the attitude you emanate will be vital during these brief encounters. Remember that first impressions are the most enduring.

Perhaps the most valuable arenas for networking are the association and club meetings you attend during your free time. These gatherings are planned specifically to further your involvement in the industry, and they are frequented by associates who can do exactly that. Catherine, a public relations specialist, believes strongly in the benefits of association meetings. "When I started my firm, I operated the company alone, and I had only two clients," she says. "But I have always been an active member of the International Association of Business Communicators (IABC). It was through the contacts I met at those meetings that I was able to build up my business. My peers were more than willing to offer recommendations and referrals, and without them, I never would have made it."

The bottom line is that while business lunches, appointments, and association meetings are outstanding occasions for networking, nearly every activity has networking potential. The person you sit next to on the plane is a potential client. The man you met Sunday night at your sister's barbecue is also a possible contact. Just about anyone you meet could represent business for your company in the future, so be ready to talk about it. Owning a home-based business doesn't have to be an isolating, lonely experience. You can actually make it work for you.

TIME OUT

Owning your own business is a time-consuming responsibility—whether it's home-based or not. You may find yourself insisting that you don't have time for a weekend trip, networking luncheon, or dinner with friends. If you don't think you have free time, make it. Time off is as crucial to your success as work time.

When you do take time out, what's the best way to spend it? Do you sit in front of the television? Read a book in your office? Relax around the house?

Because you work in your home, there is no driving force that pulls you from that location every day. A desire to stay at home is normal. However, developing a pattern of spending too much time where you live and work is counterproductive. Go out whenever you can. Maintaining social contacts and interacting with new people is as good for business as it is for your emotional stability.

John, a Laguna Beach, California, graphics designer, agrees. He reflects, "When I first began working at home, it became very easy to stay there. And after a while, it just got to the point where I rarely left—except to go grocery shopping or out for dinner on a weekend." Harrison continues, "I didn't realize what was happening at the time, but I had depleted most of my personal and professional contacts by neglecting them. It took me a long time to build them back up once I realized what I was doing, and I'll never do it again!"

Keeping up connections doesn't mean becoming a social butterfly, floating from one party to another. But don't neglect friends, family, and associates. You need their companionship, feedback, and support more than ever.

GET MOTIVATED

Discipline is one trait you must have if you're going to succeed as a home-based entrepreneur. Compared to the standard office environment, the home has thousands of distractions and temptations. There's the television— that huge black screen that's calling your name. There's the ficus plant in the living room that needs watering and the pot of spaghetti simmering in the kitchen that needs stirring. And of course, there's that overwhelming need to lie your head on the table and take a very short nap!

Unlike in an office, where peer pressure runs rampant, you are now responsible for your own motivation. Design a schedule that will prompt you to complete certain tasks at certain times, and you will find that your tendency to procrastinate will diminish. Reward yourself. When you complete a report, take a lunch break with a friend. When you successfully negotiate a contract, plan a celebration dinner. That dinner will be a motivation for future successes—and who knows who you might meet.

20

DRIVEN FROM DISTRACTIONS

COPING WITH INTERRUPTIONS AND OTHER TIME STEALERS

Your children, television, refrigerator, and spouse are potential business liabilities. Why? They will all conspire to tempt you from work. These, your beloved, are potential distractions. And your success depends on your ability to tune them out when you have to.

Sound harsh? Consider the confessions of one home-based entrepreneur: "Sometimes when I'm in my office working on administration and billing, all I can think about is my house that needs cleaning and the food in my refrigerator," says Brynne, catering entrepreneur in Nantucket, Massachusetts. "At times, the urge becomes so overwhelming that I leave my office to vacuum the family room. And once I'm actually doing that, it's like a vicious circle. I go from the family room to the kitchen, and before you know it, the day is gone."

Brynne is not alone in her distractibility. In fact, if she didn't succumb to distraction every once in a while, she would be a saint. Everyone has a tendency to give in to distractions. And at home, the distractions are many. Cleaning, eating, or chatting on the phone are only a few temptations. Watering the plants, preparing the evening meal, letting the plumber in for the neighbor, and even sleeping are also major time stealers. Ironically, when you have free time, cleaning and cooking are the last things you want to do. But when you're up to your armpits in invoices or up against an unreasonable deadline, cleaning your oven sounds like a grand time.

BE AWARE

The first step to beating temptation is being aware that it exists. Brynne came to admit that distractions were getting the better of her, but only at her husband's prompting. "My husband, Jack, is the night manager of a restaurant, so he's always home during the day. He used to just watch me strolling from room to room in search of distractions, but he never said anything," she says. "That is, until my business began to suffer. He was the one who pinpointed my problem. If he hadn't spotlighted how I spent my time, I would never have known I was procrastinating through distractions."

You can determine for yourself whether or not you are easily distracted. Think about the ways you spend your time. Do you sit at the desk in your office and work diligently for several concentrated hours at a time—then reward yourself with a break? Or do you work for fifteen minutes, then walk to the kitchen to take out some hamburger for dinner? Does the porch need sweeping? Does the toaster oven need fixing? In fact, is your whole house in need of immediate and extensive repair? If so, you either live in a disaster area or you're easily distracted.

ACT IMMEDIATELY

Fortunately, there is hope. Home-based-business owners are faced with a minefield of distractions. Compared to the standard corporate executive, home-based entrepreneurs are inundated. Your family, friends, neighbors, and pets are the primary culprits. Then there are telephones, the refrigerator, and household chores. And the list goes on.

Before digressions develop into a new habit, take steps to deal with the situation right away. If you regularly raid the refrigerator, place small snacks on your desk in the morning so that you won't be tempted to wander to the kitchen every five minutes. Put a note on the refrigerator, too: GO BACK TO WORK. Understand that the longer you tolerate your tendency to be distracted, the harder the elimination process will be.

Realizing that you have a problem is not a solution. Once you are aware of your weakness, the second step is to do something constructive about it. Start by analyzing your situation.

TAKE CARE OF YOURSELF

Why do you get up to go to the refrigerator every half hour? Could it be you're not eating properly? Are you working so many hours that you don't have time to prepare and eat three meals per day? Perhaps you aren't exercising enough and your self-esteem is low.

If this is the case, your behavior may be the result of an unhealthy approach to life. Remedy that unhealthy attitude by taking care of yourself! Resolve to start working regular hours whenever possible. Start eating right and at normal three-meal intervals, complemented by small snacks as nutrition experts recommend. Adopt an exercise pattern of some sort. Exercise helps to work out your aggressions and it gets you out of the house. You will be amazed at how significantly your overall approach to living can impact your work.

Creating a more productive atmosphere for yourself and your business can also be done by analyzing your workload and determining your limitations. Raymond, a Salt Lake City-based accountant, came to terms with distractions by taking a long, hard look at his life-style.

"I used to wake up in the morning and immediately begin to dread the day in my home office," he recalls. "I had taken on too many clients, and I was working far too many breakless hours in one day. It was so stressful for me that I would do anything just to get me out of my office."

Raymond decided that it wasn't the work itself that was stressful but rather the manner in which he approached it. To remedy the situation, he set a more realistic schedule that included lunch, coffee breaks, and a strict limit on the total number of hours he spent in the office. Unless an extenuating circumstance arises and a report is due "yesterday," Raymond works from eight A.M. until five P.M. "The results were miraculous," he reports. "The new approach to my work actually had me looking forward to facing a new day."

OUT OF SIGHT, OUT OF MIND

In addition to changing your personal habits, try to remove distractions altogether. Remember the old adage out of sight, out of mind.

For instance, if compulsive cleaning is your downfall, make an extra effort to keep your office tidy (by cleaning it after work, of course). That way, piles of files and old coffee cups won't nag at you all day. Keep your office door closed, so dirty dishes and dusty furniture can't beckon. If your compulsion is extreme, consider hiring a cleaning service. The cleaners will remove every trace of temptation, and you'll recover the money you spend by being productive, not distracted.

Also remember that giving in to a small digression is better than throwing all caution aside for a large one. Going to the kitchen for a slice of pound cake is one matter; whipping up an elaborate soufflé during work hours in another. You can give in to small distractions from time to time. Doing something unrelated to work may clear your mind and help you regain your focus. But set some limits for yourself. Taking a walk around the block is invigorating. Running a triathlon is too much.

DIAL A FRIEND

Isolation and loneliness play a big part in your tendency to be distracted. Working at home with no built-in contact or communication with others may cause you to feel bored. However, boredom doesn't have to lead to overindulgence. Instead of watching TV or eating during the day, work in breaks that are designed to incorporate interpersonal contact. Call a friend and make plans for the evening, or telephone an associate to ask for recommendations on a problem. Interpersonal contact could be what you need to get back on the right track.

Remember, though, that balance is all. Keep your conversations to a reasonable length, and don't spend the whole day dialing up your cronies. With the right balance, you can fit work and socializing into your schedule. (For more on cultivating social contacts, see chapter 19.)

DEALING WITH SPECIAL PROBLEMS

Your friends, your children, and your spouse are unique temptations. As wonderful as they are, your family and friends will undoubtedly serve as distractions in your home-based business. However, unlike the television or refrigerator, these people must be treated with love and respect.

The Kids

Dierdra, a home-based illustrator and single mother of a four-year-old girl, dealt with the "kid predicament" when she decided to quit her job with the local newspaper to launch her free-lance career.

"I used to miss Alexis so much when I was at work all day long and she was at the baby-sitter's. I called often to check on her, and I left work at lunch to visit her whenever I could. I thought that working at home would be the ultimate answer to the problem," she explains. "But when I started my own business, I was faced with a whole new dilemma. Initially, I thought I would be able to care for Alexis myself, but I learned quickly that it wouldn't be possible—she just requires too much attention."

The conclusion Dierdra reached after several weeks of testing the waters is common. Caring for a child while operating a business translates into one massive distraction. And for most busy entrepreneurs, it's one distraction that must be eliminated. If child care is your conflict, what are your options?

For home-based parents, there are several ways of taking care of the kids while working. If you want to keep the children at home with you, hire a baby-sitter. You'll be able to share some time with your children, but the bulk of the responsibility will be on someone else's shoulders.

Some businesspeople enjoy the role of parent so much that having the child in the house—even under someone else's care—is a temptation nonetheless. They float out of the office just to "check on the baby," and they allow the child to pop in regularly to visit. For these parents, hiring a sitter is not enough. Taking the children to a child-care facility is a better alternative. Another option is the child-care co-op. Because these plans require parents to take turns caring for kids, they may not work for home-based businesspeople with busy Monday-through-Friday schedules. However, if your work hours are flexible, this might be just the alternative for you.

Once your children are older than seven—the cutoff for passable maturity—you might be able to avoid formal day care. By seven, kids are usually in school for a good part of the day. During school hours, you can work, then reserve the afternoon hours for tasks that require less concentration.

Don't let your unsupervised kids run wild, however. Set some guidelines. Make it clear to your children that you love them and you're working at home in order to be closer to them. But make it clear, too, that just because you're at home doesn't mean you're available for every minor event or conflict. Explain that you will set aside break time for them but that the remainder of the time is for work and you can only be interrupted for emergencies. Spell out exactly what constitutes an emergency, and then remain firm on your policies. (For more on integrating your work and family lives, consult chapter 21.)

Your Spouse

Dealing with your husband or wife can be an even more delicate undertaking. Although your kids may not understand why you can't be with them when you're working at home, they can be taught. Adults are a different story. Spouses think of themselves as partners or helpmates—not a continual source of annoyance. Without tact and diplomacy, you could turn an otherwise balanced relationship into a battleground.

Raymond, the accountant mentioned earlier, discovered that he and his wife had different expectations about his working at home. "When Diana and I first talked about moving my business to the house, she was thrilled," he says. "She was home as well, taking care of our two-year-old son, and we both viewed it as a great way to spend more time together as a family."

But Raymond and his wife were on different wavelengths. "I knew she was happy, but I had no idea that she thought we would be together so much," he says. "During the first few weeks I was at home, she was popping in and out of the office sharing our son's new words and other progress. I had to tell her that I couldn't be bothered so often, and she was very hurt. She had been under the impression that I would be constantly available."

Diana's presumptions about her husband's availability are not uncommon. When the subject isn't addressed directly, misunderstandings are bound to occur. Discuss your expectations with your spouse. Work together to establish guidelines before a conflict arises. Make it clear that you want to spend time with your spouse but that you need to work uninterrupted as well. Ask for your spouse's suggestions so that the plan you implement is agreeable to both of you.

Don't overlook the value of quality time. You can't spend every working moment together, but you can plan special lunches, regular walks, or early dinners out.

Your Friends

The mere fact that your friends know you're home during the day may prompt them to call. Dierdra was inundated with calls from friends and neighbors when she quit her job to begin working from her Oregon home.

Requests like, "I have to run out for a few hours; would

you mind letting the television repairman into the house while I'm gone?" and, "You know, DeeDee, I'm feeling kind of low, do you mind if I come over and talk for a while?" started pouring in. Friends equated Dierdra's being at home with being available. But, of course, that's not true.

When friends call with major requests, tactfully explain that you'd love to help them out or visit but you're "on deadline" and can't tear yourself away. Then suggest a time when you can see them—in the evening, at lunch, or on the weekend. If you're firm and consistent, they'll get the message.

Some friends are extremely persistent. Despite your best efforts to discourage their calls, visits, and impositions, they are undaunted. Don't cave in to their demands. Use drastic measures if you have to: Let the answering machine screen your calls, and don't answer the door when they knock. Let them know that you are not available during work hours. In time, they'll learn to contact you when you are free.

21

FAMILY AND BUSINESS DO MIX

HOW YOUR BUSINESS AND YOUR LOVED ONES CAN COEXIST UNDER THE SAME ROOF

For many small-business owners, the decision to start a business at home is family motivated. Both men and women believe that running a business from a home office will be the answer to their prayers. No more long commutes, overtime, and unreasonable bosses. They can lavish the time they save on their previously neglected families.

However, for most home-based entrepreneurs, integrating business and family takes a fair amount of coordination. Taking the time to discuss your new roles, solve potential problems, and establish open lines of communication now could save you a lot of headaches down the road. Some conflicts are emotional; others are merely logistical. In either case, it's important to get your family working with you in your new venture. With their cooperation and support, you can all coexist peacefully in your new work environment.

Here, then, are a few tips on making your home office work for both you and your family.

ANTICIPATE CONFLICTS

Brock is a home-based speech writer in New York. When he left his job with a Fortune 500 company to work at home, he expected only positive results from spending more time with his family.

"When I reached the conclusion that I would start my own home-based business, I was apprehensive about several aspects of that decision," he says. "However, none of my major concerns centered around my family. I had no idea my family would come into play in the business so readily. I was very surprised at how strongly the business impacted my family life—but I sure learned quick!"

The first trick to business-family harmony is anticipating problems before they happen. Be realistic. Don't set up your computer in the kid's playroom. Don't get caught off guard when your spouse hits you with a list of errands a mile long. If family conflicts take you by surprise, you're likely to react irritably and irrationally—and you won't deal effectively with issues. Be prepared to set guidelines for your kids and to negotiate a new division of household labor with your spouse. By examining problems before they become the subject of emotional warfare, you'll be able to work out sensible, happy solutions.

TAKE THE INITIATIVE

You may think your home office is your castle, but remember that it was your family's home first. Just because you need peace and quiet, uninterrupted phone access, plenty of office space, and a hassle-free day doesn't mean your family is prepared to give up their usual activities. You need a place to work, but they need a place to live—to play, shout, fight, stomp, and generally wreak havoc.

Don't expect your family to adopt monklike behavior simply for your benefit. You have a right to expect consideration—but so do they. If you have three young children, set up operations in a quiet corner of the house—not in the dining room next to the TV. If your teenage offspring tie up your phone constantly, get a separate line for your business. Instead of complaining that your spouse interrupts your work with phone calls, take the initiative and call him or her at your convenience. Wherever possible, avoid confrontation by eliminating the source of the problem yourself.

You are asking your family to accommodate a demanding new intruder—your business—in their own home. Inevitably, they will have to change their ways to make room for your new concern. But you can soften the blow—and reduce the potential for conflicts—by being as considerate of their needs as you can be. If you can resolve a conflict by modifying your operations, do that. They'll be doubly cooperative with your requests if they feel you're meeting them halfway.

RECOGNIZE PROBLEMS

Working under the same roof as your spouse and/or kids is bound to be more distracting than working in an office. That isn't all bad. In fact, you don't have to deprive yourself of greeting your kids when they come home from school, enjoying a picnic lunch with your spouse in the middle of the week, or taking your long-neglected dog for a romp in the park. These distractions are welcome: They're probably one of the main reasons you decided to work at home in the first place.

But you can get too much of a good thing. You can indulge in familial distractions and make your business a success, but only if you can recognize your own limits. Are you missing deadlines? Are clients unable to reach you because you're constantly escorting the kids on outings or meeting your spouse for lunch? Do you find yourself scrambling, trying to cram as much work into a few hours as possible so you can spend quality time with your family?

Stop. When family activities interfere with your business, it's time to regroup. As soon as you detect a conflict, start working toward resolving it. The longer you live with bad habits, the more difficult it will be to get rid of them.

CALL A MEETING

If you're spending too much time with the family and not enough with your business, it's time to call a family meeting. Explain to your kids or your spouse (or both) that you love being with them and pitching in around the house but that you have to find more time for work. Then ask them for their help.

By involving your family in the problem-solving process, you avoid the role of dictator. You are not Mussolini, ordering your spouse and children about like inconsequential flunkies. You need their help. Their cooperation and support are marks of virtue. You aren't making accusations and issuing ultimatums: You're asking for their assistance, which you will appreciate. Invite their input and offer your own. This way, you have a good chance of finding solutions that everyone can live with.

BE FIRM

You went overboard; you spent too much time with your family. Now it's time to buckle down and get some work done. You are committed to your new diligence—but is your family?

Setting new guidelines isn't enough. You have to be firm in your convictions. You cannot decide that there will be no more afternoon interruptions from your children, then give in to their plea for a quick trip to the ice-cream parlor.

You can't rely on your family to provide the discipline for you. Your four-year-old daughter cannot be a model of restraint. Your wife doesn't see the mountains of work you have piled on your desk. Your business is at stake, not theirs. You must exhibit an iron will, even it it means missing out on some fun or occasionally playing the villain.

In some cases, explaining your predicament may help. For Francie, a home-based caterer in Lincoln, Nebraska, a long talk was in order. "I sat all three of my kids down and explained that although I'm home during the day, that doesn't mean that I'm always available for questions and comments," she says. "I told them to pretend I work in a regular office building, except in the case of emergencies."

CALL IN THE REINFORCEMENTS

Sometimes, despite your best efforts, you just can't juggle the demands of a growing business and a growing family. That's when it's time to call in the reinforcements.

Many home-based entrepreneurs start their business with the mistaken notion that they can supervise their toddlers, clean their home, cook elaborate meals, and keep their business thriving. With a few superhuman exceptions, this just isn't the case. Yes, you have more time to clean; but you also have more time to make a mess. Yes, you can spend more time with your children; but you probably can't spend all day playing patty-cake and changing diapers.

If you need the help of a baby-sitter, day-care center, or cleaning service, get the help you need. You cannot handle every household chore and family crisis simply because you're home. Eliminating some of the more obvious time stealers—like cleaning the kitchen or changing diapers—is one of the simplest ways of improving household relations.

TOO CLOSE FOR COMFORT?

You won't believe it, but in the course of running your own business, you may find that you're spending too much time with your family. Impossible? Take a closer look at your home-based life-style.

When you worked in an office, you left the house to do battle with the outside world. You met with clients, chatted with coworkers, interfaced with the boss. True, every day was not a picnic. But no matter how miserable your experiences at work were, you got to come home at the end of the day.

Now, you never leave the house. Your spouse comes home for lunch. Your kids rifle through your papers while you're trying to get work done. Even your dog makes off with your favorite pen. Once in a while, your family gets on your nerves. And at the end of the day, guess what? You don't leave the commotion behind. You face an entire evening with the same motley bunch.

There is such a thing as being too close for comfort. Family burnout is another good reason to limit your contact with your spouse and children during work hours. You'll appreciate your family more if you see them less. Also, make it a point to get away every so often to have lunch with friends, meet with clients, attend business seminars, or simply enjoy a night out. Your family may be the most important people in your life, but they don't have to be the only ones.

SEPARATE WORK FROM FAMILY

In large measure, your success at integrating family and business will depend on your ability to separate the two. We've already pointed out some of the pitfalls of letting your family interfere with business. Now, let us note the perils of letting your work interfere with family time.

Starting a new business is a stressful affair. You'll be putting in long hours. You'll be under a lot of pressure. Your future depends on your performance—and if you're new to entrepreneurship, that pressure can translate into serious tension. Moreover, you can't leave all reminders of work at the office. Your computer may call to you at all hours of the day or night. You may blurt out marketing schemes at Sunday dinner. The line between work and play may fade, until you find yourself always straddling both worlds.

Get off the fence. Devote your all to your business during the work week, then switch gears. Set aside some time just for the people who are close to you. Don't talk about business—don't even think about it. You expect your family to treat you like a real businessperson during the workday. On your off hours, do them the courtesy of treating them like a real family. You'll reap the rewards in your business as well as your home.

Putting your business and family in sync should be a top priority in setting up your new venture. Without the support of your family, your home-based company faces some rough going. (Of course, the opposite is also true: If your business fails, your family may find the going tough!) A family and a business are a lot to fit under one roof, but, for the home-based business owner, doing so is not only important—it's essential.

22

Enough Hours
in the Day

FINDING TIME FOR EVERYTHING YOU NEED—
AND WANT—TO DO

As an employee, you had a job. Perhaps you planned corporate meetings. You found sites, negotiated with caterers, worked out schedules. You became so good at it that you decided to strike out on your own. Now, you're a home-based meeting planner—and your job basically is the same, right?

Wrong. When you work for someone else, your work is focused. As a meeting planner, your job ended when the meeting was set. You didn't have to generate payroll, develop new marketing strategies, network on behalf of the company, or clean the corporate bathrooms. As a home-based-business owner, these additional responsibilities are yours.

How will you find enough hours in the day to complete these tasks? That's a question that many new business owners find themselves asking. Your home-based operations will probably be modest. You won't have a staff of millions to accomplish the work at hand. So in order to do everything you need to do, you must be a master of time management. Letting time get the best of you will not only hurt your productivity, but it will also increase your stress. Without the right organizational skills, you may end up a frazzled failure. For a few basic tips on making friends with Father Time, read on.

WHAT DO YOU MEAN BY WASTING TIME?

What does it mean to waste time? Generally, wasting time at work means not being productive. Experts list procrastination, indecision, daydreaming, and impulsiveness as classic time wasters.

Yet for many entrepreneurs, these activities can actually boost productivity. Catherine, a home-based portrait artist in Florida, claims that daydreaming is part and parcel of her work. "I find daydreaming very inspiring in my work," she explains. "Oftentimes, I will look at the photos I'm working from and then stare off into space in thought about the subject. That pondering is very productive for me, because it adds a new dimension to the final product."

Procrastination, indecision, daydreaming, and impulsiveness aren't necessarily enemies of the good time manager. Indulge in them with moderation and you'll probably be okay. But be aware that in excess, these activities can bring on long spates of inertia. Even Catherine admits that daydreaming can get the best of her. "I have been known to wander off in my mind for too long," she says. "I have to be careful."

WHERE DOES THE TIME GO?

You can't change your evil ways unless you first know what they are. And the best way to find out where the time goes is to put it in writing. Make a list of the things you do during a typical day that waste time. Divide your list into two columns—one for situations caused by outside forces and a second for those caused by you. This way, you can evaluate how distractions enter into your regular schedule, either through your own doing or forces beyond your control.

For Catherine, daydreaming was a minor time waster. Though she added it to her list, other elements of her daily behavior were added first. "I find that I tend to spend a lot of time on the phone and that I like to fritter my time away by completing small tasks around the house," she says. "I listed both items in the column devoted to those things I am at fault for. The opposite side of my column was almost blank!"

LIST, LIST, LIST

Your list of time wasters isn't the only list you should compile. In fact, that list is only the first of many lists that will be instrumental to the organization of your life through time management. You can keep your lists organized by filing them in a loose-leaf notebook.

Once you've completed your list of time wasters, turn your efforts toward defining your ultimate business goal. Chances are, you haven't given this one much thought. You know that you want to succeed, but you haven't envisioned what that success will bring. Knowing what your ultimate goal is will help you direct your day-to-day activities. Be as specific as possible.

For example, John, a home-based copywriter, has a clear goal for his business. "My ultimate objective is to own a highly respected advertising agency with branches all over the country," he says. "It's a challenging goal, but I know what it will take to achieve it, so everything until then revolves around that goal."

IN THE LONG AND SHORT TERM

After establishing your ultimate objective, make a list of smaller goals that will help you achieve your target. These can be both long- and short-term ambitions. For example, wanting to franchise your business in four years is a long-term goal, while increasing your July sales by 25 percent is a short-term goal. Make your list as comprehensive as possible, and use it as a reference or checklist to guide

you through your business life. Your goal list will keep
your priorities in focus.

This is important, because most time-management
decisions aren't based on what's good to do but what's
better. Deciding between an afternoon at the beach and
an afternoon in the office is easy. But choosing between a
networking lunch and having two extra hours to complete
a project is more difficult.

Before you agree to spend time on any activity—be it a
weekend seminar or a special project—ask yourself how
that activity will help you achieve your goals. If the acitiv-
ity in question will not further your cause, consider
whether or not you really have the time for it. Every
minute spent on one pursuit is time taken away from
another.

UNFINISHED BUSINESS

Now that your goals and objectives are in place, make a
"to do" list for the coming week. This will include regular
errands, like taking clothes to the cleaners and catching
up on paperwork. It will also include tasks you need to
complete for current projects: writing up an estimate for
one client, supervising work for another. Be thorough.
You can even list such banalities as brushing your teeth
and cleaning your desk.

When you're satisfied that every possible task is accounted for, it's time to prioritize. Some things cannot be
put off. Don't, for example, go without a shower for the
whole week. Schedule time for these basic chores. Even if
it seems silly to regiment your personal habits, putting
these activities on your schedule will encourage you to
finish them within a given time frame.

Give deadlines first priority. If a report is due on
Tuesday, block out enough time Monday to get it finished.
Commit your most important tasks to the calendar first,
so you'll be sure to fit them in. Then, fill your schedule
out with less important tasks.

Of course, some activities are more fun than others.
While it's tempting to pencil in the most enjoyable tasks
first, this may not be the most productive strategy. Many

entrepreneurs save the most pleasant tasks for last, as a kind of reward for hard work. Others try to intersperse fun errands with more serious ones—for instance, breaking up a grueling workday with a luncheon meeting. In any case, try to avoid putting all the fun activities toward the beginning of the week—you won't have much to look forward to.

At times, you may find that more than one project is a priority. Suppose, for example, that two projects are due at the same time. Some people have no problem juggling two projects at once. "When I have similar deadlines on several different projects, I often work on two at a time," says Joseph, a home-based accountant. "As long as I allot equal time to both, this dual-priority system works well." For other people, jumping back and forth between two projects is baffling. Find out which approach works best for you and schedule your time accordingly. Remember that in order to finish two projects on time without juggling both at once, you'll have to complete one ahead of schedule.

DELEGATING

But what if you can't possibly finish everything that needs to get done in the time you have? Learning to gauge the amount of work you can handle is one of the most important skills you'll develop as a business owner. Naturally, you want to take on as much work as possible to maximize your income. But on the other hand, contracting too much work can cut down on your effectiveness. Ultimately, you could lose accounts and create a major disaster.

Consider the option of delegating. One specialist urges businesspeople to examine the tasks at hand and divide them into three categories:

- things that you like to do but should leave to other people;
- things that you do well but that can be done by others;
- things that you have to do and that no one else can handle.

Many small-business owners believe that if they want a job done right, they should do it themselves. Your sense of responsibility will automatically tell you that you must handle everything yourself. But a quick assessment of the facts will probably indicate otherwise. Should you really spend the morning delivering a brochure to the printer when a messenger service could do it instead? Must you plow through your own books instead of handing them over to a bookkeeping service? In the beginning, your business may be so small that you will handle all these tasks yourself. As your business grows, however, your success will depend on your ability to delegate those jobs that other people can do as well or better than you can.

How can you learn to delegate? Start by hiring assistants or free lances, with the idea that you will leave them in charge of their jobs and ultimately responsible. Clearly define your expectations of them by outlining priorities and goals. Demonstrate confidence in their abilities and allow them to carry a job through to the end, despite any conflicts that may arise. Being able to delegate is an important management tool, and it will save you a lot of time in the end.

PERSONAL TIME

Creating—and keeping—a strict schedule is critical to your time-management efforts. But don't become a slave to your schedule. Even the best of us encounter occasional snags, unforeseen interruptions, cancellations, reunions, and other unexpected events. It's all right to be flexible—in fact, it's encouraged. Your schedule isn't worthwhile if it only makes you miserable.

Also remember to schedule some personal time for yourself. Experts agree that at least thirty minutes of solitude a day will help reduce stress and renew your energy for handling difficult situations. Don't feel guilty about scheduling a healthy diversion in your day, every day. You'll benefit from the escape time.

THE TOOLS OF TIME MANAGEMENT

To keep yourself on schedule, consider investing in some of the following products and services. Managing your time effectively is an ongoing battle. These accessories can help keep you on the right track:

- *Date book.* Calendar books play a pivotal role in scheduling. There are hundreds on the market—big and small. Look for one that provides a detailed accounting of hourly, as well as daily, activities.
- *Sorting baskets.* Eliminating clutter will make you feel better and more organized. You can keep your paperwork, bills, and proposals in order by purchasing several sorting baskets. Having an in and an out basket is the traditional setup. But Brynne, a Nantucket, Massachusetts, caterer has developed a more elaborate system, which she claims works wonders for her.

"I have stackable organizing trays in strategic spots around my office," she explains. "One tray is for regular clients. I have one tray for bills, and one tray for recipes, etc. It might not work for everyone, but it's been excellent for me."

- *Filing system.* In addition to sorting baskets, you will need a good filing system to keep the paper moving off your desk. Take the time to set up a system that's accessible, efficient, and neat. Plan time during each day to do your filing. Ten or fifteen minutes at the end of the day is typically the best time, because you can organize your paperwork and face the morning with a clean desk.

When setting up a filing system, don't overlook the problem of lost mail and messages. These can pile up on your desk, where they are easily lost. Experts recommend setting aside an hour to an hour and a half every day simply for returning phone calls and reading the mail. Otherwise, dealing with messages and correspondence can become a gargantuan task—one that many entrepreneurs put off indefinitely.

- *Answering machine.* If constant phone calls are a source of wasted time, find a way to screen calls. Hiring a secretary is probably the most effective, but also the most expensive. In lieu of a personal assistant, try hiring an answering service or simply setting up an answering machine.

PUT TIME ON YOUR SIDE

Many of the techniques and products we've discussed here are little more than common-sense solutions. Yet as you take on the additional responsibilities of running your own business, you may find yourself overwhelmed and in need of some common-sense approaches. The information in this chapter should enable you to get your schedule under control and make sure it stays that way.

Time-management specialists say that managing time is not an inborn trait but something you learn. With a little effort and organization, you can put time on your side once and for all.

23

IMAGE CONSCIOUSNESS

MINDING THE WAY YOU
AND YOUR BUSINESS LOOK

You're working at home. Your clients will never visit your office and they rarely see you, so you really don't need to be concerned with the appearance of either you or your office. What a relief!

Unfortunately, if you're thinking like this, it's time to rethink your philosophy—and fast! Many home-based entrepreneurs feel that working at home gives them the freedom to be lackadaisical about image. And for many, this lack of attention results in their downfall.

Believe it or not, image is even more important to home-based businesspeople than it is to operators who work from offices or storefronts. The fact that these business owners have a professional office or storefront location makes them appear professional. They had the money and smarts to get there, right? But home-based-business owners, regardless of how professional they are, are working from home. Anyone can do that, right?

While home-based businesspeople may be just as professional and effective as their office-owning counterparts, to the average person they appear less professional. As a home-based-business owner, you must compensate for your lack of professional surroundings by looking and acting as polished as possible.

START FROM THE BEGINNING

Many elements contribute to your image: your clothing and overall appearance, your written materials, your office space, your company's presentations and employees. Even your car is an instrumental part of your overall image.

Why? First impressions count. When you meet a business associate, customer, or competitor for the first time, what do you notice? Is he young and wet behind the ears? Does he appear old and stuffy or rigid? How often are your first impressions accurate? If the answer is often, that may be because first impressions don't happen by accident. They're calculated creations that people have put plenty of effort, thought, and money into cultivating.

Image doesn't stop at your appearance. Everything from your office decor to your business cards conveys something about your business—even if that something is your lack of interest in maintaining a good image. Experts recommend creating a company image even before you start your company. For example, if you are launching an interior-design business, you may decide that the most appropriate image is one of colorful creativity and openness both in your office and in your dress. On the other hand, if you're starting a home-based accounting firm geared toward lawyers and other professionals, then you would try to come across as an intelligent, straightforward professional.

Think carefully about the elements of your image. Establish a fitting image from the start and work hard to maintain that image for as long as you own your business. Don't flip-flop from one image to another. Similarly, don't come across one way in your written materials and another in person. If obvious inconsistencies exist in your overall presentation, your credibility is at stake.

LOOK AT ME NOW!

You are your own best advertisement—or, at least, you can be. After all, when you act in a business capacity, you are a direct reflection on your business. Understanding this, how can you be sure that your personal advertising is working effectively for you? Is the way you present yourself professional? Do you come across in a way that reflects positively on your business? Are clients favorably impressed with you and, as a result, your business?

The best way to determine the answers to these questions is to evaluate yourself closely—as an objective observer might. As difficult as this may seem, it must be done in order to establish the kind of positive image your business needs to be a success.

Stand in front of the mirror before you enter your office. Are you still in your pajamas? Are you wearing a ratty old T-shirt and a beat-up pair of jeans? Did you brush your hair when you woke up? If the image you see when you look in the mirror is one that you wouldn't want to see if you were a customer, go back to the drawing board. While it's not critical to don a three-piece suit every day to work in your home-based office, it is important to look somewhat pulled together.

Experts say that jeans or upscale sweat clothes are fine. Use your own discretion. Remember that even if you're not expecting a client at the office that day, there is no law that says he won't show up anyway. And if you're going out to meet a friend at a local eatery, be aware that you might run into an important client unexpectedly. If you look truly abominable, the disappointment could leave a lasting, unfavorable impression.

By all means, if you're going out to meet a client, pay special attention to your appearance. Your clients expect you to look professional. And why not? Would you want to fork over large sums of money to someone in cutoffs and a Mickey Mouse sweatshirt? Dressing properly is a sign of respect. It tells your clients that you value their opinions and that you know how to act in a business situation.

This doesn't mean you can't maintain your own style. Again, take the accountant and the interior designer as examples. If the interior designer dressed in three-piece dark suits, carried a thick briefcase, and dealt with clients in a somber manner, clients would probably find him or her a little strange. On the other hand, if the accountant wore colorful, casual sweat clothing and came across as a free spirit, he too would be projecting a jarring image. Reverse the situations and both professionals would fit the mold the public wants. Make your image fit your occupation. Otherwise, clients don't know what to think.

Take a cue from others in your profession. Cassidy, a home-based graphics designer from Austin, Texas, was pleasantly surprised when she graduated from college and plunged into the real world of advertising. "I don't know what I was expecting, but I was very surprised when I met with art directors dressed casually, even at large office buildings. When I started interviewing, I would wear nice but casual suits and carry my portfolio and a briefcase. Now, I just wear a pair of slacks and a pretty blouse, accented with my own style of accessories. I feel much more comfortable, and I fit in better too!"

ADAPTING YOUR WORK SPACE

Naturally, home-based-business owners who entertain clients in their home should be aware of their decor. Much as you love that Bruce Springsteen poster or hate to part with your table lamp made from Budweiser cans, you will probably have to keep your home decor tasteful and attractive to avoid offending your clients. Try to duplicate standard office setups: a desk, two chairs, and subdued accents are the safest bet.

Also bear in mind that normal household activities can be a nuisance to visiting clients. Don't put a pot of corned beef and cabbage on the stove before a client comes over. Coach your family on proper behavior. Generally, the less conspicuous they are, the better. Keep your toddlers out of the office; keep screaming babies out of earshot. And by all means, put your dog outside.

But suppose you run the kind of business where no one ever sees your work space. Is image still important? Yes. Nothing is more discouraging than a messy, ill-organized, unattractive work space. You won't get far in business if you have to dig your marketing materials out from under piles of laundered socks and stacks of old lunch dishes. Your home-based office does not have to be a showroom of taste and technology if you're the only one who will ever see it. But it does have to be attractive and orderly enough for you to get your work done.

WHEN MUM'S THE WORD

Your work space is tied up with image in another way. You may be perfectly happy working from your kitchen table. But experts warn that publicizing this fact is probably not a wise move. You may be just as competent working from your dining room as you would in a high-rise office, but your client may be hesitant to believe it.

Don't try to combat this prejudice: Avoid it. Give your clients the impression that you work in an office—not by lying, but by projecting professionalism. Remember that you aren't obligated to broadcast the fact that you work at home. If clients don't ask, don't mention it. Meet with them in their office or in restaurants so they don't have to visit your premises.

One way to further your professional image is to have a business-phone line installed. For the money, you will be able to obtain a listing in the yellow pages and distinguish between personal and business calls. To complement your business line, get an answering service or machine to take calls when you're not there. If you use an answering machine, keep your message simple. Silly messages make a bad impression—doubly so if your jokes bomb. Also, keep small children off your business phone. You don't expect an eight-year-old to answer when you call IBM; IBM doesn't expect this, either, when someone from there calls you.

GET IT IN WRITING

For many home-based entrepreneurs, written materials like stationery and business cards make a more lasting impression than either an office or personal appearance. Your client may never see your work space and may only see you occasionally. But your proposal may sit on his desk for weeks, and your business card may stick with him for years.

Don't skimp on stationery. For tips on developing a proper name and logo, consult chapter 7 of this book. Unless you're a talented designer, enlisting the help of a graphics consultant is probably a good idea. Shop for quality paper and printing as well. You don't need heavy, handmade cotton bond for regular correspondence, but flimsy paper and poor printing will make your business look cheap. Be sure to include business cards in your order as well. They will be a major means of publicizing your business.

Once you have your stationery, use it. No matter how informal a note you're writing, put it on company stationery and in legible writing. Notebook paper, scratch pads, and dinner napkins are not good enough. Watch out for bad penmanship, sloppy typing, and spelling errors, too. Without the watchful eye of a full-time secretary, the responsibility for neat, professional correspondence is yours.

ALSO KEEP IN MIND

In some businesses, cars are image builders (or destroyers!). Do you visit clients at their offices? Are they likely to ride in your car? Is delivery an important element in your business? If so, your car affects your image. You probably don't need a luxurious auto to conduct simple business. But you do need clean, reliable transportation. At the very least, you should have a car that doesn't prompt gasps of horror or derisive laughter from your clients.

Another aspect of image that is often overlooked is punctuality. Every time you are late for an appointment, you make a negative impression. Not only is it annoying to wait around for a tardy person, but it also calls into question that person's competence. Are you this careless with deadlines? Are you always inconsiderate of other people's time? Punctuality—and good manners in general—can go a long way toward demonstrating your ability to meet your commitments and your eagerness to work with a particular client.

A MATTER OF HABIT

As an employee, you probably spent a good portion of each day trying to impress the boss. You scrambled to get to work on time. You lived up to the corporate dress code. You tried to keep your office neat (or, at least, clear of debris). In short, you tried to look like a diligent, ambitious, capable worker—even when your solid work record and excellent performance should have made these efforts unnecessary. Why? Because if you cruised in late every day, wore sloppy clothes, and worked in a pigsty, you wouldn't look like a good employee. And you were judged, in part, on what the boss perceived.

As a home-based businessperson, you're in much the same position. You could be the most amazing, efficient, wonderful professional around, but if your clients can't see that, they won't give you the chance to prove it.

Projecting a proper image starts with simple consciousness. Make it a habit to run an image check—on your clothing, your personal appearance, your office, your stationery, and every aspect of your business. Be aware of how you and your business look to others. At one time, your image may have been a question of personal style. Now that you're a home-based-business owner, it's a question of your livelihood.

V

GROWTH AND EXPANSION

24

HIRING LINE

HOW TO RECRUIT AND TRAIN QUALIFIED EMPLOYEES

Most small-business owners look forward to the day when they can hire their first employees. While that day may seem far off now, you may need help sooner than you think. No decision you make will affect your overall success more than choosing who you hire, both in the office and out in the field. Your employees will perform tasks that you alone cannot. Ideally, they will duplicate your enthusiasm and complement your skills. Without good employees, your business will never reach its full potential.

Yet hiring employees is scary. How can you be sure they're qualified? What if they aren't honest? Will they ever be able to take over the tasks you've so lovingly assumed as a business owner? Your new employees probably won't be perfect (and, remember, neither are you), but if you follow some basic guidelines and use common sense, you can find associates who are bright, reliable, helpful, and competent. It all starts with you.

ESTABLISHING REQUIREMENTS

One of the biggest problems in hiring employees is preparing yourself for the process—that is, fully understanding the requirements of the job being filled. What is going to be required of the job applicant? What kind of personality, experience, and education are needed for the job? Assemble a job description that covers the following main areas:

- physical and mental tasks involved (ranging from judging, planning, and managing to cleaning, lifting, fabricating, etc.);
- how the job is to be done (the methods and equipment used);
- the reason the job exists (including an explanation of job objectives and how they relate to those of other positions in the company);
- the qualifications needed (training, knowledge, skills, including personality traits and employee characteristics needed).

Putting together a job description is simple if the aspects of the job are well researched. One method of obtaining information is to interview employees and supervisors at other companies or workers in similar positions within your own firm. You can then incorporate the information into a job-analysis form listing the job title, the person to whom the employee will report, employee tasks, how the work will be done, and why the position exists. Also allow three or four lines each for job duties, background requirements, and personal qualifications. The more thoroughly you define the job, the more successful the overall hiring process will be.

Suppose you're hiring a salesperson. It seems obvious that this person needs to be outgoing. He or she must be fairly intelligent, have a quick mind to be able to answer questions about your product or service, and enough memory to retain information about what you are selling. If you're going to hire a bookkeeper, you are seeking somebody who enjoys math and detail—a perfectionist, if possible. You don't need a dazzling personality from someone who does books. In fact, a chatty bookkeeper may not be as diligent as you'd like.

Of course, personality does count in the hiring process. You are looking for someone to share your home eight hours a day. Don't hire someone who will make you irritated or uncomfortable. However, whether or not you like a person is less important than whether you feel he's qualified and reliable. The personality traits you evaluate should relate to the job you are filling—not only to your likes or dislikes. Judging a potential employee solely on personality is one of the quickest ways to hire the worst employees.

RECRUITING

Once you've established firm guidelines, how do you find the right people and bring them to you? This is where a lot of people fail. They don't spend enough time or money on advertising. Your ads can make or break your recruitment efforts, so take heed. Your job is to sell the position you're trying to fill.

As an employer, you may feel that you are the buyer, not the seller. Prospective employees should be seeking you out, not the other way around. That's partly true. But you won't attract top-notch candidates if you present a job as bland, boring, and a waste of time. Good employees are looking for interesting, rewarding, enjoyable work. To catch their attention, stress the positives about the position.

What Do You Have to Offer?

If you read the classified ads, 75 percent or more don't indicate what employers have to offer. Once in a while, you'll see an ad suggesting challenge, the chance for advancement, an exciting atmosphere, informality, a dynamic, growth-type organization. This job will be in high demand.

Don't say, "Typist, must type 50 words per minute, good pay." You'll draw the dregs of society, the people who have been turned down for every other job in town and are shooting for anything. Compare this: "Fast-growing video company needs self-starter who types 50 wpm. Great benefits and salary. A real stepping-stone for the right person. Call Ed, 555-5555."

A survey of three thousand executives around the country revealed that salary was of secondary importance. The challenge of the job and the achievement of business goals were more important. All of us at one time or another have done boring work. Most people don't want work in which they act as little more than a machine. They know they'll be bored to death. Rather, they want something exciting, which will encourage thought and creativity. Remember this in writing up job descriptions and ads. Let applicants know that innovation and initiative are valued at your firm.

Set Realistic Requirements

Be exciting but not excessive. In the advertisement, don't include requirements other than educational or experience-related ones. Don't demand certain personality characteristics. If you give away the traits you are looking for (e.g., outgoing, detail-oriented), the person is going to come in and imitate those characteristics immediately. Do say a word about your company (e.g., fast-growing, dynamic). Convey the excitement and challenge of the job—the money, the opportunities, and the rewards. You have to sell people on the idea of coming to see you. That's the important thing.

Don't require what you don't need when you advertise for a job. Don't ask for a college education if the job really doesn't require it. For example, some business owners demand that their salespeople have a college degree, believing they can make a more intelligent pitch. Yet their salespeople may not be calling on clients with degrees, so their education is extraneous. Often when degree-conscious owners change their demands, their turnover rates (always a factor in sales-oriented businesses) decrease significantly. Anybody who has been in business realizes that a degree may not mean anything other than the ability to graduate from college. Gear your demands to the requirements of the job.

Important as salesmanship is in attracting good employees, never sacrifice your honesty. Don't advertise for an office administrator when you really want a receptionist. Don't call your offices plush if they're really informal. You want employees who fit in and are comfortable in your firm—not people who are shocked and dismayed at the realities of their work. Stick to being positive and honest. It really is the best policy.

Some Like It Small

Being a small company may or may not be a plus. People have varying tastes. Some like large offices with a lot of people around. Others prefer smaller offices. This can be a positive or a negative, depending on the personality of the prospect. One thing seems clear, however: Many people like an intimate work environment, where politics are kept to a minimum. The bigger the company, the more likely that politics are involved. In this sense, a small business has an advantage over the larger office.

Good Titles Are Free

Even the title of the position you are offering can be important. For instance, one business owner was complaining that he couldn't find a typist. He had been trying to hire someone, but no one would respond to his ad. The owner rechecked the ad and found it bland. Even the title—clerk-typist—sounded dreary.

Reasoning that the new person was going to be taking on clerical tasks associated with administrative duties in addition to typing, he decided to advertise for an administrative assistant instead. He also jazzed up the ad by referring to the benefits of working in a lively, intimate business environment.

Changing the title to administrative assistant was the key. Many people don't want to be secretaries or typists these days, and the business owner was smart enough to realize this. After the ad ran, the owner interviewed thirty people and ended up with a great employee. This story illustrates how an attractive job title can widen your field of applicants.

Most people are concerned with their job title. If you want somebody to work on a production line, don't call it "assembly-line work," but something like "electronic-connector work, no experience necessary." Be aware of the psychology of prospective employees, and gear your employment ads toward their thinking. Do not worry if the first ad you place doesn't give you the results you seek. Every business experiences peaks and valleys in ad response. Hang in there. Vary your advertising with a view toward improving that response, and hold out until you find the right person. Personnel turnover is expensive. If you stop in the middle of the recruiting process, settling for what you can get rather than for what you need, you'll inevitably have to start all over again.

Society Pages

For many people, a job is a social experience. In fact, many people don't have a social life outside their work environment. They go home, come back to work, and see nobody in between. Many people would rather meet new people on the job than in other social environments. Studies indicate this is particularly true of women. Due to this, when you advertise a job, you may want to stress that it is a nice, friendly place to work, where new employees can get to know and meet people (that is, if it is accurate).

Location Points

The location of your home will play some part in who decides to apply for the position. Driving distance may be a critical factor for potential employees. This is demonstrated by the experience of a desktop-publishing owner whose home was located near Buffalo, New York. He advertised for workers but found that many Buffalo residents who called about the job were reluctant to commute even a short distance.

The problem was that when the entrepreneur first placed his ad, he did not specify that his company was located in Williamsville. If he had been specific in his ad, he could have saved himself the time and effort of talking to people who did not want to travel to the job.

SCREENING APPLICANTS

Your time, as owner of your own business, is extremely valuable. If you have hired before, you know that a lot of people who respond to an ad are not qualified. They may have no background. They may have zero skills. As a small-business owner, you may have a hard time training employees. Because your margins are often thinner than what big companies have, you may prefer to go with experienced people. In many cases, small businesses are not set up to train employees, while large companies have built-in education programs. For that reason, it's critical that you weed out the qualified prospects from the uninitiated. Here are a few options to consider.

Phone Screening

To minimize the time you spend with unqualified people, screen applicants by phone. Pre-interview them regarding their experience. If they don't have it, say very directly, "I am looking for someone more experienced. I don't have the resources to train an inexperienced person." This will cut down on the number of people you interview in person.

Of course, if you are looking for trainees, you will not do much screening by phone. If you run an ad that indicates you are willing to train, the majority of applicants will be young people. And in most cases, young people haven't matured to the point where they can sell themselves over the telephone. You can weed out people who sound belligerent, slow, or overly nervous, but you probably won't be able to detect subtler qualities over the phone.

If you are hiring sales personnel, one effective method is to tell the person, "Look, you are a salesman. Persuade me to interview you." You'll be amazed at the performances you get. Almost all sales are done over the telephone. At the very least, an appointment for a sales call has to be set up over the phone. Asking a prospective salesperson to sell himself on the phone is a powerful screening tool. If the applicant on the other end of the phone can come up with something good, he or she is probably qualified.

Résumé Screening

Employers are divided on the question of résumés. Some think a résumé is little more than an advertisement—and about as revealing. They would rather see the applicant fill out a good four-page application in his own handwriting. That way, they have some control over the information provided.

Other employers like the idea of résumés. They can review an applicant's background before he or she comes for the interview. They can use the résumé as a screening device, to determine whether or not to call the applicant for a personal interview at all. The résumé becomes a permanent part of the personnel file if the applicant is hired and is kept on file as a record if he is not.

The changing legal climate, where applicants sometimes sue prospective employers who do not hire them, provides a good argument for retaining résumés and job applications even after you've selected a candidate. You can purchase employment-application forms from an office-supply store. You should make sure that any application form you use conforms to EEOC (Equal Employment Opportunity Commission) guidelines.

INTERVIEWING CANDIDATES

Big companies will pre-interview hundreds of applicants, and out of that group they will pick ten to come back for a second interview. You are running a small business. You don't have time for two and three interviews for each applicant. Ask applicants specific questions about their work experience, and make sure you can recognize false claims and exaggerated experience.

Setting up an employment interview correctly is an important aspect of the hiring process. In the typical hiring interview, you have twenty to ninety minutes to size up prospective employees. The length of the interview depends on the importance of the job. In any case, you have to find out as much as you can about that person in a short period of time.

Being able to identify and hire good employees can mean the difference between a successful and unsuccessful business. But for many employers, hiring is a daunting, hit-and-miss process. They hire the wrong people because they don't know how to identify the right ones. The most important part of the hiring process is the personal interview. If you know how to conduct an efficient interview, the chances are much improved that the right people will be hired. Though anyone can run an interview, it takes planning and know-how to do it correctly.

Interview Dos and Don'ts

If you sit at a big desk and look down on everybody, you are going to intimidate your applicants. They're not going to talk to you. They're not going to open up. How in the world are you going to learn what they are really like if you scare the personality out of them? Set up your interview so that it is relaxed.

Don't sit at your desk: A desk is intimidating. It symbolizes authority and causes people to tighten up. Take two chairs, set them side by side, sit down and talk to the person.

You, too, have to open up and show the person you are interviewing that you care about him or her. If, for example, the applicant tells you something negative, you have to be willing to show what psychologists call unconditional positive regard, not extreme shock. This has to be a purposeful action on your part. Your willingness to open up will let the applicant open up. You can't feel uptight and expect to conduct a revealing employment interview.

Privacy is important. If you don't have a private office in your home, schedule the day so you can get some privacy in the house. You don't want other people in the house or on the phone interrupting you. When the person walks in for the interview, it should be understood that you are not to be disturbed unless it is an emergency.

Making the Interview Work

When you interview job applicants, take notes. You'll be talking with several people. Unless you have an incredible memory, you're going to forget things. You don't want this to happen, not only for the welfare of your company, but also for legal reasons we will detail later. For now, just recognize that when you talk to a lot of people, they can run together in your mind. So take notes.

But isn't note taking intimidating? To minimize this, put the interviewee's application on a clipboard. Each time you make a note, pick up your pencil, then put it down when you're finished. Make the note quickly, between comments, and never write anything down when the applicant says something negative. This does not mean that you don't make negative notes. It does mean that you write negative notes down when the applicant says something positive. This will keep the applicant open and at ease throughout the interview.

This might seem like a lot of work—and it can be taxing psychologically. It's all going to happen fast, particularly if you ask specific questions that are related to the job. The idea is to move the interview forward to get as much information as you can as quickly as possible.

The interviewer is most effective when he or she has already defined the job and its needs, as mentioned earlier. In addition, the well-prepared interviewer will try to learn, prior to the interview, as much about the applicant as possible—including studying application forms, résumés, and test scores.

If you see the résumé for the first time when the applicant arrives in your office, take the time to familiarize yourself with its details, reading it carefully for clues to the candidate's qualifications. But you can see that becoming familiar with the candidate before the interview is better. It saves you the time of asking questions for which answers were readily available beforehand. It also enables the interviewer to prepare pertinent questions, ones that might be missed if the interviewer had to improvise.

The planning process should include a list of points to be covered during the interview. This has two parts.

One is getting the information the interviewer wants from the applicant. The other is imparting the information he wants to give.

Remember that a good employer-employee match can only occur if you each understand what the other has to offer. Ask interviewees for their questions about the job and/or your company. Don't be offended if they're blunt. Good employees are bound to be picky, so be prepared to answer a lot of questions.

What They Say, What They Signal

During the interview, you walk a thin line between comfortable informality and serious business. The applicant should be comfortable but not too casual—and it's up to you to set the pace.

When the interviewee first enters the office, say something like, "Make yourself comfortable," or, "May I get you a cup of coffee?" Be pleasant and courteous, but avoid too much small talk. It wastes time and can create an atmosphere that discourages serious discussion. Break the ice by talking first. Explain what the job is and describe the company—the business, history, and where it is going. Being enthusiastic about your own business is important if you expect your employees to have enthusiasm for it.

Let the interviewee talk. Listen to what the person says and doesn't say. For example, if a person talks about what a lousy boss he has now and complains about what poor bosses he's had in the past, it's possible this person has trouble getting along with people—especially authority figures (i.e., you). If an applicant has gone from one job to another looking for "just the right thing," he probably gets bored in a job easily. Look for personality cues as well. Is the applicant too dull for phone work? Too hyperactive for a desk job? Is he or she dressed appropriately? You can learn as much from these clues as you can from questions and answers.

Whether you take notes during the interview or wait until the applicant has gone to do so, record the person's responses and your own impressions as soon after the interview as possible, before you forget the details. Even if you take notes during the interview, allow yourself time to record your impressions after it is over so you don't forget what you discussed. You'll want as much accurate information as possible to make your final decision.

ASK THE RIGHT QUESTIONS

When you interview a prospective employee, you're going to ask a lot of questions. Your purpose in asking these questions is not just to gain information but to elicit a response that will answer questions you (deliberately) haven't asked.

What does this mean? Often, a person's attitude toward his work is as telling as the work itself. For example, if you are hiring an office manager, it is less important that the person seeking the job has worked in the field for six years than what that person's attitude toward fellow workers is. You may be hiring someone who knows how to order office supplies but alienates colleagues to the point that they don't submit orders.

Here's a list of questions that will help you uncover applicants' attitudes toward work, authority, integrity, and so on:

- *Tell me about the first job you ever had. What was it like? What was your boss like? What about the company?*
- *Of all the job's you've had, which one did you like best? Why did you like it?*
- *What's the worst problem you've ever had on a job?*
- *What are some of your greatest accomplishments on the job? Have you ever won an award or bonus?*
- *Have you ever had to confront another employee about poor job performance? What happened and how did you resolve it?*
- *Have you ever worked with an unreasonable boss? What was he like and how did you deal with him?*

Through these questions, you should be able to determine whether an employee is petty and resentful or hardworking and reasonable. This is critical because in a small business, you don't have time to deal with difficult people. Look for loyal, flexible employees who can move forward with you.

In addition to exploring your potential employee's attitudes, ask him or her about duties and responsibilities at previous positions. In some positions, descriptions will be short: "I picked up and delivered pizza." For executive or managerial positions, more illumination will be warranted. Here are some sample questions to get the conversation rolling:

- *What tasks do you enjoy most? Why?*
- *Some people like creative jobs, jobs where they have to use their heads. Other people like to deal with people, supervising them to make sure they're doing their jobs right. How would you categorize yourself, as a people mover or an idea person?*
- *What do you consider your primary skill or talent?*
- *Which aspect of the job do you consider yourself weakest at?*

Personal Questions

Legal restrictions govern some of the personal questions you can ask of prospective employees. You cannot, for example, ask questions that have to do with a prospect's race, religion, number and age of children, or sexual preference—either directly or indirectly. For this reason, as you read this section, bear in mind that questions you direct toward the candidate must be free of the possibility of interpretation in those terms. What you can do, however, is elicit information that will give you clues to the personality of the candidate and how it matches the personality you need in the job you are offering.

In this regard, you can ask questions about the person's earlier life—perhaps asking if there was anything in the person's life that particularly helped form his or her attitude toward work. Asking what somebody's father did for a living will give you a clue to his or her socioeconomic background. Some employers believe this shows whether the applicant was a spoiled kid and never had to work for a living, as well as the value he places on money. If you ask whether the applicant's father and mother were strong disciplinarians, you will get an indication of how he feels about accepting criticism. If you ask whether the applicant was the oldest child or the only child, you may find out how well he assumes authority and responsibility.

Because questions about an applicant's personal attitudes, family background, and so on are tricky—and because they can lead to legal complications when they depart from reference to the work situation—many personnel experts believe they should be eliminated altogether. People do get a little uptight about answering personal questions. But some veteran entrepreneurs believe that asking these kinds of questions can pinpoint an applicant quickly. This is an area that requires great care and should only be handled with reference to state and federal employer guidelines.

You can discuss the educational experiences of the candidate. This will be particularly necessary if you are talking to someone who has never had a job before. Ask the candidate what his major or favorite subject was. That should give you a handle on whether the candidate is a "people person" (an English or P.E. enthusiast) or a detail-oriented individual (math and science majors, for example). Ask about school activities. Someone with a background in speech and drama might do very well in public relations, while someone involved in student government might make a good manager. Academic study and extracurricular activities may not qualify anyone for skilled employment, but they do shed some light on a person's character.

Probe the applicant's armed-forces record if it is on the résumé or application. Many people dislike the armed forces because of the discipline required. On the other hand, the military is a well-known training ground for leadership. Did the applicant progress through the ranks? Did he or she receive any special training?

The applicant's interest in hobbies can reveal a tremendous amount about him. Many job seekers list hobbies on their résumé. Explore them in detail. Is the applicant athletic? Artistic? Community-oriented? These are all attributes that can make a good employee. Look for hidden skills as well. A woman who heads a Girl Scout troop is likely to make a good day-care aide even if she has no paid experience.

Interview Dynamics

When you are conducting an interview, don't hog the whole conversation. Let your applicant do the talking. People think that when they are talking, they are in control. Encourage the job seeker to talk freely, remembering that the person talking is not always in control. The person directing the conversation is the one in control—and it's your role to direct the conversation toward getting the information you need.

Let the applicant run on until you think you have enough information to make a judgment. Do not interrupt if he is developing a thought. Interrupt only if he is rambling, and go on to the next question.

Don't ask leading questions. For example, don't ask, "Do you consider yourself a conscientious person?" You already know how the applicant will answer. Rather, assume you already know the answer and ask the question from that perspective, seeking amplification of a basic thought. You would say, "How has your conscientiousness as an employee benefited your work situation in the past?"

THE LONG ARM OF THE LAW

You've finally chosen the right employee. He's intelligent, capable, reliable, congenial, and ambitious. Screening hundreds of résumés, conducting dozens of interviews, agonizing for days over your choice—it was all worthwhile to get this gem of a worker.

But wait. The EEOC is conducting an investigation of your business because someone has filed a $150,000 sex-discrimination suit against you—and the person isn't even an employee! How can this be? The applicant who's filing suit claims you passed her over because she's a woman.

By now, the selection process is a blur. You think you rejected her because she didn't have enough experience—

or was it because she couldn't work a computer? You search for the résumés, then remember that you threw them out weeks ago. You become even more confused. Who was this woman? How can you defend your decision when you don't even remember who she is?

Don't put yourself in this position. Bone up on state and federal equal-employment regulations, and run your business in accordance with them. This isn't as difficult as you might think. And it certainly isn't new.

Equal-employment-opportunity legislation first appeared on the books in 1966. But equal-employment legislation actually began with President Kennedy's executive order 10925, in the early 1960s. The statutes grew with the Equal Pay Act of 1963, the Civil Rights Act of 1964, the Federal Age Discrimination in Employment Act of 1967, executive orders 11141 and 11246, the Fair Credit Reporting Act of 1971, the Vocational Rehabilitation Act of 1973, and the Vietnam Veteran's Readjustment Act of 1974. Most states also have fair-employment-practices laws. Equal Employment Opportunity Commission (EEOC) is the name given to the whole range of legislation and regulation covering fairness in hiring, personnel policies, and firing in the American business community.

What do these regulations come down to? EEOC prohibits discriminatory employment practices because of age, sex, race, national origin, religion, or handicap. EEOC tells you as an employer to base your hiring, wage, promotion, and firing policies solely on the needs of a particular job. Its aim is to prevent you from using any of the covered factors as determining factors in your personnel policy.

Well, you say, I'm not worried about any investigation. I've only got a handful of people working for me, and as a matter of fact, I know every one of those folks. They're local people. They'd never take me to court. After all, I gave most of them their first chance to get in on the ground floor and grow with me.

Well, you should also know that employees are becoming more and more aware of their rights under the law and exercising them. Suits alleging discrimination in small businesses are skyrocketing nationwide. Some attorneys are even specializing in EEOC cases for a percentage of the amount collected. There is also a program known as the Early Litigation Investigation that every small-business person should know about. The ELI management procedure is aimed at small-business employees, rather than zeroing in on the big boys of the business world. This demonstrates that the government bureaucracy is willing to take aim at the so-called little guy, too.

It's critical that you maintain the highest standards of nondiscrimination in your business. Avoid even the appearance of it. Defending yourself against an EEOC suit could mean the end of your business. By adhering to the standards set forth by the government—and keeping up good relations with your employees—you and your staff can enjoy a long, happy relationship.

WHEN FOREVER IS TOO LONG

Using permanent employees may not be the best solution to a labor problem. If you have a rush order, if your workload increases suddenly but will drop in a few weeks, if a key employee is sick or on vacation, or if you need extra help during a seasonal period, hiring temporary help may be more cost-effective than hiring a permanent employee or increasing the workload of your current employees.

To arrive at a decision, weigh the pros and cons. Is it financially beneficial to offer overtime pay to your present employees? Under the Federal Labor Standards Act, hourly employees must be paid one and one half times their basic pay for overtime. Salaried and commissioned employees are not subject to this stipulation, but if you want them to work overtime, there should be some incentive. Long hours without reward can sap anyone's motivation.

If paying overtime proves to be a financial drain, if the work isn't getting done fast enough, or if your present employees are already working overtime, then start hiring temporary help.

Finding an Agency

Temporary-help services exist in most metropolitan areas. Look under the yellow pages headings "Employment — Temporary," or "Employment — Contractors." Temporary-help services also advertise in the classified sections of newspapers, trade journals, or by direct mail.

Prescreen the agencies before making any phone calls. Ads will usually indicate what fields of employment they specialize in. For example, most agencies staff clerical temporary help, but only a select few will advertise help that can work in dBASE III or Lotus 1-2-3. Some may specialize in temporary medical, legal, or executive personnel, as well.

Before calling a temporary-help firm, prepare a list of questions. How quickly can the firm provide you with help? What skills can it guarantee? Does the contract allow you to ask for another employee if you are dissatisfied with the choices you were offered? (Remember, the reason you are using their service is to not only get quick help but also professional help.) And most importantly, what will using the service cost you? This method of employment is supposed to save you money in the long run.

You should also prepare all the necessary information about the jobs you need filled. Make sure the firm knows what the job requirements are, what talents you are looking for in an employee, and the length of time required for the job. Provide the temporary-help firm with a detailed description of the job(s) so you can get the most qualified person at the lowest possible cost. Don't ask for someone with higher qualifications than what you actually need. You will only be wasting money.

The more background information you provide the agency with, the easier it will be for the firm to find you the exact person you are looking for. Do you need a skilled computer operator or someone with a pleasant phone voice to cover for your sick receptionist?

One advantage to using a temporary-help service is that at the end of the workday, if you are not satisfied with the employee's work performance, you can either ask for another worker or switch agencies. This saves you the money you would have to pay a bad permanent employee while you searched for a replacement.

How Temp Services Operate

The temporary-help agency tests and interviews applicants on a daily basis to obtain a wide range of experienced personnel. The more variety in their applicants' skills, the more they have to offer their clients. Established agencies carefully screen their applicants and weed out the "flakes." They know that each temporary employee is a walking advertisement for their company. One bad egg could give their agency a poor reputation in the business community.

A temporary employee's hourly wage will be higher than what you pay a normal employee, because you will be responsible for payroll taxes, Social Security, worker's compensation—and the profit margin of the temporary-help firm. Depending on the experience of the employee and your requirements, the cost runs anywhere from $7.50 to $25.00 or more per hour. Filing clerks work at the low end of the scale; managers and supervisors or those with specialized skills, such as nurses or data-processing professionals, work at the high end.

Temporary employees usually carry their own time cards, are on the agency's payroll, and are usually covered by its insurance. You will be billed by the agency not long after the employee has finished the term of the contract. Be sure to keep your own record as to the hours performed by the temporary helper.

When considering whether or not to contract for temporary help through an agency, do some figuring in hard dollar amounts. Calculate how long the temporary help is needed and the hourly rate to arrive at the total cost. Will hiring a temp be cost-effective? Could your current staff handle the additional work? Can a temp furnish skills no one else at your company has? Temporary help can be an effective way to boost productivity when you aren't ready to make the commitment to hiring a permanent staff.

25

MANAGING JUST FINE

KEEPING YOUR EMPLOYEES HAPPY, PRODUCTIVE, AND MOTIVATED

Now that you've hired the employee of your dreams, don't think your work is done. Even the best employees can be soured on work if they aren't managed properly. As the owner of a growing business, your job is to motivate and challenge employees—or risk lowering productivity and increasing turnover.

Few entrepreneurs get into business for themselves because they're excellent managers. Yet most find they need managerial skills to succeed in business. How can you keep your employees enthusiastic, dedicated, and working hard? Experts have many theories on employee motivation ranging from strict authoritarianism to shared-power, democratic styles. But most agree that the common goals—high productivity and low turnover—are only reached when employer and employee work together, either as boss and underling or as cooperators.

MANAGEMENT: MORE IMPORTANT THAN EVER

It's no secret that American productivity has been on the decline in recent years. Though several factors contribute to this trend, among them is a slowdown in personal productivity. According to current estimates, only four of every eight hours of work is used efficiently among white-collar workers in the United States.

Whatever the reasons for this widespread efficiency lag, one fact remains clear: Good work habits are not a given, even among good employees. You must find the right balance of strictness and sympathy, the right blend of challenge and reward, to keep your staff working at its peak.

Management can be a small-business owner's biggest nightmare—or greatest asset. Many entrepreneurs get into business without the slightest notion of how to supervise and motivate employees. For them, managing is an uphill battle. With a little practice and thought, however, you can provide even better management than large companies. Studies show that management in large companies is inflated—as much as 20 to 30 percent larger than necessary. The system becomes bogged down in bureaucracy. In smaller companies, employees can have a greater impact on management. Done properly, this will lead to increased job satisfaction and productivity.

WHAT DO YOU WANT?

The first step toward helping your staff be more effective is determining your expectations. This may be harder than you think. Here are two examples of expectations gone awry, each with its own bad consequences.

Bill, the owner of a computer-repair service, was a chronic workaholic. Along with his duties, he emptied wastebaskets, wrote ads, and stocked shelves. He regularly cleaned the work areas of his two repair people and his receptionist. His staff was perfectly capable of handling these mundane tasks—in fact, they expected to. Bill's insistence on doing everything himself revealed his low expectations. Clearly, he didn't trust his employees to handle even the smallest jobs. Not only did he waste his own time, but he also discouraged them from showing responsibility or initiative.

By contrast, Kyle, a business consultant, created unrealistic expectations for his employees. On one occasion, Kyle asked his assistant, Craig, to get a dozen quotes on meeting sites within a half hour. When Craig complained that he'd need more time, Kyle reasoned that dialing each number and asking ten questions should take no more than three minutes, perhaps even less. He didn't take into account the possibility of being put on hold, not being able to reach the right person, or having to negotiate a good rate. Faced with an unreasonable demand, Craig didn't try very hard. His initiative was squelched, and Kyle got poor results.

The trick to setting effective goals for your employees is balance. Don't condescend. If you've hired capable people, they can and will rise to a challenge. In fact, studies show that employees like challenges on the job. On the other hand, don't expect your employees to perform superhuman tasks. Be reasonable. If you don't know what a reasonable expectation is (perhaps you've never done their job), ask them for their input. Look at their past production and try to gauge whether they've been working slowly, at capacity, or on overload.

SIMPLE ECONOMICS

Once you have realistic goals in mind, you must communicate those goals and help your workers reach them. Many managers use the bullying technique: Employees will meet their standards "or else." They believe workers are "lucky to have jobs." Perhaps you know a manager like this. Perhaps he or she caused you to quit being an employee and to start your own business.

You can try the old Me Boss, You Servant routine, but most experts agree that these tactics are tired. Strong-arming your employees into compliance will only foster resentment. Bad relations are harmful in any business, but in a small home office they're deadly. You have to work in close quarters with your employees. Wouldn't you prefer a congenial atmosphere to awkward silence day after day? Moreover, if the mood is really bad, your staff will seek employment elsewhere, and that's disruptive and expensive to your business.

View the situation as simple economics. You want your employees to be productive, diligent, efficient—and happy enough with their jobs to stay at your firm. To create this kind of environment, you will have to meet some of their demands. You exchange consideration for consideration. By providing the kind of workplace that your employees want, you will win their cooperation and support.

WHAT EMPLOYEES VALUE

Often, small-business owners see themselves at a disadvantage where employee satisfaction is concerned. After all, big companies can offer great benefits packages, profit sharing, company cars, luxurious offices, and a host of corporate perks. Most small companies—especially home-based businesses—aren't in a position to shower employees with extras. Yet you can provide employees with a pleasant work environment by taking note of what most employees want. Following is a brief rundown of common employee desires:

- *Responsibility:* In most situations, employees prefer acting on their own initiative to being told what to do. Give your employees guidance, but don't hover over their every move.
- *Recognition:* When a staff member does something outstanding, be generous with your thanks. They'll appreciate the gesture, and you'll set a good example for other employees.

  Don't go overboard, though, or give praise when you don't mean it. People know when you're being insincere. If they catch you making a fulsome comment, they won't believe you when you really mean it.

- *Respect:* Never treat your employees like idiots or they'll oblige you by acting the part. All good employees deserve your respect.

- *Reward:* Commissions, overtime bonuses, and frequent raises for good performance give employees incentive for reaching your established goals. Raises don't have to be large, by the way, if they're frequent and clearly reward hard work. In fact frequent, small raises are preferable to infrequent but substantial ones.

Interestingly enough, it can be just as damaging to overreward as it is to underreward. When employees feel they're being overpaid, they're likely to improve the quality of their work but decrease the quantity of work they accomplish.

- *Fairness:* Most employee gripes center around unfairness. An employee may feel that he or she is not being adequately compensated for his work. Or he may believe that another employee is getting preferential treatment, either by being allowed to shirk or by getting extra benefits.
- *Consideration:* Business owners like to believe they know everything about their business. But in the case of your employees' jobs, this may not be so. Open up communications to employee complaints, requests for new procedures and/or equipment, and general suggestions. You'll boost employee morale and maybe even find new, improved ways of running your business.
- *Opportunity:* Giving employees the chance to move up the corporate ladder (even if it has but a few rungs) makes excellent sense. Reward good work with additional responsibility and a better title. Also, splurge on training or seminars for your best employees. They may learn technical skills that will keep your business on the cutting edge—and they'll be grateful for the opportunity to better themselves.

SHARING THE POWER

Research shows that companies that set employee goals are generally more successful than those that don't. What's more, research indicates that it's better to err on the side of difficulty. Employees enjoy a genuine challenge, and you want them to stretch. To that end, never condescend.

Yet as we already mentioned, the degree of challenge has to be carefully balanced. Too difficult, and the goal is seen as unrealistic and unfair, producing a backlash. Imagine yourself in a union negotiation. If your goals are accepted, you'll win a significant rise in productivity. But if they're rejected for being unrealistic, you're facing a strike. Goal setting works best in climates stressing achievement and less well in companies that emphasize power.

You can get your employees involved in the goal-setting process through participatory management. By bringing them into this phase of planning, you can raise group norms, increase productivity, and enhance your chances of reaching accepted goals. You will, on the other hand, have to share some of your power with employees.

Some business owners can't bear to give up their power—even marginally. If this describes you, consider another method of managing. It's more damaging to ask employees for input and ignore it than never to ask at all.

If you opt to try participatory management, decide ahead of time how much decision-making input employees will be allowed. You might want to limit power sharing to reaching set goals, certain equipment purchases, idea consideration via a suggestion box, etc. These, incidentally, are the kinds of decisions into which employees want input—not major strategy or investment decisions. Keep in mind that participatory decision making for its own sake won't increase productivity, just goodwill. Productivity rises only when participation is tied to setting and achieving challenging objectives.

This system works even if you have only a few employees. George, the owner of a mobile-bookkeeping service, wanted his salesperson to bring in more business. To encourage improvement, George and his salesperson worked out a reasonable goal: two new clients per month and an increase in commission after the quota is met. Not long afterward, George added another van and hired additional staff to deal with the increase in business.

VIRTUE'S NOT ITS OWN REWARD

Don't let good work go unrewarded. Start by paying your employees fair salaries. For outstanding performance, consider giving bonuses, gifts, extra days off, awards, or other incidental perks. You don't have to hand out ribbons for each hour of overtime or every completed project, but you should provide employees with some incentive to keep up the good work.

Of course, as a small-business owner, you don't have unlimited resources. Just because you want to give your assistant a raise doesn't mean you'll be able to do so. If finances are tight, explain at the outset that you won't be able to provide raises for at least a year (or whatever you think is appropriate). Even when they aren't your fault, misunderstandings are costly.

Johnny worked at a miniblind-cleaning service, where he dispatched cleaners to various locations. Hoping to get ahead, Johnny taught himself to program the personal computer. He was soon designing spreadsheets for financial reports and databases to keep track of customers. All this helped the business run more smoothly and efficiently, so Johnny approached his boss for a raise. He figured that the extra work he had been doing and the money he had saved the company made him a shoo-in for more money.

However, the boss did not agree. Despite Johnny's efforts, the company was still struggling and the boss could not afford to give him a raise. He promised to give Johnny a raise as soon as he could, but for Johnny, this wasn't enough. He didn't argue, but he became resentful. From that day on, his output decreased steadily. He rarely did anything outside his minimum duties. Once he perceived that his hard work was not going to be rewarded and that he was underpaid, he let up on his work.

Johnny's expectations were established unilaterally. He did not discuss his ambitions with the owner but assumed that working hard would bring financial rewards. When it did not, Johnny became disillusioned and unproductive. Though this misunderstanding wasn't really the owner's fault, it could have been avoided by his stating clearly that no raises could be granted, even for exceptional performance. This might have slowed Johnny down a bit but wouldn't have caused the motivational crash that eventually occurred.

DEALING WITH POOR EMPLOYEES

Some employees require more managing than others. What do you do when an employee doesn't meet your standards, even after a reasonable training period? You have three basic options:

1. Reassess your standards. Are you expecting too much? Can you lower standards without making major sacrifices in productivity or quality? Can you modify that employee's duties so that they're more suitable to his or her talents?

2. Provide additional incentives for good work. Are your objectives clear to your staff? Could a program of rewards, bonuses, or quotas help stress your priorities?

3. Terminate the employee. Have you discovered ingrained personality traits that just don't fit in with your company (belligerent behavior, chronic tardiness, dishonesty)? Have you given the employee ample opportunities to change?

Firing an employee is probably the least attractive option. Not only is the task itself unpleasant, but you'll also spend plenty of time hiring and training a replacement. You may even face legal problems if the employee feels he or she has been wrongfully terminated or the subject of discrimination. However, if you're certain that all hope is lost, terminate the employee as quickly and painlessly as possible. Trying to work with a hopelessly inadequate employee is a waste of time.

In most situations, though, motivating slow employees is better than firing them. Here are a few steps for setting employees on the right track, and keeping them there:

- Tell workers at the outset what you expect and what they can expect to gain by living up to your standards.
- Make rewards dependent on behavior.

- Reward each person differently, based on the level of performance.
- Do not over- or underreward.
- Advise workers as to what they're doing wrong before the behavior is ingrained.
- Avoid punishment and correction in front of others.
- Keep in mind that a lack of response to a bad behavior is in itself a kind of reinforcement.
- Explain any negative consequences that will occur as the result of poor performance. If salespeople will be fired for not meeting quotas, let them know in advance.
- Provide feedback. Poor performers should be alerted to problems—and successes—so they know where they stand.
- Reward intermittently. Reward (and punishments) are more effective if they're provided sporadically. Constant praise or criticism doesn't seem genuine. Intermittent feedback is more compelling. This is the psychological basis for gambling: If you won at poker every time, it wouldn't be nearly as addictive.

THE ART OF MANAGEMENT

Managing people is not a science but an art. In addition to some of the techniques we've discussed here, you'll also need a fair measure of tact, honesty, perceptiveness, wisdom, and understanding.

Also, remember that one of the best ways to inspire hard work is to work hard yourself. As the owner of the business, you set the tone for the company. Be the first to meet new challenges, consider other people's suggestions, and find workable solutions to problems. Leading by example will not only help your staff, but it will also benefit your business.

26

MOVING OUT

WHEN YOUR HOME-BASED BUSINESS
LEAVES THE NEST

I t's the home-based entrepreneur's dream: expanding your business to the point that your home office just can't hold everything. While this is a sure sign of success, it also presents a dilemma. Do you stifle your business's growth so you can stay at home? Or do you move your business to new facilities?

Faced with continuing expansion, many home-based entrepreneurs opt to move. While your home may have been the ideal incubator for your new business, pitfalls like limited space, restricted access for deliveries, low visibility, and the general chaos that accompanies running a growing business and a growing family under the same roof may force you to look for new environs. The question is, where do you start?

ARE YOU READY?

Before you even think about signing a lease, packing a box, or calling a mover, create a moving budget. The cost of setting up a new office may be higher than you think. In addition to basics like rent and moving fees, you should allot funds for a telecommunications system, utility deposits, architects or interior designers, new stationery, new business cards, computer upgrades, a security system, furniture, and packing plans. Don't overlook hidden costs, either, like feeding employees on moving day.

The costs of making a move may be compounded by the addition of new employees (a common reason for leaving home). Can you afford the additional salaries and the new office? Changing locations will also cost you manpower. Someone in the office will have to shop for a location, negotiate a lease, coordinate the move itself, and set up the new office. Can you or your current staff handle this overload? If not, factor in the cost of additional help to get you through the transitional period.

Moving into a new office is inherently stressful.

Even the most extensive planning doesn't guarantee a smooth move. George, the owner of a desktop-publishing business, encountered a few major roadblocks. Before the move, he arranged for the water, electricity, and phones to be turned on. He checked all three companies several times to confirm dates and times. Yet when George and his employees arrived at the site, the phones and the electricity had not been turned on. Only the faucets and toilets worked, and it was too dark to use them. George's company remained without electricity and phones for two days.

This little setback didn't ruin George's business, but it did provide some premium stress. You can expect similar mishaps in your move—despite your best efforts. With advance planning and the right person in charge, you can move your business without serious problems. But don't count on it being a breeze. Relocating a business takes several months of planning—sometimes more than a year—and lots of hard work.

PUT SOMEONE ON THE CASE

The first order of business when you're making a move is to put someone in charge of the transition. You may decide to handle this yourself. However, be prepared to spend long hours following leads, getting quotes, and ironing out details. In the meantime, you may find you have no time to run your business. Alternatively, you can assign the project to someone in your office. A reliable, efficient employee can take the legwork off your hands.

In either case, don't underestimate the time and effort required to supervise a move. If you assign your top assistant to the task, make sure his or her regular work is being covered. Coordinating your move may not be a full-time job, but it's not something that can be done in a few hours, either. There's much more to a move than simply packing boxes and carting them to a new location.

Most business owners don't realize the incredible amount of stress that's placed on the person who is responsible for the move. According to one expert, more than two thirds of the people responsible for a move are demoted, fired, or resign within months after the move. And many more suffer stress-related illnesses due to the responsibilities.

Lynn owned a greeting-card company that she ran out of her basement. While exhibiting her cards at a trade show, she landed an especially large order. After reviewing the order and delivery times, Lynn realized she would need at least two additional employees, for which there was no room in her basement. She and her two employees were already stepping all over each other. Lynn decided to move to an office.

Although she wanted to handle the move herself, co-ordinating the production of the new order required a great deal of her time. So in her place, she assigned the project to her most trusted and responsible employee, Erika. Lynn believed Erika could find a new location, coordinate the move, and keep up with her regular work with no problem.

Over the next few weeks, Erika became increasingly harried. She could not find an appropriate location, and she fell behind in her work. Lynn also was having problems. The production schedule was suffering. Erika's inability to find a decent location and get her work done frustrated Lynn. After a month, it became apparent the move would not be completed in time to make the delivery. Lynn confronted Erika. They argued, and Erika quit.

Suddenly, Lynn was without both her best employee and a new location. Eventually, she had to tell her customer she could not deliver on schedule. A week later, he canceled his order and sued for breach of contract.

OUTSIDE HELP IS ON ITS WAY

If you or your best staffer can't take on much additional responsibility comfortably, don't resign yourself to long hours and killer anxiety. Being in charge of a move doesn't mean doing everything yourself. Some of the burden can be alleviated by delegating tasks to various employees, who then report back to the person in charge.

There are business-relocation-planning systems that include a checklist and task cards you can hand out to others. These systems can be invaluable in the mayhem of moving from your home to an office. They help order what is otherwise complete chaos.

Another way to ease the stress and enormous burden of moving is to hire a relocation consultant, who can assess your needs, then find the right moving company for the best price. Relocation consultants will help you find a moving company that has experience moving the type of equipment you have, whether it's heavy machinery, mainframe computers, or complicated equipment.

Can't find a relocation specialist in your area? Consider hiring a temporary employee just to coordinate your move. Contact your local temporary-help service to find someone reliable and organized to get the job done. Or advertise in the paper. As long as you can communicate what you want done, you can probably find outside help to do it.

WHERE TO?

Before you can move, you have to find a new facility. And in today's real estate market, you have several options. Don't think that your choices are limited to a high-rise complex. You might try a mobile office, a strip center, an industrial park, or a free-standing building. Consider what has worked well in your home and what you would like to improve, then look for the combination of those things in your new office.

The type of business you run will partially dictate the kind of space you seek. Although they are rare, home-based retail operations do exist. An expanding retail operation may consider relocating to a mall. But remember that mall space is generally expensive (between $4 and $5 a square foot per month) Before signing a lease for mall space, calculate your operating costs and sales projections. If you won't be bringing in enough profits to cover the increased rent, reconsider your move.

Joan and her husband, Bob, operated their needle-point shop out of a converted home pantry. This worked out for a while, but as the business grew, the shop became too small to hold all the customers and inventory. Joan and Bob decided it was time to move.

They spent several weeks researching regional malls, strip malls, and free-standing buildings, considering the costs versus consumer traffic of all three. They decided to lease space from a regional mall. Although the level of business they had done in their home would not cover the increase in overhead, they counted on a considerable increase in volume because of additional traffic.

Unfortunately, that was not the case. Although the shopping mall brought more customer volume, it did not substantially increase sales, thus leaving Joan and Bob short each month. Improved sales did not cover the increased overhead. After four months of losing money, Joan and Bob subleased the mall space and moved their shop back into their home.

In addition to fixed operating costs (like rent), you should consider any up-front construction fees for building out your new space. Before you sign the lease, ask the landlord who provides the following:

- heating, air conditioning, and ventilation
- toilet facilities
- the concrete floor slab

- the demising wall (the wall between you and your neighbor)
- the ceiling and general lighting
- a sprinkler system, if one is required

You should also ask your landlord the following:

- Are there any special design considerations relating to the storefront, the store interior, or the signage that will add significantly to construction costs?
- Are there any other construction factors that would affect the build-out costs?
- Will the landlord provide any kind of building allowance to help pay for items such as store fixtures or floorcovering?

If you cannot cover the added costs, you'd better look elsewhere. A strip center might be the answer. Strip-center rents are less expensive than malls (from $1.50 to $4 per square foot a month), but watch out for exorbitant marketing and maintenance fees that may go along with the lease.

Entrepreneurs in service businesses will probably be looking at office space, whether it's in an industrial park, a high-rise building, a strip center, or even a mobile van.

Look for office space that has all the features you need without expensive extras. For instance, only if your business relies on foot traffic for customers should you consider an expensive strip-center location. Otherwise, the most important factors are space, lighting, convenience (for you, your customers, or your staff).

THE MOVING EXPERIENCE

Once you've found that ideal space, start looking for movers. But what if you only have light office equipment and a few desks? Do you really need to hire movers? Many small-business owners manage to move themselves easily and inexpensively. By taking a good look at the type of materials you need to move, you can determine whether or not you require professional movers.

Be realistic about doing it yourself, though. Don't expect your already overworked ninety-pound secretary to help you haul desks and cabinets to your new locale. Paying professional movers isn't cheap, but then again neither is the time you lose trying to get everything done yourself.

When hiring vendors, solicit a minimum of three bids from each one. Look out for the low-ball bidder, whose service may not be up to par. Experts concluded that the average cost of a move should fall between 75 cents and $1 per square foot of the old facility. So if your home office is 500 square feet, you should plan on paying somewhere between $375 and $500.

Look out for unexpected hitches. For example, if you plan to hit the road while crowds are leaving a football game, your move could take hours longer than it should. And that can cost you double, even triple, what it should.

DRESSING UP THE OFFICE

What you put into your new office is a prime consideration. For tips on buying office furniture and equipment, review chapter 8 of this book. Remember that the right furniture will make the most of your new space and help your employees stay productive. You may even want to enlist the help of an expert.

That's what Janet, owner of a garage-based gift-basket business, did. After several months in business, her baskets caught the fancy of the town, boosting sales dramatically. To handle the increase in orders, Janet had to hire two more employees in addition to the two she already had.

Furthermore, she needed space to store gift items, plastic grass, and cellophane wrap. The garage was so full of people and supplies that there was little room for movement. And when the baskets were completed, Janet had trouble finding a place to store them without damaging them.

Janet contacted an ergonomics specialist. She explained the kind of work she and her staff did and asked if there was any way to improve production. After discussing it, they decided to divide the new space into work stations and a supply station. They found a retail shop that had space enough for displaying the baskets as well as a back room large enough to put the baskets together.

Next, Janet brought in an interior designer to decorate the interior of the store, as well as the work area in the back. In fact, Janet insisted the back work area be every bit as attractive as the front.

After they moved into the store, Janet and her employees went right to work creating baskets. In fact, the new space was so conducive to work that three employees could arrange more baskets than four could do in the garage.

Hiring professional help can make a world of difference. But how do you choose the right specialist?

Barbara Waldman, owner of Designer Previews, a San Francisco-based designer referral service, suggests shopping around. "You should look for a designer who can give you the look that you want," she says. "Find someone who has worked with your type of space before. For example, a designer of a law firm wouldn't be the one to call for your funky advertising agency. And someone who has worked mainly on huge office complexes may not know the needs of a small retail space."

The design you choose for your new office can have a direct impact on productivity. Studies show that colors affect productivity levels. According to color specialist Naomi Tickle at the Institute of Colour & Design, your choice of colors "should depend on the lighting. If there's no natural light, grays and rose colors work best. With a lot of natural lighting, warmer colors like beiges and peaches work well." And whatever you do, she warns, "Stay away from olive green, yellow-green, and orange."

THE HUMAN ELEMENT

Moving into a new office is exciting. For you, it may represent the success you always dreamed of. But moving is also a major change, and with that change comes emotional upset.

Let's face it, moving is upsetting. It requires a lot of

work—boxing up supplies, carting things from one place to another, setting up a new work space. In between, your company has to produce a product or render a service just as it always does. You and your employees will have to change commute patterns, lunch spots, dry cleaners—the host of people and places you visit on your off-hours. All this is bound to have an effect.

If you're making a major move, you may even lose employees. Your rapidly expanding business may take a wrong turn if your best salespeople quit instead of moving with you. No matter how minor you think a move will be, the best strategy is to warn your staff in advance. As soon as you know that you are going to relocate, let your employees know. Find out how far they're willing to drive and what their limitations are. If you know in advance that your production staff won't follow you to the next county, you can plan your move accordingly.

Whatever you do, don't be dishonest or secretive. Always communicate new information concerning the move to everyone in your employ. This will cut down on office rumors and will help employees make a smoother transition to the new facility. Hiding information from your employees will result in bad feelings, especially in a small company, where staff members feel close to one another. By being up-front in your intentions you'll keep the respect and support of your staff. And keeping your key employees with you is one of the most important factors for continued success.

VI

OPPORTUNITIES

27

TWENTY-ONE BUSINESSES YOU CAN START FROM HOME

NEED IDEAS FOR YOUR NEW HOME-BASED BUSINESS? START HERE.

Are you sold on starting a business from home but short on ideas for businesses to start? Look no further. In this chapter, we profile a handful of opportunities for the home-minded entrepreneur. Some are long-established industries; others may be new to you. But they're all making serious inroads across the country.

Of course, this list provides only a sampling of potential home-based businesses. All sorts of businesses can be tailored to the home—from business consulting to dog grooming, commercial printing, book publishing, and more. The following pages offer just a few of our suggestions on home-based opportunities that look promising for the years to come.

GIFT-BASKET SERVICE

When it comes to gift giving, do you find yourself filling a gym bag with golf tees, tennis balls, and tickets to next week's football game for your brother the sports fanatic? Do you prefer making your own gifts to simply buying something off the shelf? If so, you could be earning an income selling gift baskets.

Suddenly, creative people all over America have become basket cases! A quiet cottage industry called gift-basket making (taking an attractive basket or container and filling it artistically with special products) has emerged and has already attracted a huge following of gift givers. For them, the search for that perfect gift is over.

Selling just ten baskets per day at an average price of $35 to $50 can mean substantial profits. As a home-based business, with part-time help and few equipment needs, a gift-basket service could bring in as much as $120,000 in gross annual revenues.

DESKTOP PUBLISHING

Not since Gutenberg invented movable type has publishing experienced such a dramatic revolution. Now, with page-composition software and laser printers that produce typeset-quality pages, personal computers can be turned into profitable desktop-publishing centers that can get you out of the rat race and into real money.

Only $10,000 provides all the equipment you need for this high-tech home-based business. Then you can put together a desktop-publishing system that churns out camera-ready typeset pages at about 1 cent a page, compared to an average of $20 a page using traditional typesetting. With desktop publishing, you have a vast profit potential—plus freedom of the press—at your fingertips.

WEDDING-PLANNING SERVICE

From the moment Prince Charming pops the question, cash registers across the nation start ringing up sales. In their quest for the best values in wedding apparel and services, the future bride and groom have yet one more check to write—to the wedding consultant.

American couples spent more than $27 billion on weddings in 1988, and the bridal consultant is sharing a larger piece of the pie each year. The return to big, traditional weddings has brought with it the problem of staging this complex and costly event. Busy couples are saving time and headaches by delegating the nitty-gritty details to a wedding planner. And since wedding planners earn an average of $2,500 for each event, you can do just two a month and still make $60,000 in one year.

PERSONAL-SHOPPING SERVICE

Personal-shopping services emerged about ten years ago, at about the time women were swelling the ranks of the work force in unprecedented numbers. New priorities were being placed on ways to save time instead of money. Busy executives, doctors, and realtors utilize shopping services to take care of their client and employee gift lists. And men as well as women are turning to personal-shopping services to help them get the job done.

If you're looking for a business with an extremely low start-up cost and a healthy profit potential, this is it. Personal shoppers can begin with virtually nothing but a telephone, an answering machine, and business cards and do very well. As little as $500 can get you started on a small scale.

CHILD-CARE SERVICE

Who's watching the kids? These days, it's not their parents. As mothers enter the work force in droves, child care has become the business phenomenon of the 1980s. Where to leave the kids from eight A.M. to five P.M. has become a major concern for parents nationwide.

According to the U.S. Census Bureau, more than 90 percent of children under the age of five receive day care from someone other than their own parents. Family day care and in-home child care dominate the $11 billion child-care industry. Providing in-home care has proven to be one of the most viable and inexpensive ways for people who love kids to get into this thriving industry.

With the original baby boomers creating their own "baby boomlet," the demand for child care is far from reaching its peak. Experts in the industry estimate that there will be in the neighborhood of 20 to 21 million children in need of child care by 1990. That's why taking care of the small fries can mean big business.

TEMPORARY-HELP SERVICE

Don't confuse this with an employment agency that matches the unemployed with full-time jobs. What the temporary-help service does is place qualified workers in positions for a limited period of time. Temporary services aren't just growing, they're branching out. What was once the exclusive domain of the clerical worker has become the new frontier for a herd of various professionals.

Since 1970, the number of employees in the temporary work force has grown from roughly 400,000 annually to 5 million. Every day, hundreds of thousands of temporary employees invade the workplace, providing more than a hundred services that range from word processing to marketing advice to accounting. Today, nine out of ten businesses use temporary help at one time or another.

With a temporary-help service, there's no inventory to maintain, no stock to buy, and no sales tax to fuss with. All you need to do is find qualified temporary employees who can get the job done.

MAIL ORDER

Shopping is one of America's favorite pastimes, but time constraints are making us abandon trips to the mall in favor of less time-consuming ways to shop. For a fast-paced society that can't find enough hours in the day to get everything done, what could be more convenient than shopping from home?

Bringing everything from power tools to prom dresses right to shoppers' doorsteps, mail-order catalogs are taking the hassle out of shopping while bringing in billions of dollars every year. Today, this $117 billion industry is attracting hundreds of entrepreneurs thanks to its low overhead and easy operation.

Think of mail order as having your own retail store

without having to pay for all that equipment, inventory, labor, and space. With a mail-order catalog, you can offer hundreds of items for sale that you couldn't possibly squeeze into a small shop in a mall or strip center. And you don't have to rely on local sales. You can take your wares nationwide without ever stepping outside your house. Despite mail order's increasing popularity among aspiring business owners, there are still plenty of opportunities in the field.

EVENT-PLANNING SERVICE

Have you ever attended a party where everything ran so smoothly you wondered how the hostess managed to pull it off without a hitch? Chances are your hostess turned to an event planner to organize that gala affair.

Event planners are part of the booming service industry that's cashing in on the fact that Americans are often too busy to plan thir own events, whether they're social or corporate. Weddings, parties, reunions, meetings, conventions, and fund-raisers alike are all part of the event planners' domain. Because event planning is a home-based operation, your overhead costs are kept to a bare minimum.

Normally, planners will charge clients a percentage of the total cost of an event, which assures a profit. Percentages usually range from 10 to 20 percent, and with conventions costing upward of $100,000, profits can add up quickly.

AUTO DETAILING

With car prices looming near the $20,000 mark, Americans are taking better care of the cars they already own instead of buying new ones. This increasing interest in car care is fueling a new industry—auto detailing. Today, approximately 7,000 detailers nationwide gross nearly $2.5 million per year making people's cars shine inside and out.

Requiring only a modest initial investment, the least expensive way to get into this lucrative field is a mobile detailing service, which doesn't require a commercial location. With a truck or van, you can visit clients at the office or at home, adding extra convenience for the customer.

For about $150, a detailer will give a car a thorough cleaning—washing, waxing, polishing, vacuuming, even taking a toothbrush to the nooks and crannies. And doing just three to four detailings each day can put your income into high gear.

CATERING SERVICE

Looking for a high-profit, low-risk alternative to starting your own restaurant? Try catering. Catering, currently the fastest-growing segment of the food-service industry, is no small potatoes. According to the National Caterers Association in Akron, Ohio, caterers made an impressive $5 billion in 1987. And their statistics show that of the 40,000 caterers in the United States, only about one third gross less than $100,000 a year.

Even if you're just a weekend caterer, the profits can be high. Catering even one party of a hundred people may gross as much as $3,000; so if you cater four events a month, that's $144,000 a year! And don't think that you have to be a *cordon bleu* chef to start a catering business. Offering a limited menu is one way for entrepreneurs who aren't the best chefs in the world to make a living as caterers. One such caterer has found a niche in the market by offering a roving sundae bar that he takes to children's birthday parties.

MOBILE BOOKKEEPING

Mobile bookkeepers have given a new twist to an old business. By providing small-business owners with a bookkeeping service that is faster, cheaper, and more convenient, mobile bookkeepers are stealing the small-business market from their office-bound competition.

Mobile bookkeepers eliminate most of the problems associated with traditional bookkeepers: long delays in getting work done and keeping financial books and data for extended periods of time. By equipping vans with all the amenities of an office, the mobile bookkeeper can arrive at the business, complete the books, print the reports, and discuss them with the owner all in a matter of hours.

While this industry is still young, it is expected to expand rapidly over the next ten years. Most mobile book-keepers charge a flat fee, based on the client's activity, which includes the number of employees, the number of checks written, and the number of back accounts. Most mobile bookkeepers charge a minimum monthly fee of $75 and average about $40,000 in pretax net profits.

PROPERTY INSPECTION

The home-inspection industry has experienced phenomenal growth over the past decade. According to the American Society of Home Inspectors (ASHI), home inspectors barely impacted 2 percent of the homes sold in the country ten years ago. Today, they impact more than 40 percent. And that number is expected to double over the next five years.

To meet the increasing demand, the number of home inspectors continues to grow. Over the past two years, ASHI's membership has jumped from five hundred to more than a thousand. Today's high cost of housing has fueled the home-inspection boom. With the median price of a new home hovering at $89,000, buyers cannot afford any major catastrophes like cracks in the foundation, leaks in the roof, or dry rot in the wood. That's why they're paying home inspectors approximately $200 to search homes from top to bottom before they sign on the dotted line.

INFORMATION BROKER

Normally hired on a per-project basis, the information broker finds information in published and/or electronic sources, organizes it in a form that best suits the client's needs, and sells it based on the time expended and the expertise involved.

Information brokering, previously dominated by a few big corporations, now accounts for approximately $1.6 billion in revenues and is expected to grow at 10 to 15 percent annually through 1990. However, according to the Department of Commerce's *U.S. Industrial Outlook*, close to 80 percent of total revenues are generated by the industry's twenty largest companies. The remaining 20 percent of revenues are generated by small firms, which often specialize in one or two fields of information.

To become an information broker, you'll need a microcomputer, a printer, a modem, and research skills. The equipment can be obtained for about $2,500, but you may also have to learn the skills of electronic research in specific databases, and over a period of time the cost of doing this can add up to several thousand dollars.

BED-AND-BREAKFAST INN

Established around 3,000 B.C., the earliest inns offered little more than a crude meal and cot to weary travelers. Over the centuries, inns gained sophistication and eventually developed into the high-rise hotels we know today. But in today's society, inns are enjoying a resurgence as travelers shy away from the commercial hotels in favor of more homey, rustic bed-and-breakfast inns.

This age-old industry is undergoing a rapid revitalization. As more and more travelers seek out a unique traveling experience, innkeepers can see occupancy rates average as high as 70 to 80 percent. With most inns charging approximately $55 to $60 a night and some going as high as $200 a night, innkeepers are bringing in tidy profits. Depending on the number of rooms you have available and how much you charge, it's possible to bring in upward of $100,000 a year.

MAID/JANITORIAL SERVICES

One segment of the service industry that's really cleaning up these days is maid and janitorial service. With some 35,000 janitorial services in the United States, the janitorial industry grosses about $25 billion in annual sales and employs over six million people.

Seem incredible? Just think that every time a building is built, it has to be professionally cleaned. This is where the janitorial service steps in. And since all buildings need ongoing maintenance, independent janitorial services are enjoying a sweeping success.

In the private sector, maid services are busy helping individuals, working couples, and senior citizens keep their homes sparkling. Traditionally in charge of keeping their homes clean, women no longer have the time to straighten, dust, vacuum, sweep, wash the dishes, and do all the other little things that go into keeping a home neat and tidy. And since there's no end in sight to the rising percentage of women working outside the home, maid services should continue to thrive throughout the 1990s.

BUSINESS BROKERAGE

In only five years, the number of business brokers has more than doubled from 3,000 to over 7,000. But even this increase has barely put a dent in the market. Approximately 2.5 million businesses change ownership each year, representing sales of more than $200 billion. Yet fewer than half of those business sales are conducted by brokers.

Even though the start-up costs appear to be relatively low, you'll need about $50,000 to $60,000 for daily operations and living expenses to cover the extended start-up period. But this initial investment can pay off. Selling just one business for $100,000 (the average selling price) at a 10 percent commission, you earn $10,000.

LAWN-CARE SERVICE

Every family has experienced the dread of waking up Saturday morning knowing that the lawn has to be mowed and the leaves raked. These days, people are affording themselves the luxury of a little free time by paying professionals to do these chores. The high demand for lawn care has turned this business into a $25 billion industry that keeps on growing. The Professional Lawn Care Association estimates that the industry is expanding at about 15 to 20 percent a year.

Today's lawn care includes much more than just mowing the lawn, however. Chemical lawn care, including fertilization and weed killing, is capturing an increasing share of the market, although maintenance, which specializes mostly in mowing and edging, still makes up the lion's share of the market.

With demand for lawn care at an all-time high, independent services that keep lawns looking lush and verdant are raking in revenues. And revenues for this industry should continue to grow throughout the coming decade, since more and more people are turning to the service industries to lighten the burden of everyday chores.

IMAGE CONSULTING

Millions of people want to improve their image but aren't sure how to go about it. This is where the image consultant comes in. As an image consultant, you can make money teaching people how to make the best of themselves and how to make the best impression on others.

According to the Association of Fashion Image Consultants, Americans spent about $148 million on image consultants in 1985 (the last year for which figures are available). Experts estimate that there are about five to eight thousand image consultants currently in business, working either as independents or for another company. And some of these consultants are making a lot of money.

Image consultants who have built a good corporate and individual client base are grossing $100,000 to $200,000 a year. Add to that a relatively low initial investment of $10,000 to $20,000, and you've got a business that's looking good!

INTERIOR DESIGNER

If you think interior designers spend their days at the drawing board sketching fabulous homes and offices, you're living in the Dark Ages. As a matter of fact, designers spend only about 15 to 25 percent of their time developing and drawing concepts for interiors. The rest of the time they're seeking out clients, tracking down suppliers, supervising installations, and doing general troubleshooting. And since designers typically work on a variety of projects at one time, just keeping track of what needs to be done—and when—can be a mind-boggling task.

Within the design field, you can specialize in residential design or commercial design. While both can prove lucrative, there is definitely more money to be made in the commercial field. Commercial designers who have been in business less than two years generally handle between twenty and forty small or medium-size projects per year and gross between $300,000 and $500,000. And with most designers making net profits of 10 to 20 percent, few of them are complaining.

PUBLIC-RELATIONS AGENCY

The job description of the public-relations consultant varies depending on whether the consultant is a generalist, who tackles a client's entire marketing strategy, or a more specialized public-relations adviser, who handles only clients in a particular field—say, fashion, finance, or high technology. Celebrities aren't the only ones who consult independent public-relations agencies. Corporations, nonprofit organizations, and even the government hire the services of PR agents.

According to a 1987 International Association of Business Communicators (IABC) survey, the number of self-employed PR consultants jumped 44 percent between 1985 and 1987. Currently, the U.S. Department of Labor estimates the total number of both private and corporate public-relations specialists at 142,000. A 1988 survey by the Public Relations Society of America indicated that 88 percent of consultants who were partners in a private PR firm earned more than $45,000.

Getting started in this industry is inexpensive. Many consultants start up with as little as $1,000. The PR agent's best friend: the telephone. Whether you're calling to cultivate new accounts or to get placements for existing clients, the PR agent must learn to live with a phone in hand.

PRIVATE INVESTIGATING

Have you ever thought about being a PI?—living the glamorous life, racing your way through high-speed chases in a Ferrari, slowing only for a shootout with this week's bad guy? Well, real PIs dream of this type of a life-style, too—because theirs doesn't resemble this at all.

While the image we hold of PIs does not portray the real life-style or job functions of the contemporary PI, it is one of the reasons why this industry is growing at such a quick pace. Experts say that the number of investigations in the U.S. is increasing at a rate of 10 to 15 percent annually. Today, there are about 22,000 PI agencies throughout the U.S. And with the average agency employing three investigators, that adds up to over 60,000 PIs in the nation. But that doesn't mean that the competition is getting stiff; there's plenty of business for everyone.

All that business means that PIs are bringing in good profits for their investigative talents. Today's average agency grosses about $75,000 to $100,000. And since overhead is low in this business, independent PIs can bring in net profits of approximately 75 percent.

HOME-BASED FRANCHISES AND BUSINESS OPPORTUNITIES

AEROWEST/WESTAIR WASHROOM SANITATION SERVICE, 25100 S. Normandie, Harbor City, CA 90710, (213) 539–6104; washroom-sanitation service

ALOETTE COSMETICS, 345 Lancaster Ave., Malvern, PA 19355, (215) 644–8200; direct sales of cosmetics and skin-care products

AMERICLEAN CLEANING & RESTORATION SERVICES, 6602 S. Frontage Rd., Billings, MT 59101, (800) 342–2345 x430/(406) 652–1960; liquid dry cleaning/restoration of carpeting/upholstery

AMERICAN LEAK DETECTION, 1750 E. Arenas Rd., #7, Palm Springs, CA 92262, (619) 320–9991; concealed water/gas leak-detection service

AMERICAN POOLPLAYERS ASSOCIATION 1000 Lake Saint Louis Blvd., #325, Lake St. Louis, MO 63367, (314) 625–8611; recreational billiards league

AMERISEAL INC., 3060 Leon Rd., Jacksonville, FL 32216, (800) 356–0991; asphalt-pavement maintenance

BATHCREST INC., 2425 S. Progress Dr., Salt Lake City, UT 84119, (801) 972–1110; porcelain resurfacing

BIO-CARE, 2105 S. Bascam Ave., #240, Campbell, CA 95008, (408) 559–7500; restaurant-grease maintenance service

BUILDING INSPECTOR OF AMERICA, THE, 684 Main St., Wakefield, MA 01880, (800) 321–4677; prepurchasing home inspections

BUNDLE OF CONVENIENCE INT'L., 8956 Ellis Ave., Los Angeles, CA 90034, (213) 839–1114/(818) 376–1114; home-delivery service of baby products

CEILINGS BEAUTIFUL, 100 Industrial Dr., Ivy Land, PA 18974-1481, (215) 357–7800; spray-on texture ceilings

CEILING DOCTOR, 2200 Lakeshore Blvd. W., #105, Toronto, Ont., Can. M8V 1A4, (416) 253–4900; commercial specialty cleaning

CHEM BROOM INT'L INC., 674 Enterprise Dr., Westerville, OH 43081, (800) 292–2436/(614) 433–0579; carpet, ceiling, and drapery cleaning

CHEM-DRY 3330 Cameron Park Dr., #700, Cameron Park, CA 95682, (800) 841–6583/in CA: (800) 821–3240; carpet, drapery, and upholstery cleaning

CHILDSCAPES, 375 E. Elliot, #2, Chandler, AZ 85225, (602) 892–1464; interior design for children

CLASSIC CARE OF AMERICA, 10190 Belladrum Dr., Alpharetta, GA 30201, (404) 475–8961; window-cleaning service and carpet-cleaning service

CLASSY MAIDS, 1180 S. Spring Centre Blvd., #115, Altamonte Springs, FL 32714, (800) 445–5238; residential-cleaning services

CLEANSERV INDUSTRIES INC., 3403 Tenth St., 8th Fl., Riverside, CA 92501, (714) 781–0220/(213) 692–0220; commercial cleaning

COLOR-GLO, 7111 Ohms Ln., Minneapolis, MN 55435, (800) 328-6347/(612) 835–1338; fabric redyeing and restoration

COMPLETE MUSIC, 8317 Cass, Omaha, NE 68114, (800) 843–3866/(402) 391–4847; Disc-jockey music service for special occasions

COUSTIC-GLO, 7111 Ohms Ln., Minneapolis, MN 55435, (800) 328–6347/(612) 835–1388; ceiling/wall cleaning and restoration

COVERALL, 3111 Camino Del Rio N., #1200, San Diego, CA 92108, (619) 584–1911; commercial office cleaning

CRITTER CARE, P.O. Box 95003-143, Baton Rouge, LA 70895, (504) 291–7244/(504) 273–3356; in-home pet-care service

CRITTER CONTROL, 32932 Warren, Ste. B, Westland, MI 48185, (313) 522–6888; urban wildlife management

CUSTOM MAID, 1608 N. Miller Rd. Ste. #5, Scottsdale, AZ 85257, (800) 888–6876; residential cleaning/maid service

DEBIT ONE MOBILE BOOKKEEPING, 43739 Belleview, Kansas City, MO 64112, (800) 999–8160; mobile bookkeeping, accounting, and tax services

DECORATING DEN, 4630 Montgomery Ave., Bethesda, MD 20814, (301) 652–6393; full-service interior decorating

DEKRA-LITE FRANCHISE CORP., 17945 Sky Park Cir., Irvine, CA

92714, (714) 852–9977; exterior Christmas-lighting decoration service

DOMESTICAIDE INC., 6400 W. 110th, #205, Overland Park, KS 66211, (800) 533–9684; home cleaning and home care

DR. VIDEO, 1131 Bay Ave., Pt. Pleasant, NJ 08742, (201) 892–7400; VCR/Nintendo maintenance and repair

DR. VINYL, 13665 E. 42nd Terra, Independence, MO 64055, (800) 531–6600; mobile vinyl, leather, plastic repair and dyeing

DURACLEAN, 2151 Waukegan Rd., Deerfield, IL 60015, (800) 251–7070/(312) 945–2000; carpet, furniture, and drapery cleaning/restoration, building-maintenance services

EDUCATIONAL RESOURCE CENTER, 315 Golfview Dr., Boca Raton, FL 33432, (407) 391–2033; tutoring and test-preparation services

EGAL "AMERICA'S HOME INSPECTION SERVICES," 12345 W. 95th St., #203, Lenexa, KS 66215, (913) 541–1862; property-inspection services

FOLIAGE DESIGN SYSTEMS, 1553 S.E. Fort King, Ocala, FL 32671, (904) 629–7351; interior foliage plants, maintenance

FRANKLIN TRAFFIC SERVICES INC., 5251 Shawnee Rd./P.O. Box 100, Ransomville, NY 14131, (716) 731–3131; transportation consulting service

GUARANTEE GIRLS INC., 6210 Hollyfield Dr., Baton Rouge, LA 70809, (800) 735–4475/(504) 293–8682; residential and commercial cleaning services

HAUNTED HAYRIDES INC., 3520 W. Genesee St., Syracuse, NY 13219, (315) 488–2824; entertainment/recreation

HOUSEMASTER OF AMERICA, 421 W. Union Ave., Bound Brook, NJ 08805, (800) 526–3939; home-inspection service

HOUSESITTERS, THE, 530 Queen St. E., Toronto, Ont., Can. M5A 1V2, (416) 947–1295; pet, plant, home child care; maid service

INTERCLEAN SERVICE SYSTEM INC., 1325 10th Ave., Greeley, CO 80631, (303) 352–8100; janitorial service/carpet cleaning

JANI-KING, 4950 Keller Springs, #190, Dallas, TX 75248, (800) 552–5264; janitorial service

JANTIZE, 19306 Ecorse Rd., Allen Park, MI 48101, (313) 386–9500; commercial cleaning service

KNIGHTRIDERS INC., 33 Boston Post Rd. W., #210, Marlboro, MA 01752, (508) 460–0148; restaurant cleaning

LANGENWALTER DYE CONCEPT, 4410 E. La Palma, Anaheim, CA 92807, (800) 422–4370/(714) 528–7610; carpet- and color-restoration services

LIEN CHEMICAL CO., 501 W. Lake St., Elmhurst, IL 60126, (312) 832–6500; restroom risk management

LIQUI-GREEN LAWN CARE CORP., 9601 N. Allen Rd., Peoria, IL 61615, (309) 243–5211; lawn and tree care

· LUBE ON WHEELS, 150 S.W. 12th Ave., Pompano Beach, FL 33069, (800) 234–5823; on-site oil changes

MAID BRIGADE SERVICES, 850 Indian Tr./P.O. Box 1901, Lilburn, GA 30226, (800) 722–6243; residential maid service

MAID EASY, 33 Pratt St., Glastonbury, CT 06033, (203) 659–2953; residential maid-search service

MAID OF GOLD, 917 Western America Cir., #101, Mobile, AL 36609, (800) 451–5371; maid service, carpet cleaning, commercial cleaning

MERCHANT ADVERTISING SYSTEMS INC., 4115 Tiverton Rd., Randallstown, MD 21133, (301) 655–3201; merchant advertising display centers in markets and malls

MERRY MAIDS, 11117 Mill Valley Rd., Omaha, NE 68154, (800) 345–5535/(402) 498–0331; maid service

MINI MAID, 1855 Piedmont Rd., #100, Marietta, GA 30066, (404) 973–3271; residential cleaning service

MIRACLE METHOD BATHROOM RESTORATION, 3732 W. Century Blvd., #6, Inglewood, CA 90303, (800) 444–8827; bathroom/kitchen fixture and tile repair/refinishing

MOBICARE, 115 Airport Dr., #100, Westminster, MD 21157, (800) 277–6333/(301) 875–5823; mobile car care/quick oil change and lube

MORTGAGE SERVICE ASSOCIATES, 21 Brock St., North Haven, CT 06473, (800) 637–5459/(203) 624–2025; property-inspection service and maintenance

MR. ROOTER, 8130 W. Reno, Oklahoma City, OK 73127, (405) 946–3000; sewer and drain cleaning

NATIONAL MAINTENANCE CONTRACTORS, 18001 130th Ave. N.E., Bellevue, WA 98005, (206) 881–0500; janitorial service

NATIONAL PROPERTY INSPECTIONS, 236 S. 108th Ave., #3, Omaha, NE 68154, (800) 333–9807; home and commercial property inspections.

NATIONAL TENANT NETWORK, P.O. Box 1664, Lake Grove, OR 97035, (503) 635–1118; computerized tenant performance reporting/retail credit/extended services

NOVUS PLATE GLASS REPAIR, 10425 Hampshire Ave. S., Minneapolis, MN 55438, (800) 328–1117/(612) 944–8000; plate-glass repair

OFFICE ANSWER, THE, 8445 Keystone Crossing, #165, Indianapolis, IN 46240, (317) 254–9040; personalized telephone-answering service

ON-SITE DRY CLEANING DRAPERY SERVICE, 16400 Ventura Blvd., #312, Encino, CA 91436, (818) 501–8798; on-site drapery dry cleaning

OUTDOOR FUN SIGNS, 138 River Corner Rd., Conestoga, PA 17516, (717) 872–6916; all-occasion lawn signs

PERMA CERAM INT'L., 327 Village Pl., Wyckoff, NJ 07481, (800) 645–5039/(201) 670–8379; tub, sink, and tile resurfacing

PERMA-GLAZE, 7310 E. 22nd St., #167, Tucson, AZ 85710, (602) 722–9718; bathroom/kitchen fixture restoration and refinishing

PETS ARE INN, 27 N. Fourth St., Ste. #500, Minneapolis, MN 55401, (800) 248–7387/(612) 339–6255; pet-boarding service at private homes

PET NANNY, 1000 Long Blvd., #9, Lansing, MI 48911, (517) 694–4400; in-home pet care

PRICECHECK, 32 Sixth St., Toronto, Ont., Can. M8Z 3A2, (416) 251–5986; market-research network

PROFESSIONAL CARPET SYSTEMS, 5182 Old Dixie Hwy., Forest Park, GA 30050, (800) 735–5055/(404) 361–9362; carpet-redyeing service

PROVE, 4806 Shelly Dr., Wilmington, NC 28405, (919) 392–2550; mystery shopping and seminars

RAINBOW INT'L CARPET DYEING & CLEANING CO., 1010 N. University Parks Dr., Waco, TX 76707; (817) 756–2122; carpet/furniture/drapery dyeing, cleaning, repair, and restoration

REPELE, 219 Newbury St., Boston, MA 02116, (617) 353–1884; flameproofing stain protection

ROTO-ROOTER, 300 Ashworth Rd., West Des Moines, IA 50265, (515) 223–1343; sewer- and drain-cleaning service

ROTO-STATIC INT'L., 6810-I Kitimat Rd., Mississauga, Ont., Can. L5N 5M2, (416) 858–8410; carpet/upholstery cleaning and related services

RUG DOCTOR PRO, 2788 N. Larkin Ave., Fresno, CA 93727, (209) 291–5511; carpet-, upholstery-, and drapery-cleaning service

SCREEN MACHINE, THE, P.O. Box 1207, Sonoma, CA 95476, (707) 996–5551; mobile window screen/screen-door repair and service

SERVPRO, 575 Airport Blvd., Gallatin, TN 37066, (800) 826–9586; cleaning and restoration services

SHADE SHOWER, P.O. Box 54713 Phoenix, AZ 85078–4713 (602) 996–6143; window-blind cleaning

SPARKLE WASH INT'L., 26851 Richmond Rd., Cleveland, OH 44146, (800) 321–0770/(216) 464–4212; mobile power cleaning and restoration

SPECIAL SELECTIONS INC., P.O. Box 3243, Boise, ID 83703, (208) 343–3629; personal-shopping service

SPORT IT, 8960 Springbrook Dr. N.W., #150, Coon Rapids, MN 55433, (612) 784–0490; sporting-goods equipment and apparel

SPOTLESS OFFICE SERVICES, 4040 Brockton Cr., No. Vancouver, B.C., Can. V7G 1E6, (604) 929–4432; building-maintenance broker

SPRING-GREEN LAWN CARE, P.O. Box 2828, Naperville, IL 60567 (815) 436–8777; lawn- and tree-care service

STANLEY STEEMER CARPET CLEANER, 5500 Stanley Steemer Pky., Dublin, OH 43017, (800) 848–7496/(614) 764–2007; carpet and upholstery cleaning

STEAMATIC INC., 1601 109th St., Grand Prairie, TX 75050, (800) 527–1295/(214) 647–1244; cleaning and restoration service

ULTRA WASH, 2335 Naomi St., Houston, TX 77054, (713) 796–2431; power washing and restoration

UNICLEAN SYSTEMS INC., 642 W. 29th St., No. Vancouver, B.C., Can. V7N 2K2, (604) 986–4750; office-cleaning services

UNIMAX BUILDING SERVICE OF AMERICA INC., P.O. Box 70251, Riverfront Plaza, Louisville, KY 40270–9998, (812) 944–0360; janitorial services/carpet cleaning

USA CLEANING SYSTEMS, 1542 Edinger, Ste. C., Tustin, CA 92680, (800) 552–3242; residential/commercial cleaning

VACCU-FORM, 23281 Vista Grande Dr., Ste. B, Laguna Hills, CA 92653, (714) 770–2316; Vaccu-formed replacement bathtubs

VIDEO 5000, 211 E. 43rd St., New York, NY 10017, (212) 371–7050; videotaping service specializing in weddings

VIDEO DATA SERVICES, 24 Grove St., Pittsford, NY 14534, (716) 385–4773; video photography

WEE WATCH PRIVATE HOME DAY CARE, 25 Valleywood Dr., #20, Markham, Ont., Can. L3R 5L9, (416) 479–4274; private home day care

WEED MAN, THE, 2399 Royal Windsor Dr., Mississauga, Ont., Can. L5J 1K9, (416) 823–8550; lawn-care service

WORD HANDLERS, 1605 N. Wilmot, #104B, Tucson, AZ 85712, (602) 722–8768; desktop publishing/word processing services

WORLDWIDE REFINISHING SYSTEMS INC., 508 Lake Air Dr., Waco, TX 76710, (800) 369–9361/(817) 776–4701; porcelain/fiberglass refinishing and repair

WOW, OF ORLANDO, 5401 S. Bryant Ave., Sanford, FL 32773, (800) 345–1969/(407) 321–4010; mobile power cleaning; carpet, drapery, and upholstery cleaning/restoration

YARD CARDS INC., 2940 W. Main, Belleville, IL 62221, (618) 233–0491; 8-ft. greeting-card rental

RESOURCE GUIDE

ASSOCIATIONS

AMERICAN HOME BUSINESS ASSOCIATION
397 Post Rd.
Darien, CT 06820
(203)655–4380/(800)433–6361

AMERICAN FEDERATION OF SMALL BUSINESS
407 S. Dearborn St.
Chicago, IL 60605
(312)427–0207
for membership information

ASSOCIATION OF ELECTRONIC COTTAGES
P.O. Box 1738
Davis, CA 95617–1738
(916)756–6430

MOTHERS' HOME BUSINESS NETWORK
P.O. Box 423
East Meadow, NY 11554
(516)997–7394
(send S.A.S.E. for information)

NATIONAL ASSOCIATION FOR THE COTTAGE INDUSTRY
P.O. Box 14460
Chicago, IL 60614
(312)472–8116
(send S.A.S.E. for information)

NATIONAL ASSOCIATION OF HOME-BASED BUSINESSES
10451 Mill Run Cir., #400
Owings Mill, MD 21117
(301)363–3698

NATIONAL ASSOCIATION OF HOME BUSINESS OWNERS
P.O. Box 423
East Meadow, NY 11554
(516)997–7394

NATIONAL SMALL BUSINESS UNITED
1155 15th St., N.W. #710
Washington, D.C. 20005
(202)293–8830

PUBLICATIONS

Electronic Cottage Handbook, Lis Fleming (Fleming Ltd.), 1989

Entrepreneur Magazine
2392 Morse Ave.
Irvine, CA 92714
(714)261–2325

Entrepreneurial Woman
2392 Morse Ave.
Irvine, CA 92714
(714)261–2325

Help for Your Growing Home-Based Business, Barbara Brabec
    (Barbara Brabec Productions), 1989

Home Occupation Ordinances, Joann Butler and Judith Getzels
    (American Planning Association)

Homemade Money, Barbara Brabec (Betterway Publications, Inc.),
    1987

National Home Business Report (Quarterly Report)
P.O. Box 2137
Naperville, IL 60567
write for catalog

New Business Opportunities
2392 Morse Ave.
Irvine, CA 92714–6234
(714)261–2083

Office at Home, Robert Scott (Scribner's), 1985

Planning Your Own Home Business, Coralee Smith Kern and
    Tammara Hoffman Wolfgram (VGM Career Horizons), 1986

Women Working Home, M. Behr and W. Lazar (WWH Press), 1983

The Work-at-Home Sourcebook, Lynie Arden (Live Oak
   Publications), 1987

Working from Home, Paul and Sarah Edwards (Jeremy P. Tarcher),
   1985

ON-LINE SERVICES SPECIFICALLY FOR THE HOME-BASED ENTREPRENEUR

GENERAL ELECTRIC INFORMATION SERVICES
888 S. Figueroa St., #700
Los Angeles, CA 90017
(213)236–0200

HOME OFFICE BUSINESS NETWORK
Dial Direct
44 Monterey Blvd. #1400
San Francisco, CA 94131
(415)239–6162

WORKING FROM HOME FORUM ON COMPUSERVE INFORMATION
   SERVICE
(on-line network of people involved in home-based business)
CompuServe Subscription
5000 Arlington Centre Blvd.
Columbus, OH 43220
(800)848–8990

RADIO

HOME OFFICE RADIO
Weekly local business network (Sunday Evenings)
(800)321–2468

GOVERNMENT ASSISTANCE

SMALL BUSINESS ADMINISTRATION
1441 L Street, N.W.
Washington, DC 20416
(202)653–6600

165 Guides to Help You
Start Your Own Business

ANIMAL-ORIENTED BUSINESSES

Business Guide No. ....Reg. Price/Sub. Disc.

1033.	Pet Hotel & Grooming Service	$69.50/59.50
1007.	Pet Shop	$69.50/59.50

APPAREL BUSINESSES

Business Guide No. ....Reg. Price/Sub. Disc.

1161.	Children's Clothing Store	$69.50/59.50
1272.	**Large-Size Women's Apparel Store**	**$29.50**
1152.	Lingerie Shop	$69.50/59.50
1290.	``Sweats''-Only Retailing	$69.50/59.50
1043.	T-Shirt Shop	$69.50/59.50
1229.	Used/Consigned Clothing	$69.50/59.50
1333.	Women's Accessories Store	$69.50/59.50
1107.	Women's Apparel Shop	$69.50/59.50

AUTOMOTIVE BUSINESSES

Business Guide No. ....Reg. Price/Sub. Disc.

1076.	Car Wash	$69.50/59.50
1268.	Cellular Phone Service	$69.50/59.50
1146.	Detailing, Automobile	$69.50/59.50 †
1224.	Limousine Service	$69.50/59.50
1054.	Oil-Change, 10-Minute	$69.50/59.50
1197.	Parts Store, Auto	$69.50/59.50
1018.	**Sales, Consignment**	**$29.50**
1108.	Used-Car Rental Agency	$69.50/59.50
2330.	Used Car Sales	$69.50/59.50 ‡
2329.	Vehicle Leasing	$69.50/59.50 ‡

What's inside an Entrepreneur
How-to Business Guide:

Imagine having a group of business owners unselfishly confide the details of their success in the kind of business you want to start. They reveal profits and operating costs. They share their solutions to typical problems. They give you their own secrets for making the business "hum".

That's what it's like inside an Entrepreneur Business Guide. You get inside information compiled, analyzed and categorized by our staff and put in a form that's easy to read and understand. It gives you the equivalent knowledge of many years of experience in your new business even though you're just starting out.

Each Guide is approx. 200 pages in length, and comes full tabbed for easy reference in its own handsome, vinyl-covered loose leaf binder.

YOU LEARN–

■ The profit potential for this business ■ The specific start-up costs ■ The size and scope of the market ■ How many hours a week it will take ■ How to easily manage this type of business ■ Site selection and lease negotiation ■ What kind of equipment you may need ■ Anticipated sales volume ■ Sample floor layout of your operation ■ How and where to buy supplies ■ How to set prices ■ How to set up an accounting system ■ Licenses and permits you may need and where to get them ■ How to hire and set up payroll when you're ready ■ How to advertise and promote your type of business.

Each guide comes with an unconditional 90-day money back guarantee (from date of purchase, less shipping and handling).

**CALL TOLL FREE 1-(800)421-2300
in California 1-(800)352-7449**

COMPUTER-ORIENTED BUSINESSES

Business Guide No. ....Reg. Price/Sub. Disc.
2335. Bookkeeping Service $69.50/59.50
1221. Consulting &
      Temporary-Help Service, ...$69.50/59.50
1288. Desktop Publishing $69.50/59.50
2333. Diet & Meal Planning.................$69.50/59.50
1084. Hardware Store, Computer $69.50/59.50
1265. Home Computer,
      Making Money With a $69.50/59.50
1237. Information Broker $69.50/59.50
1256. Repair Service, Computer $69.50/59.50
1253. Software Locator Service $69.50/59.50
1261. Software Store $69.50/59.50
2332. Tax Preparation Service...............$69.50/59.50

CRAFT & MANUFACTURING BUSINESSES

Business Guide No. ....Reg. Price/Sub. Disc.
1304. Craft Businesses $64.50/54.50
1262. PVC Furniture Mfg $64.50/54.50

EMPLOYMENT SERVICES

Business Guide No. ....Reg. Price/Sub. Disc.
1051. Employment Agency $69.50/59.50
1228. Executive Recruiting Service $69.50/59.50
1260. Resume Writing &
      Career Counseling $69.50/59.50
1189. Temporary-Help Service $69.50/59.50

FAST-FOOD BUSINESSES

Business Guide No. ....Reg. Price/Sub. Disc.
1270. Chicken, Flame-Broiled $29.50
1083. Cookie Shop $69.50/59.50
1126. Donut Shop $69.50/59.50
1073. Hamburger/Hot Dog Stand $69.50/59.50
1187. Ice Cream Store $69.50/59.50
1056. Mobile Restaurant/
      Sandwich Truck $29.50
1006. Pizzeria $69.50/59.50
1279. Restaurant Start-Up $69.50/59.50
1079. Yogurt (Frozen) Shop $69.50/59.50

FOOD & SPIRITS, RETAIL

Business Guide No. ....Reg. Price/Sub. Disc.
1158. Bakery.......................................$69.50/59.50
1202. Coffee & Tea Store. $69.50/59.50

1173. Convenience Food Store $69.50/59.50
1296. Health-Food/Vitamin Store $69.50/59.50
1024. Liquor Store $69.50/59.50
1295. Muffin Shop......................................$29.50

HOMEBASED BUSINESSES

Business Guide No. ....Reg. Price/Sub. Disc.
1278. Bed & Breakfast Inn $69.50/59.50
1288. Desktop Publishing $69.50/59.50
1258. Freelance Writing $69.50/59.50
1306. Gift Basket Service ....$69.50/$59.50
1265. Home Computer,
      Making Money With $69.50/59.50
1092. Import & Export $69.50/59.50
1015. Mail-Order Business $69.50/59.50
1308. Silk Plants ....$67.50/59.50 †

HOME FURNISHINGS

Business Guide No. ....Reg. Price/Sub. Disc.
1212. Used/Consignment Furniture Store $69.50/59.50

PERSONAL SERVICES

Business Guide No. ....Reg. Price/Sub. Disc.
1194. Dating Service $69.50/59.50
1170. Hair Salon, Family $69.50/59.50
1264. Image Consulting $69.50/59.50
1274. Nail Salon $69.50/59.50
1239. Tutoring Service $29.50
1330. Wedding Planning Service $69.50/59.50

PHOTO-RELATED BUSINESSES

Business Guide No. ....Reg. Price/Sub. Disc.
1209. One-Hour Photo Processing Lab $69.50/59.50
1204. Videotaping Service $69.50/59.50

PUBLISHING BUSINESSES

Business Guide No. ....Reg. Price/Sub. Disc.
1067. Newsletter Publishing $69.50/59.50

RECREATION & ENTERTAINMENT BUSINESSES

Business Guide No. ....Reg. Price/Sub. Disc.
1242. Balloon Delivery Service $69.50/59.50
1186. Bar/Tavern $69.50/59.50
1269. Bowling Center $69.50/59.50
1308. Compact Disc-Only Store $69.50/59.50
1132. Hobby Shop $69.50/59.50

1342	Mobile DJ	$69.50/59.50
1124	No-Alcohol Bar	$69.50/59.50
1100	Pinball & Electronic Game Arcade	$69.50/59.50
1226	TV & Movie Production	$69.50/59.50
1192	Videocassette Rental Store	$69.50/59.50

RESTAURANTS, SIT-DOWN

Business Guide No. ....Reg. Price/Sub. Disc.

1289	Diner	$69.50/59.50
1279	Restaurant Start-Up	$69.50/59.50
1156	Sandwich Shop/Deli	$69.50/59.50

RETAIL BUSINESSES, MISC.

Business Guide No. ....Reg. Price/Sub. Disc.

1318	Baby Store	$69.50/59.50
1277	Beauty Supply Store	$69.50/59.50
1293	Bookstore, Children's	$69.50/59.50
1331.	**Character Merchandise Store**	**$29.50**
1135	Cosmetics Shop	$69.50/59.50
3361	Buying Products From Other Countries	$59.50/49.50
1143	Flower Shop	$69.50/59.50
1144	Framing Shop, Do-It-Yourself	$69.50/59.50
1306	Gift Basket Service	$69.50/59.50 †
1218	Gift, Specialty Store	$69.50/59.50
1323	Kiosks & Cart Business Opportunities	$69.50/59.50
1222	Multilevel Marketing Sales, How to Develop	$69.50/59.50
1316.	**Off-Price Retailing**	**$29.50**
1283	Party Goods/Gift Store	$69.50/59.50
1325	Print/Poster Store	$69.50/59.50
1214	Religious-Gift/Book Store	$69.50/59.50
1340	Sock Shops	$69.50/59.50
1337	Silk Plants Shop	$69.50/59.50 †
1322	Sports Memorabilia Store	$69.50/59.50
1117	Used-Book Store	$69.50/59.50
1182	Wedding Shop	$69.50/59.50

SELF-IMPROVEMENT BUSINESSES

Business Guide No. ....Reg. Price/Sub. Disc.

| 1172 | Physical-Fitness Center | $69.50/59.50 |
| 1046 | Self-Improvement/Insight-Awareness Seminars | $69.50/59.50 |

SERVICES TO BUSINESS

Business Guide No. ....Reg. Price/Sub. Disc.

1223.	Advertising Agency	$69.50/59.50
1292.	Advertising, Specialty	$69.50/59.50
1236.	Apartment Preparation Service	$69.50/59.50
1317.	Business Brokerage	$69.50/59.50
1307.	Business Development Center	$69.50/59.50
1207.	Collection Agency	$69.50/59.50
2328.	Construction Cleanup	$69.50/59.50 ‡
1329.	Construction Interior Cleaning, New	$69.50/59.50
1151.	Consulting Business	$69.50/59.50
1232.	Coupon Mailer Service	$69.50/59.50
1328.	Freight Brokerage	$69.50/59.50
1237.	Information Broker	$69.50/59.50
1336.	Instant Sign Store	$69.50/59.50
1034.	Janitorial Service	$69.50/59.50
1098.	LiquidatorSelling Distressed Merchandise	$69.50/59.50
1332.	Mobile Bookkeeping Service	$69.50/59.50
1962.	Money Broker	$84.50/74.50
1031.	Parking Lot Striping & Maintenance Srvc	$69.50/59.50
1280.	Pest Control	$69.50/59.50
1324.	Public Relations Agency	$69.50/59.50
1339.	Referral Services	$69.50/59.50
1136.	Secretarial/ Word-Processing Service	$69.50/59.50
1150.	Surface Cleaning, Mobile	$69.50/59.50
1148.	Telephone-Answering Service	$69.50/59.50
1157.	Trucking, Cross-Country	$69.50/59.50
1012.	Window-Washing Service	$69.50/59.50

SERVICES TO THE HOME

Business Guide No. ....Reg. Price/Sub. Disc.

1053.	Carpet-Cleaning Service	$69.50/59.50
1215.	Catering Service	$69.50/59.50
1291.	Closet Customizing	$69.50/59.50
1334.	Home Inspection Service	$69.50/59.50
1275.	**House Sitting/In-Home Care**	**$29.50**
1314.	Interior Designer	$69.50/59.50
1105.	Kitchen Remodeling	$69.50/59.50
1198.	Lawn-Care Service	$69.50/59.50
1343	Mini-Blind Cleaning	$69.50/59.50
1160.	Maid Service	$69.50/59.50
1249.	Painting, House	$69.50/59.50

CALL TOLL FREE 1-(800) 421-2300
in California 1-(800) 352-7449

| 1285. | Pool Cleaning & Repair | $69.50/59.50 |
| 1012. | Window-Washing Service | $69.50/59.50 |

SERVICE BUSINESSES, MISC.

Business Guide No.		Reg. Price/Sub. Disc.
1309.	Check Cashing Service	$69.50/59.50
1058.	Child-Care Service	$69.50/59.50
1037.	Dry-Cleaning Shop	$69.50/59.50
1313.	Event Planning Service	$69.50/59.50
1306.	Gift Basket Service	$69.50/59.50
1298.	Instant Print/Copy Shop	$69.50/59.50
1326.	**Instant Shoe Repair Shop**	**$29.50**
1162.	Laundromat	$69.50/59.50
1042.	Mini-Storage Facility	$69.50/59.50
1287.	Packaging & Shipping Service	$69.50/59.50
1310.	Personal Shopping Service	$69.50/59.50
1341.	Pet Sitting	$69.50/59.50
1320.	Private Investigator	$69.50/59.50
1147.	Private Mailbox Service	$69.50/59.50
1335.	Senior Day Care	$69.50/59.50
1150.	Surface Cleaning, Mobile	$69.50/59.50
1154.	Travel Agency	$69.50/59.50
1077.	**Vinyl-Repair Service**	**$29.50**

SPORTS BUSINESSES

Business Guide No.		Reg. Price/Sub. Disc.
1022.	**Bicycle/Moped Shop**	**$29.50**
1286.	Sporting Goods Store	$69.50/59.50
1322.	Sports Memorabilia Store	$69.50/59.50

STREET-VENDING BUSINESSES

Business Guide No.		Reg. Price/Sub. Disc.
3360	Sourcebook of Products for Flea Markets	$59.50/49.50
1127.	Shrimp Peddling	$64.50/54.50
1299.	Vending Businesses	$69.50/59.50

MISCELLANEOUS BUSINESSES

Business Guide No.		Reg. Price/Sub. Disc.
1091.	Burglar Alarm Sales/ Installation	$69.50/59.50
2327.	Buying Foreclosures	$69.50/59.50 †
1227.	Government Contracts, How to Obtain	$69.50/59.50
1282	Herb Farming	$69.50/59.50
1222.	Multilevel Marketing Sales, How to Develop	$69.50/59.50
1153.	Real Estate Company, Flat-Fee	$69.50/59.50
1284.	Real Estate, Complete Investment Guide	$69.50/59.50
1071.	Seminar Promoting	$69.50/59.50

IMPROVING YOUR BUSINESS ABILITY

Business Guide No.		Reg. Price/Sub. Disc.
3402.	Business Plan, Developing A	$59.50/49.50
7205.	Calif. Business Start-Up	$64.50/54.50
3370	Complete Government Resource Guide Complete Set	$99.50/89.50
3371	Western Region	$49.50/39.50
3372	Midwestern Region	$49.50/39.50
3373	Southern Region	$49.50/39.50
3374	Eastern Region	$49.50/39.50
1321.	Credit Consulting	$69.50/59.50
7000.	Incorporation Kits for Any State (Specify State)	$59.50/49.50
1327.	Lessons From America's Successful Entrepreneurs	$54.50/44.50
1312.	Personal Financial Planner	$84.50/74.50
1111.	Promotional Gimmicks	$69.50/59.50
1999.	Complete Library of All Business Guides	$5,450/$4,450
1315.	SBA Loan Guide	$74.50/64.50
1319.	Standard Business Forms for the Entrepreneur	$59.50/49.50

‡ Audio Cassettes Plus Reference Book

† Supplemental Video available

Satisfaction Guaranteed

You have nothing to lose. If you follow the instructions and they do not work for you, return the business guide within 90 days with a simple note, telling us where we went wrong. Yes, return the business guide within 90 days and we'll return the purchase price, less shipping and handling.

Place your order by mail or phone.

To order by phone:
Call TOLL FREE: 1(800)421-2300
CA residents call: 1(800)352-7449

For rush shipments:
Please call our toll free number:
6a.m.-8:30p.m. Monday-Friday
7a.m.-3p.m. Saturday Pacific Coast time.

For customer service or billing inquiries call:
1(800)345-8614
In CA call: (714)261-2325 • 8a.m.-5p.m. • Monday-Friday

To Order by phone: ☎

In order to save you time when ordering, please have the following information ready:

1. Completed order form.
2. Credit card number and expiration date.
3. Customer code number: **9N184**
4. Please note: We do not take C.O.D. orders.

To Order by Mail: ✉

1. Be sure to fill out the order form completely.
2. Please check all your entries for legibility.
3. Please include a home <u>and</u> work phone number in case we have a question about your order.
4. Be sure to include your complete street address for parcel deliveries. U.P.S. will not deliver to P.O. boxes.

**CALL TOLL FREE 1-(800) 421-2300
in California 1-(800) 352-7449**